ESCAPE ROUTES

ESCAPE ROUTES

FURTHER ADVENTURE WRITINGS OF **DAVID ROBERTS**

THE
MOUNTAINEERS

Published by
The Mountaineers
1001 SW Klickitat Way
Seattle, WA 98134

10 9 8 7
5 4 3 2 1

Published simultaneously in Canada by Douglas & McIntyre, Ltd., 1615 Venables Street, Vancouver, B.C. V5L 2H1

Published simultaneously in Great Britain by Cordee, 3a DeMontfort Street, Leicester, England, LE1 7HD

Manufactured in the United States of America

Edited by Karen Parkin
Cover design by Helen Cherullo
Book design by Alice C. Merrill
Book layout by Ani Rucki

Cover photograph: *Looking at the Coast Range in British Columbia.* Photo © James Martin, Tony Stone Images.
Cover photo research: Mark Hipple, Tony Stone Images.

The following stories in this collection first appeared in other publications in their present or in slightly different form:
Storming Iceland (*Outside*); First Down the Tekeze (*Men's Journal*); Lechuiguilla: A New Mexico Marvel (*Smithsonian*); Rambling through the Winds (*Outside*); The Race Diabolique (*Men's Journal*); Bleau (*Outside*); Wandergolf in the Tirol (*Men's Journal*); A Mountain of Trouble (*Men's Journal*); The MoabTreehouse (*Men's Journal*); Ed Viesturs: Confessions of an Altitude Junkie (*Men's Journal*); The Hearse Traverse (*Summit*); Quiet Days in the Brooks Range (*Chicago Tribune*); The Gunks Revisited (*Smithsonian*); Bandiagara: The Dogon and the Tellem (*National Geographic*); Campaign in the Clouds (*Men's Journal*); Lost City of the Lukachukais (*Discovery Channel Online*); La Provence Ignorée (*Men's Journal*)

Library of Congress Cataloging-in-Publication Data
Roberts, David, 1943–
    Escape routes : further adventure writings of David Roberts.
       p.   cm.
    ISBN 0-89886-509-3
    1. Mountaineering. 2. Adventure and adventurers. I. Title.
GV200.R619   1997
796.5'22—dc21   96–52175
                                                                                            CIP

To my mother, Janet Roberts,
Who named me after Stevenson's David Balfour,
Who read me Alice in Wonderland,
And who taught me never to split my infinitives.
With Love

CONTENTS

FOREWORD

I first laid eyes on David Roberts in September 1972, on the grounds of Hampshire College in Amherst, Massachusetts, where I had just enrolled as an eighteen-year-old, fresh off the turnip truck from small-town Oregon. Strolling across campus, I noticed a shaggy-haired guy holding forth to a large gathering of students on the steps outside the dining hall. Impressed by the crowd, I stopped to see what the ruckus was about.

The guy with the hair was named Dave, and he was recruiting participants in the college Outdoors Program, of which he said he was co-director. He was a persuasive speaker. Within a few minutes I found myself blowing off the rest of the day's appointments in order to join Professor Roberts and several van loads of other freshmen for an impromptu rock-climbing session at a local crag called Rattlesnake Gutter.

By the conclusion of that Indian summer afternoon, I'd belatedly come to realize that my climbing tutor was none other than *the* David Roberts: the renowned Alaskan alpinist who'd authored *The Mountain of My Fear*, one of the finest mountaineering books ever written. Although it would be some years before I recognized it, my life had just veered to an incautious new heading. Thanks to the considerable force of the Roberts personality, thereafter my existence revolved increasingly around the twin poles of climbing and the written word. Two and a half decades later, to an astounding degree I'm still chugging doggedly along that same implausible orbit.

When I graduated from college and moved back west, I watched dubiously from afar as Dave abandoned the security of academia and dove headfirst into the snake pit of freelance writing. Against long odds, he thrived—and a few years later the silver-tongued bastard badgered me into taking the reckless dive as well. It would never have occurred to me that one could actually write for a living had Dave not demonstrated that it was possible.

He also demonstrated what good writing is. Year after year he hammered out a remarkable body of work. Some of it appeared as books—about the dazzling, troubled writer Jean Stafford; about fraudulent explorers; about Geronimo; about the enigma of the Anasazi—but most of Dave's stuff was published as magazine features, a lamentably ephemeral medium. In 1986 The Mountaineers preserved twenty of Dave's articles for posterity by publishing them as the collection *Moments of Doubt,* the title essay of which has been widely lauded as one of the finest things ever written about climbing. Now, eleven years later, we owe thanks to The Mountaineers for rescuing another twenty pieces as *Escape Routes*.

Dave is a complicated man: short-fused, brilliant, mechanically inept, incorrigibly pedantic, intensely loyal, witheringly critical, extravagantly generous, politically incorrect, a swinger of birches, a burner of bridges.

He has never been afraid to tell it like it is, the consequences be damned. Indeed, Dave's best writing has always been characterized by a ruthless—even brutal—candor. It has won him his share of enemies over the years, to be sure, but honesty is a rare and valuable attribute. In this volume, readers will find a bountiful dose of it.

—*Jon Krakauer*

INTRODUCTION

"Do you still climb?"

I get asked this question, it seems, about once a month—sometimes by climbers, but more often by new acquaintances who find out that I once pursued expeditions to little-known ranges in Alaska, or that when I "became" a writer, it was the glories of ascent that I first hymned.

The question never fails to induce a pang of guilt. "Yeah, but not like I used to," I usually answer, then launch into one of three pat explanations calibrated to the apparent sensitivity of the inquirer. The guilt, however, puzzles me: Why should I feel guilty for not climbing as hard or as well as I once did? Perhaps it is simply regret that life turned out to be a more vexed and muddled business than one dreamed it would be at twenty-two. When I was twenty-two, I conceived of the future only in terms of an endless succession of daring jaunts to shining mountains all over the globe.

"I go out three or four times a year with old buddies and do moderate stuff," I say to the least curious, hoping to end it there. That formula is true enough, but sometimes I add, "Climbing's simply too dangerous, and too scary to keep up, unless you're in great shape." That too seems true—though God knows a whole younger generation of sport climbers toiling on bolted crags and artificial walls has yet to discover that their pastime has anything to do with risk or fear.

But if I feel like really talking about it, I'll say, "You know, the kinds of adventures I write about now—and the writing itself—take the place of the mountaineering I did when I was young." I can go on and on in this vein, almost convincing myself, until the mocking imp that perches on the shoulder of every writer's conscience—what Hemingway called the "built-in shit detector"—reminds me that I'm spinning an elaborate fib. Nothing that I'm likely to do in the rest of my life will have the diamond intensity, the tightrope walk on the margin of life and death, that my best mountain expeditions did.

For the last seventeen years (but for a one-year hiatus as an editor at *Horizon* magazine), I've made a living as a writer. My first collection

11

of essays, *Moments of Doubt,* gathered together what I hoped were my best adventure writings, from an account of our Mount Huntington climb recorded when I was twenty-two through magazine assignments completed in my forty-third year. Virtually all of those pieces had to do with mountaineering.

Escape Routes, which collects my favorite adventure essays from the last eleven years, ranges far from mountaineering, as I go caving in New Mexico; rafting in Ethiopia; biking in China; probing prehistoric mysteries in Mali; and rambling happily through France, Argentina, Iceland, and Italy. Contemplating my decade of vagabondage—all of it on assignment for magazines—I am confronted with the crucial question every would-be explorer must face as he ages: Have I kept my life adventurous? Is there indeed something out there that takes the place of the adamantine climbs of youth?

There are mountaineers who keep tying in to the sharp end among the great ranges well into their fifties; I think of Jim Donini and Doug Scott, among others. The example of that peerless Brit, H. W. Tilman, who turned from mountaineering to polar exploration in small sailboats, who regarded the very notion of mellowing as anathema, and who was lost at sea in his eightieth year, gives pause and admiration to us all.

For me, however, climbing at the hardest level ceased to be alluring in my midthirties. Nine years of teaching the craft to beginners at Hampshire College burned me out. Doubts I had always harbored about climbing—about its solipsistic cult of the heroic deed performed in a cultural vacuum, its worship of narcissistic self-control validated by grade ratings—came to the surface. My own ambivalence on the crags was trying to tell me something. And I made a genuine discovery of new kinds of adventure. Most recently, the quest for obscure Anasazi ruins in the backcountry of the Southwest, and for an understanding of the Puebloans who are the descendants of the Anasazi, has driven me to years of passionate prowlings on the Colorado Plateau, and to the writing of a book I think of as my most lyrical, *In Search of the Old Ones.* In southern Utah today, I can set off down a new canyon looking for thousand-year-old petroglyphs with all the brimming joy I used to taste pushing the first lead on an unclimbed granite wall.

Thanks to my mountain obsessions, I was for years a narrow specialist in the art of wandering, and in that respect a singularly unadventurous traveler. At the age of thirty-eight, I had never been to Europe (I've gone more than fifty times since). My smattering of junior-high German and my two years of high-school French lay dormant in my brain, since I had never found the need to speak a single phrase in a foreign language. The Third World, insofar as I dimly granted its existence, loomed as a squalid, incomprehensible wilderness. (Climbers as a breed, I would venture, are ethnically squeamish.) I read many books about the Inuit, but toured such forlorn outposts as Barrow and Nome only on brief, disheartened visits.

If "Have I kept my life adventurous?" remains the crucial question, it clings, for the freelance writer, like a barnacle to the hide of a far more pragmatic concern: Can I make a living doing this stuff? The vast majority of magazine articles in my field celebrate "adventures" that a stressed-out yuppie can fit into a long weekend. The obligatory "If you go" sidebar postulates excursions that come packaged with 800 numbers and frequent-flyer bonus miles.

In the 1980s, a phenomenon called "adventure travel" took America by storm. Companies sprang up right and left, offering bike tours of Tuscany, treks in Kashmir, rafting in Turkey, Christian fundamentalist dogsled trips across the Brooks Range. For the writer, these were some of the easiest assignments to scam up: the tour operators had already filled our editors' ears with gooey hype, and magazines love "replicable" journeys—i.e., ones their readers might actually be able to perform themselves.

The slick marketing of adventure travel neatly disguises the fact that these trips have very little to do with adventure. Over the years, I've joined about a dozen such excursions, always on assignment. Often I had a good time, and my articles earnestly praised the stupas of Ladakh or the Inca walls of Cuzco, but I found that these were not essays I was eager to push onto potential readers two or three years later. The rare exception usually came when something went wrong, allowing adventure to creep in, as in "Biking through Tiananmen Square."

Because the tour operator makes all the decisions, down to where you eat breakfast on Day Four; because you never have to risk ordering dinner in Spanish; because the sixth head count of the day precludes the possibility of your getting lost; because just when a folk dance or street melee begins to get interesting, it's time to take the bus back to the hotel—for all these and other reasons, adventure travel bears a closer resemblance to a QE2 cruise than to a walk on the wild side.

Often—at least as often as I'm asked, "Do you still climb?"—I hear, on the lips of some friend or acquaintance who's envious of my latest junket to Andalusia, "You lucky bastard, you have the best job in the world." In the winter of 1991, Matt Hale visited Jon Krakauer and me at the Kleine Scheidegg beneath the Eiger Nordwand. Jon and I had been lodged under Frau von Almen's stern regime for weeks, as we waited for Jeff Lowe and the weather to get their acts together, and we were grumpy. On the second night, over yet another epicurean dinner, Matt pointed out, "Do you realize that this whole business that you keep complaining about—food and

13

wine, skiing in Switzerland, watching Jeff on the Eiger—all this stuff that you guys are getting paid to write about and take pictures of, is exactly what I'm spending thousands of dollars to do, on my vacation?" Jon and I traded sheepish grins, and stopped bitching.

On the other hand, occasionally someone with a closer familiarity with the freelance game (often an editor turned friend) will let down his guard and sympathize with my plight in tones of unfeigned pity. I was once introduced at a publishing course by Anne Fadiman, then an editor at *Life*, as "the only happy freelancer I know." Certainly writing for a living is one of the loneliest professions known to humankind, and one of the most insecure. If you don't have a hide as thick as a rhinoceros's, the sheer rejection will do you in.

When you start out as a writer, you must come up with all the ideas and persuade editors to buy them. You may even write "on spec," hoping to sell a finished piece to an unwary journal. (From Mike Curtis at the *Atlantic Monthly*, in my first years, I received what I still consider my favorite rejection slip. Afire with a summer's National Endowment for the Humanities (NEH) study at Stanford, where I had read all I could about nineteenth-century British expeditions in the Arctic, I wrote a piece on spec that I called "The Myth of the Fat Eskimo." It was my thesis that a collective Victorian fantasy of the Arctic had dictated seeing Eskimos as cherubic children, hence fat and cute, in defiance of their actual physiques and temperaments. Mike sent the piece back with a one-line note: "This is a marvelous answer to a question no one has asked.")

The writer's first benchmark of success comes when magazines begin to assign him pieces of their devising. Today, between one-third and one-half of the articles I write are of this sort. And yet, when I look over the debris of my scribblings, I find that it is only rarely these assignments that result in pieces I'm proud to save. Of the twenty pieces collected here, only two originated as assignments suggested by magazines ("The Gunks Revisited," for *Smithsonian* and "The Race Diabolique" for *Men's Journal*). All the others were my idea. If this bespeaks anything more than one writer's vanity, maybe it is the stubborn fact that, to find the true thread of adventure, one must draw one's own maps.

At the core of the exploratory journey there must be some spark of the unplanned, the unforeseen. It is still not so hard, after all, to find adventure in this postmodern rat race of a world: simply set off down a river in Ethiopia that has never been run, or try to climb Iceland's Snaefellsjökull in winter. At a lecture about one of his trips, H. W. Tilman was approached by an earnest young man who asked, "But, sir, how does one get on an expedition such as yours?" "Put on your boots and go!" Tilman thundered.

The passion that drove me to climb for thirteen straight years in Alaska and the Yukon was an insatiable itch to probe the unknown, to go where no one had been. The first time in my life that I ventured onto ground never before trod by human feet came on Denali's Wickersham Wall, when I was twenty. I still remember the acute, imperishable taste of that moment, the druglike rush of conviction that here was a deed that turned the barren world into crystalline joy.

Yet climbing is among the most literal—and, in Lionel Terray's felicitous epithet, the most "useless"—of ways of confronting the unknown. Of course no one had ever touched the brown granite slabs of the south ridge of a peak we called The Angel in a range we named the Revelation Mountains: the place, in 1967, was too obscure for anyone before us to have cared about.

In the proud and angry adolescent who became an Alaskan mountaineer at age twenty, there was a strong streak of the loner. Climbing seemed to me the perfect escape from the frightening tangle of human relations, from the need for love and the burden of dependency. On unexplored walls under a subarctic sun, my chosen partners and I could pretend for a month at a time that no one else existed, that nothing mattered beyond the next pitch.

Decades later, the siren song of the unknown still rings in my ears. But as I have mellowed into middle age, my instinct for the adventurous has made a diametrical shift. Now, rather than fleeing society to perform arcane deeds in a world of sterile rock and ice, I find my challenges in plunging into the mysteries of human passage on a globe still far from fully discovered. Anthropology and archaeology, which at twenty seemed to me of chiefly academic interest, have become my new passions, though I remain an amateur in both.

The unknown embodied in a trackless mountain wall is of a relatively ephemeral sort. Much of its mystery is solved by the first ascent. For me, at fifty-three, the ideal adventure requires difficult travel of my own devising into the heart of a cultural mystery in some remote place. Somewhat immodestly, I might point to one piece in this collection, "Bandiagara: The Dogon and the Tellem," as epitomizing what I seek in a current-day adventure.

My month in Mali with three companions was a layman's quest to unravel an archaeological riddle—one posed by the Tellem, who may have been the finest prehistoric climbers the world has ever seen. Throughout the Bandiagara, in alcoves as high as 200 feet up overhanging sandstone walls, these herders and hunters, who vanished in the fifteenth century, had built granaries and buried their dead. We visited many Tellem caves that no westerner before us had seen; others defeated our best efforts to reach with modern climbing gear. Each night in camp, the four of us renewed our ceaseless debate: How had the Tellem done it, and why?

At the end of our month, we were more baffled by the Tellem achievement than we had been when we arrived in Mali. An unclimbed mountain wall had always seemed to ask me a simple yes-or-no question: Will it go, or not? The Tellem phenomenon goes beyond yes or no, to the heart of the human condition. That we made no real dent in the enigma only deepens it. We had ventured into the unknown, coming home not with answers so much as with a renewed sense of wonder. What more can one ask from a journey?

RAMBLES AND ESCAPADES

STORMING ICELAND

Who travels widely needs his wits about him.
The stupid should stay at home.
            —from "The Words of the High One,"
                 a medieval Icelandic poem

I woke at 2:00 A.M. when the tent began to smother me. We had gone to bed five hours earlier in perfect calm; the candle flame by which I wrote in my notebook had not even flickered. When we pitched the tent on the bare shoulder of the road, we were unable to anchor one side of it, a detail that seemed unimportant at the time. But now a hard gale was whipping off the Bay of Faxaflói, slinging horizontal snow. One of the tent poles, designed to arch gracefully on the showroom floor, was buckling inward. The window, through which happy campers were supposed to peer at the moonrise, clung to my face like a dank towel. The nylon walls sang with the steady hum of buckshot sleet.

I had already woken earlier in the night to discover that my inflatable sleeping pad had gone flat, rudely interrupting a dream in which Larry Bird had found me open for the winning three-pointer. I had then improvised a lumpy mattress out of spare clothes, day packs, and soggy paperbacks, and muttered my way back to sleep.

Now, in the blizzard, I jackknifed in my sleeping bag to get my head downstream, next to the door. Fifteen minutes later the wind shifted 180

18

degrees and the door crumpled. I sat up, cursing, and Jon cursed in response. There was some comfort in knowing he couldn't sleep, either. "How fast is this mother blowing, do you think?" I asked. "Fifty or sixty," said Jon.

During the next two hours, the wind actually picked up speed while it veered neurotically through most of the points of the compass. We would get a weird lull of ten seconds, then the tent wall would snap with the sudden return of reality. For most of an hour around 4:00 A.M., we held the upwind wall in place with our backs or feet, for fear the poles would snap. It wasn't a life-or-death situation, since we had camped next to our rented Land Cruiser, to which we could dash in an emergency. "If we do, though," said Jon, "the tent's gone." What was more, the road was drifting over, and it could be days before a snowplow stumbled along.

Bleary-brained, I pondered the possibility that we had no business being out here at the tip of an Icelandic peninsula in the dead of winter, a degree and a half south of the Arctic Circle. Maybe Dóra was right. Where was Bárðr when we needed him?

Around 5:00 A.M. the wind slacked off to a steady forty miles an hour. The tent pole, bowed but not broken, stood by itself once more. Exhausted, I let drowsiness creep over me, but just before I went under I murmured to myself the eternal motto of the ambivalent climber: Oh well, at least we won't have to get up and do anything in the morning.

WE HAD BEEN HOPING TO ASCEND Snæfellsjökull, Iceland's most famous mountain, a peak wreathed in history and myth. Four years earlier, I had traveled through Iceland in July, retracing the 1936 path of the poet W. H. Auden. Like Auden, I had been mesmerized by the scenery, bathed in what he called "the most magical light of anywhere on Earth." I had also grown fond of the locals, most of whom were on their annual midsummer spree, worshipping the old Norse gods with outdoor chess marathons, all-night drunks, and subarctic sunbathing in their underwear. Why not return in winter to see the other side of what I presumed to be a manic-depressive culture? And, while we were at it, why not ski to the summit on which Jules Verne's heroes had found the secret passage that led to the center of the earth?

"Is that up there near Alaska?" a woman in Cambridge, where I live, had asked me prior to our departure. Icelanders touring the United States are routinely greeted with similar tokens of our geographic ignorance. "Is that part of Canada?" "Are you one of the British Isles?" You would think all the vagabond travelers flying cheapo to Europe in the 1970s who stopped over at Keflavík Airport might have put Iceland on their mental map. Reykjavík, after all, is closer to Boston than San Francisco is.

On the other hand, only 28,724 Americans visited Iceland last year*, a decline of 7,000 from the year before. (Compare this number with the 4,690,959 who in 1988 elbowed their way into tiny Acadia National Park in Maine.) Maybe it's the name that scares people off. If in labeling Greenland Erik the Red indulged in an all-time piece of real estate hype, then Flóki Vilgerðarson, who climbed a mountain one day in the ninth century and saw ice floating in a distant bay, pulled off quite the opposite trick when he named Iceland. Warmed by the Gulf Stream, the island is in summer one of the greenest places in Europe. It is also the most volcanic place in the world: One-third of all the lava that has burbled to the earth's surface since 1500 has done so here. Lush with summer meadows, rife with moss and wildflowers, Iceland's 40,000 square miles are nonetheless almost treeless.

It is the only place on earth with no prehistory, in the sense that its first settlers—Irish monks in the eighth century, Norwegian Vikings after 874—left written records of their arrival. Today, Iceland has only 250,000 inhabitants, a good half of them in and around Reykjavík. Thus a country the size of Hungary supports a smaller population than Corpus Christi, Texas. And it is perhaps the most literate population in the world. There are twenty times as many books published per capita in Iceland as there are in the States. The language has changed so little in a millennium that Icelandic teenagers can—and do, for pleasure—read the medieval sagas and Edda with little difficulty. (It is as if an American adolescent switched off "NYPD Blue" and picked up *Beowulf*.) Iceland is also supremely democratic. It has the world's oldest standing parliament, and until recently you could look up the president (a woman) in the phone book. There is little poverty in Iceland, and there are no millionaires.

JON KRAKAUER AND I HAD ARRIVED in the beginning of March, as Iceland was crawling out from under one of its stormiest winters in decades: an official meteorological report noted that Reykjavík had enjoyed two sun hours in January. We expected hibernal stupefaction, but the natives seemed every bit as jazzed up as they had been in July. For one thing, just six days before our arrival, beer had become legal for the first time in seventy-seven years.

The story is a curious one. In 1912, Iceland became the first country to enact prohibition. With repeal in 1933, wine and spirits became legal, but an old distrust of beer as the true demon drink kept it outlawed in

---

*Written in 1989.

concentrations of greater than 2.2 percent alcohol. For five decades, Icelanders either smuggled in European beer or swilled what Auden called the "weak and nasty" local brew. Five years ago, a pub called Gaukur á Stöng launched a craze by mixing the 2.2 percent draft with vodka, right in the tap. In 1988 the parliament nixed this concoction but voted to make real beer legal in a year's time.

As we wandered into Gaukur on a Tuesday evening in March, we were unprepared for the euphoria that was washing in on waves of Löwenbräu and Budweiser. For three nights running—weeknights, no less—the patrons closed Gaukur by dancing on the tables as waitpersons danced on the bar; one evening the owner mooned the congregation as he pirouetted above the rafters. Each night the floor became a carpet of broken glass, but the mood was one of dedicated ebullience. Even a fistfight seemed good-natured, earnest youths throwing errant haymakers like bear cubs swatting mosquitoes.

One afternoon, hearing disco music from the closed dining room of our hotel, we peered in to see a parade of beautiful women striding down a stage runway in bathing suits and high heels. We had happened upon the rehearsals for the Miss Reykjavík contest. As journalists intent on plumbing the cultural life of the city, we wangled a private press session with the candidates the next day. Iceland takes beauty contests seriously. Last year's Miss Iceland won Miss World, as had the 1985 entrant; in 1986, Miss Iceland placed third. I asked Gróa Asgeirsdóttir, who organizes the pageants, if it had been obvious last year that Linda Pétersdóttir, soon to become Miss World, would win hands down in Iceland. "No," she said thoughtfully. "There were three or four women who could have won." And how had celebrity affected Linda, who hailed from the tiny town of Vopnafjörður and had worked in a fish plant? "She has a wonderful personality," said Gróa. "The title has not changed her."

So we were finding Reykjavík hard to leave. We had stretched our bedtimes to help Gaukur shut its doors at 1:30 A.M., but by the standards of Icelandic nightlife we were callow weenies. On Friday night we resolved to run the full gauntlet of Nordic excess. At closing we crunched our way out of Gaukur and headed for Casablanca, one of the trendier discos. There we fell in with a quintet of local artsy types, whose blithe spirit was a ravishing exhibitionist named Iris. Iris was wearing a fez, a black leotard, and what looked like a high school letter jacket with white felt falsies stuck to the front, in the style of a Wagnerian Valkyrie. When I complimented these appendages, she gave me a kiss and told me she had sewn them on herself.

Casablanca seemed a whirl of excitement to us, but Iris declared it slow. We piled seven in one car and headed for Tunglið, a three-story disco where

Iris knew all the patrons, half of whom were making out in androgynous permutations on the sofas. After Tungliꝺ closed around 3:30 A.M., we found our way to the apartment of Iris's boyfriend, who was out of beer. A collection was taken, a black-market taxi driver was called, and in half an hour we had a pristine bottle of vodka before us.

The rest I remember only hazily. Snorri, whose brother had attempted Mount McKinley, was delighted to meet a pair of climbers who had been on the same peak. As luck would have it, I had gotten up McKinley twenty-six years before, while Jon had been stormed off it in 1987. This discrepancy Snorri could not fathom. "I can see that he could climb McKinley," he said to me five or six times, indicating the bearded and still hard-looking Krakauer. "But you?"

Iris and her boyfriend, who had had a little spat earlier, were in the bedroom making up. All evening, the articulate but hostile Dóra had been telling Jon and me, "Darlink, I love my country. And I am sick and tired of fucking American journalists who come here and . . . " But it was never quite clear what we journalists came and did. Now, around 5 A.M., Dóra said, "Darlink, I was born under the glacier." (The idiom is peculiar to natives of towns like Olafsvík, in the shadow of Snæfellsjökull.) "I know the glacier as the back of my hand. And I say, if you climb the glacier to the top in March, you are fucking lucky or you are fucking good."

BY SUNDAY—AFTER A HEALING IMMERSION in the Blue Lagoon, a carbonated lake in the middle of nowhere heated by an Orwellian power plant—we had recuperated sufficiently to make our getaway. For seven hours, as we drove north to Borgarnes, then snaked along the south shore of the rugged Snæfellsnes peninsula, we watched snow squalls alternate with sunbursts dancing on the bay. The farther we went, the worse the going. Without every erg of four-wheel drive and every stud on our Land Cruiser's heavy tires, we could not have navigated the road. We would drive for an hour without seeing another vehicle. Every few miles, a farmhouse would loom into view, set far back from the road in a snowdrift. Perhaps half of these dwellings were abandoned; in the other half, the age-old life of rural Icelanders spun out its Spartan thread.

To travel anywhere in Iceland is to plunge into history. Not even Greece so imprints the deeds of its heroic age on the very landscape. I had been reading the sagas, those plain but vivid prose narratives that, mixing myth and fact, detail the exploits of the Vikings who settled, farmed, warred, and wooed in Iceland from A.D. 930 to 1030. On Snæfellsnes we were deep in the Eyrbyggjasaga, crossing paths with the ghosts of such men as Helgi the Lean and Steinolf the Short, Bolverk the Rash and Illugi the Black,

Thorolf Lamefoot and Thorir Woodenleg, Odd the Bold and Bork the Stout. In my mind, as I stared at the snow-stricken countryside, I saw the berserkers Halli and Leiknir speared in their scalding bath; Bjorn shivering in his three-day cave bivouac; Katla stoned to death as a witch; Alf and Ospak fighting over the rights to a beached whale.

All of Snæfellsnes is mountainous, so it is somehow fitting that the highest peak of all is the one farthest out, at the western end, which is very nearly the westernmost point in Iceland. Snæfellsjökull (pronounced "sny-fells-yokel") is a 4,744-foot volcano that springs directly from the ocean and is covered by an ice cap. On a clear day you can see it from Reykjavík, a disembodied beacon gleaming in the northwest, seventy-five miles across the water.

According to the sagas, Snæfellsjökull was named by Bárðr (pronounced "bowr-thur"), who sighted it from his ship as he looked for a place to land on the Icelandic coast. The name, prosaically enough, means "snow-mountain-glacier." The events of the Bárðar Saga take place on the tip of the peninsula, "under the glacier." Few of the sagas mingle the supernatural and the historic so effectively. Woven through the tale are the dark doings of trolls, monsters, dwarfs, and elves. Bárðr himself is descended from a giant and a troll. (Icelanders remain superstitious: a recent survey found that fifty-five percent believe in elves.)

The Bárðar Saga's central event occurs when Bárðr's strong, beautiful daughter Helga is roughhousing on the beach with her two male cousins. They push her onto an ice floe that drifts out to sea and carries her all the way to the coast of Greenland. Erik the Red rescues her from the ice floe, and she falls in love with a married man named Skeggi.

At his daughter's disappearance, Bárðr flies into a rage. He grabs his nephews about the waist and carries them up onto Snæfellsjökull, where he dumps one into a crevasse and throws the other off a cliff, killing them both. Later, in a wrestling match, he breaks his brother's leg. In remorse, Bárðr flees human society, climbing the mountain to a hidden cave. Yet instead of "reverting to trolldom," in the saga's pithy phrase, he becomes one of the landvaettr, or protective supernatural beings. Throughout the rest of the saga, Bárðr makes fugitive appearances to aid humans in trouble. Always he appears in a gray cloak with a walrus-hide rope for a belt. He carries a two-pronged staff with feather blades that he uses to cross the glacier.

I had been unable to discover who made the first ascent of Snæfellsjökull. Jules Verne, who never visited Iceland, supplied the details of his fictional 1864 ascent in *Journey to the Center of the Earth* by consulting books and maps. His German adventurers, having come across ancient runes that tell of the secret tunnel down to the bowels of the earth, happen upon a miraculous basalt staircase that paves their way to the summit. (Mount Sneffels in Colorado—which I had also climbed in winter—is named after the Icelandic mountain, as spelled by Verne.)

The nonfictional Charles S. Forbes, a plucky Victorian mountaineer, made an attempt in 1859 or 1860, at which time the mountain was still thought to be unclimbed. The locals in Olafsvík warned Forbes that the ascent was impossible, and when he hired two men as guides, their relatives mourned them as goners. Befuddled by crevasses and an August snowstorm, Forbes pulled out all the stops: "I attached the party Alpine-fashion; and leading the way, occasionally encourag[ed] my companions with brandy and snuff." Still, the effort failed. Forty years later another fine Victorian traveler, W. G. Collingwood, was content to gaze at the mountain from Olafsvík, "inaccessible as it is—and except by the crazy foreigner unattempted."

Nowadays Snæfellsjökull is an easy summer climb. The only obstacles it presents are the crevasse fields two-thirds of the way up and the 100-foot tower of ice and rock that forms the summit. But it is rarely climbed in winter, especially in bad weather, when—as Jon and I had discovered with our tent crumpled around us and the blizzard shrieking off the Faxaflói—the mountain can be as nasty as a berserker on the loose.

"DAVE, WAKE UP! IT'S CLEARED OFF. Let's give it a shot!"

From the bliss of deep sleep, I struggled with the malediction ringing in my ears. Putting on my glasses, I peeked groggily out the tent door. Yes, technically, I suppose you could say that it had cleared off, but what about those ominous banks of cloud here, those snow plumes blowing off the ridges there?

"It looks cold," I mumbled.

"It's late already," Jon nonsequitured. "Let's hit it."

It took a while to round up the debris of our car camp, turn snow into hot chocolate, put skins on our skis and film in our cameras. We didn't get off till 9:45 A.M.. It was about twenty degrees Fahrenheit, with a stiff southwest wind blowing in our faces. But I had to admit that the yellowish stuff sparkling on the snow was indeed sunlight, and as I settled into the creaky swing of uphill skiing, I actually began to enjoy myself.

We angled toward the col between Stapafell, a sharp and lovely satellite peak to the south, and the formless reaches of Snæfellsjökull, whose summit lurked in clouds. In summer there is supposed to be a jeep road hereabouts, but all we could see was an endless plain of wind-carved snow punctuated by spiky lumps of congealed lava. The texture underfoot varied from bare ice to soft snow dust. At the col we turned to the right. Somewhere near here was Sönghellir, the cave where Bárðr, in his first days ashore, had heard echoes that he knew were dwarf-talk and where he and his men held all their councils. Even today you can supposedly see ancient inscriptions scratched in the walls, but we had no time to look for the cave.

Jon was raving about the light, zigzagging back and forth on his skis as he photographed everything in sight. Older, wiser, and feebler, I conserved my strength in a steady plod. For about fifteen minutes, Snæfellsjökull cleared off completely, and we could see the spiky, remote tower of the summit. Then the cloud cap returned, and as the hours crept by, it darkened and spread.

I had been sweating in my Gore-Tex suit, and when we stopped at 12:30 P.M. for a dispirited lunch in the snow, I got chilled right away. We guessed we were halfway up. The wind was sharper here, the temperature distinctly lower, and the cloud cap was descending to meet us. I took a quick compass bearing on Stapafell, behind and below us to the southeast. We swigged from our slushy water bottles and started on.

Soon we were in a complete whiteout. Route-finding was mindless—just head upward. By far the inferior skier, I switched to crampons, while Jon glided along on his alpine-touring skis. Still cold, I pulled my balaclava down over my face and put on my down jacket, until I was wearing everything I owned. Ages passed with no change in the tangible universe. My glasses fogged up; Jon became a yellow-suited blur ahead of me, an automaton working out on the same tedious white treadmill that I was.

I began to lose a certain perspective. The precise identity of the yellow automaton became a vague, academic question, but I spent a good deal of thought trying to gauge whether I could close the jacket snap under my chin with my mittens on or would have to take them off. And in either case, while I continued to move, or only by coming to a stop? With my ski poles dangling from my wrists, or disengaged? I spent an equal effort trying to calculate the logistics of taking a leak, an inquiry that was muddled by having to decide whether I needed to. A tune I had not heard since third grade played 117 times straight on what seemed to be a xylophone.

I was jolted out of my funk when I stuck my left leg up to the knee in a hole. "Jon!" I shouted over the wind. "Crevasses!" I drew a line with a mitten across my knee. Thereafter, Jon performed a diligent charade of poking with his poles at faint depressions, but I knew that he figured there was no way he'd fall in with 180-centimeter boards on his feet.

It was getting very rough out, and I was getting very tired. The wind, which struck us from the left and front, had increased to at least fifty miles

25

an hour, and the temperature was about ten degrees. It was after 2:30 P.M., and I was beginning to worry about getting down before dark. I complained to Jon about the situation. "It can't be far," he said. We resumed the ordeal.

I started to feel sorry for myself. It wasn't my fault that Jon had been born on skis, while I had first strapped the things on only in my thirties. It was his sheer good luck that he was eleven years younger than I, still at an age when even NBA players could cut the mustard. Where was the respect due my vast funds of judgment and experience? After all, when he had been a young upstart setting his eye on the great ranges, I had taught him— what?—fifteen percent of what he knew?

I was tired, cold, depressed, and edgy. "Jon, look," I said. "I've about had it. I'm ready to go down." He stopped and turned. He looked like a berserker, with rime in his beard and a wild glint in his eye. "Ten more minutes, Dave, then we'll bag it."

We clumped on. Through my fogged-up lenses, the world was a tedious smear of gray. Suddenly Jon lost his cool. "There it is!" he yelled. "It's the summit!"

"Where?" I could see nothing.

"Right in front of us! We're there!"

I wiped my glasses with my thumbs and saw a hint of black rock and blue rime. Jon was tearing off his skis and putting on crampons. We got out our ice axes. All at once I was full of new energy. I had never come so close to giving up on a mountain while still having a chance for the summit. We circled the 100-foot tower to attack its north ridge. My God, what fun it was to climb again, to kick crampon points into ice and claw away with the axe! How perfect that the only technical bit was the last! We galumphed our way up the final ten feet and sprawled joyously in the nothingness. It was 3:15 P.M.

THE DESCENT WAS EERIE, A BLIND STAGGER ruled by the compass. One of us would stare at the jiggling needle while the other tried to walk in a straight line. It was astonishing how naturally we proceeded in circles when we forgot to consult our magnetic guide. Jon skied in a knee-wearying snowplow while I stumped down in my crampons. It was whiteout all the way, and only at the end, when we could hear the sea crashing on the invisible shore and nearly bumped our noses on Stapafell, did we know that our compass work had brought us straight to our starting point.

We threw our gear into the Land Cruiser, turned on the engine, and powered up the heater. With Jon at the wheel, we drove a hundred yards and plowed to a halt in a deep drift. I got out and started digging with our plastic avalanche shovel. After ten minutes, Jon could drive another ten feet. I postholed down the road, trying to see how far the drift stretched. At fifty yards, it showed no sign of shallowing out.

It was late and dim, and the wind was bitter. How long would it take to shovel to the next drivable roadway? Hours? Days? Our marooned Land Cruiser was costing us $200 per diem. They were tapping the kegs at Gaukur á Stöng; the future Miss Reykjavík was combing her hair. Instead of celebrating, would we have to hike to a farmstead, sleep on the floor with a family who spoke no English, and wait for the apocryphal snowplow?

Suddenly we heard a whine from the east; looking up, we saw headlights. A Land Rover with chains was gunning its way through the yards of deep drift, straight for us—the first vehicle besides our own to force this stretch of road in the last twenty-four hours. Two tough Icelanders jumped out and put their shoulders to our rear door. Our wheels shuddered and caught, and we surged forward. The plowed trough flew in our wake.

From his cave on the glacier, Bárðr raised his two-pronged staff in benediction. If asked back in Reykjavík, I would swear that I had seen it with my very eyes.

FIRST DOWN THE TEKEZE

T hings were looking grim on the Tekeze. It was 100 degrees in the shade; the only doctor on our trip was out of his mind with fever; the anopheles mosquitoes that cause malaria were biting my ankles, while the sand flies that carry leishmaniasis were nestling in my ears; crocodiles had begun charging our rafts; it was at least a five-day walk to the nearest road, assuming we could find natives willing to guide us; at the moment, however, the solemn-looking men wading the river to check us out were brandishing AK-47s.

And to top it all off, a techno-weenie named Kevin was leaning over my shoulder, reading my e-mail.

The Tekeze River (pronounced Talk-ah-zay), which rises in the highlands of northern Ethiopia and flows northwest into the Sudan, is one of the three most important tributaries of the Nile. Midway through its upper course, as it carves a long bend around the Simien Mountains, the Tekeze flows through the deepest canyon in Africa, 7,000 feet beneath the surrounding plateaus. Remarkably, by 1996 no one had ever boated the Tekeze, nor had anyone, as far as we could ascertain, even attempted such a journey.

Our first three days on the Tekeze had passed in a lazy, floating trance. Troops of Gelada baboons, bright red splotches on chest and rump, ran barking up the hillsides away from our boats. Verraux eagle owls and hammerkop water birds stared gloomily from dead branches. Colonies of yellow weavers flitted in and out of softball-sized nests that hung from willow branches over the river. We camped on lordly sandbars, stretching our blue tents up and down the beach. The cool morning hours, before the sun found us, were the best of the day, with shadows angling the canyon and the air full of birdsong. But the stretch from eleven to four o'clock was deadly, an ordeal by iron heat; we poured plastic buckets full of river water over ourselves, but dried out in minutes. By evening it had begun to cool off again, but with dusk black hordes of insects gathered to buzz and bite and crawl.

Then George Fuller, our expedition doctor, suddenly fell ill. He was up all through the night vomiting; by morning he could barely walk. We loaded him on a raft and headed downstream, but at lunch, his temperature had risen frighteningly over 105 degrees Fahrenheit and he was shaking uncontrollably. We called it a day and set up camp on the nearest sandbar.

Before the trip, George—a melancholic pessimist by temperament—had had serious premonitions about the Tekeze. Two or three times he had backed out, only to sign on again a week later. Now he was too delirious to offer a coherent guess as to what was wrong.

We had a satellite phone. Just conceivably, we might be able to call for a helicopter rescue. Two of George's oldest friends sat beside him and asked, "George, do you want to be flown out? We can try to do it."

Still trembling, his eyes closed, George mumbled, "No. It'll pass." Then he reached for the plastic bucket and threw up again.

TWENTY-THREE YEARS EARLIER, a small crew of American river rats had descended on Ethiopia, looking for new worlds to conquer. With the pluck of true pioneers, they blazed the first descents of three great streams, the Awash, the Omo, and the Baro. But they paid a heavy price: one rafter drowned on the first attempt on the Baro, another on a disastrous assault on the Blue Nile.

Chastened by their losses but still hungry for first descents, these maverick idealists incorporated their passion as an adventure travel company called Sobek, named after the Egyptian crocodile god. During the next two decades, Sobek guides made the first descents of more great rivers worldwide than all their international rivals put together.

The Tekeze had been high on Sobek's list, but in 1974, before the rafters could get to the river, a fierce civil war seized the northern half of Ethiopia, rendering the countryside far too dangerous for *faranji* (foreigners, in Amharic) to visit. The war ended in 1991, but it took five years for a Tekeze expedition to coalesce.

When it did, it was thanks to the scheming of Richard Bangs. Now forty-six years old, tall, soft-spoken, endlessly imaginative, Richard had put on a few pounds and lost a few hairs since the Omo. In the early days, the impecunious Sobek guides had grabbed their boats, a few dry bags, three weeks' worth of food, and rowed off into the unknown. But in September 1996, our Tekeze expedition comprised not only eight expert rafters, but an Ethiopian interpreter, a film crew of eight, and a squad of five of us entrusted with sending nightly texts, photos, and audio and video bites via satellite phone to a brand-new site on the World Wide Web.

Ours was thus a postmodern expedition with a vengeance. In Richard's mind, a twenty-two–person media circus bombing down an unknown river was not a necessary evil, but rather a fine and altruistic way of bringing the wilderness to an audience far larger than the gaggles of affluent pilgrims who might actually betake themselves to Ethiopia.

And Richard had another idea up his sleeve: to concoct the Tekeze trip as a reunion of those visionary river rats who had first landed in Ethiopia in 1973. Over the years, they had gone their separate ways, drifting into careers that left them rusty behind the oars. But so alluring was Richard's siren song that in the end, five of the six surviving Sobek pioneers gathered at the headwaters of the Tekeze.

Richard had convinced the film crew, from Turner Original Productions, to finance most of the trip as they built a movie around the reunion of this Gang of Five. Then, in March 1996, Richard had been plucked away from Sobek by the richest man in America, Microsoft's Bill Gates. Richard's charge was to invent an online adventure magazine. Mungo Park, as Richard cryptically named the enterprise (after the doomed Scottish discoverer of the Niger River), instantly became, with our "Expedition Ethiopia," one of the sexiest sites on the Web.

This electronic tour de force was no easy stunt. Beforehand we had been so leery that we met at Microsoft to discuss how we might fake our way through the potential fiasco we nicknamed "the seventeen-day blackout." But on the river the wizardry worked, enabling viewers around the world to read about, see, and even hear our adventure each day only hours after it unfolded.

Over the years, Richard had become a formidable promoter of bagatelles such as ours. Now, online, there was a certain pressure to match our dispatches to Richard's predeparture hype: the Terrible Tekeze, he had called it, the World's Last Great First.

I HAD SIGNED ON FOR SEVERAL REASONS. In 1983, Richard had talked me into joining another first-descent-cum-film, on the Tua River in New Guinea. The crew of BBC cinéastes who joined the Sobek guides got so freaked out by the wilderness that, rather than camp out with us, they commuted daily by helicopter from a highland hotel. This did serious violence to the integrity of our journey. The river had its say, too, thrice flipping our rafts before we pulled out in the face of unrunnable Class VI rapids.

Yet when all was said and done, the New Guinea trip had been a memorable adventure. Thirteen years later, I was ready for another plunge into aqua incognita, and I had always longed to visit Ethiopia. In 1983, Richard had said, "Don't worry, David, any rapids you don't like the looks of, you can walk around"—a baldfaced lie, in the event. This time, after an airplane scout of the Tekeze in 1995, Richard declared, "It looks a lot like the Colorado, very straightforward. Maybe big rapids, but nothing too weird."

Although this would be my fourth bout of writing "in real time" for the World Wide Web, I remained a skeptic about the medium—not to mention an electronic nincompoop. My home office sported neither fax machine nor e-mail, and to see my own stories online I had to go to a nearby cyber cafe. A writerly qualm continued to nag me: were "sites" such as Mungo Park destined by their very nature to remain superficial and ephemeral?

During the first three days on the Tekeze, we had seen not a single *tukul*, or thatched hut, along the river. Only a few natives, goggling in disbelief as they tended their herds, had witnessed our passage. These, we knew, were Amhara, Emperor Haile Selassie's people, Christians who have dominated modern Ethiopian history and government (Amharic is the country's official language).

About these backcountry Amhara, we knew very little. In my pre-trip research, I had come across a favorite Amhara chant that gave me pause:

Kill a man! Kill a man! It is good to kill a man!
One who has not killed a man moves around sleepily.

The only consistent reports of human presence on the Tekeze that I had been able to dig up had to do with *shiftas*—bandits who waylaid, robbed, and murdered passing travelers. As late as the 1950s, *shiftas* caught at their trade were hanged from trees on the spot after summary trials.

Now, on our fourth morning, as we stayed put and waited for George Fuller's fever to abate, we had our first visitors—fit-looking young men wading the river, AK-47s slung over their shoulders. As they walked warily toward camp, Daniel Mehari, our Ethiopian interpreter, greeted them in Amharic. We had pondered but rejected the option of taking armed guards with us on the river; we had not a single firearm among us. Now, after a parley shouted across fifty feet of no-man's land, Daniel reported that some locals had seen us pull into camp the afternoon before. Rather than approach, they had sent runners to alert their best warriors, who were sent to check us out and attack if they had any doubts.

These Amhara, it turned out, thought at first that *we* were *shiftas*, or at least enemies of some kind sent to punish them. Only a few years before, their remote villages had seen bloodbaths, as these rebels, sympathetic to the Tigrean guerrillas who ultimately toppled Mengistu's brutal dictatorship, fought government troops. The AK-47s were the spoils of war.

Once they were convinced we were harmless, the numbers of visitors swelled through the day until nearly a hundred men and boys (though not a single woman) stood staring at our mysterious possessions. A fiberglass kayak was far more interesting than a laptop computer or a movie camera, but our cook stove was the most dazzling artifact of all. On other Ethiopian rivers, veterans Jim Slade, John Yost, and Bart Henderson had seen, from season to season, unacculturated natives turn into beggars and petty thieves. Now they urged us to keep an eye on our belongings, told us not to give the locals any gifts, and through Daniel, kept shooing the visitors away from our goodies. This seemed to me churlish and capitalistic, but I kept my peace.

Meanwhile Richard, the born schmoozer, got the men clapping and singing some of their traditional songs—most of which had to do with the Tekeze. One translated as:

Our village is Abia,
Our river is Tekeze;
We can shout and jump
And nothing will happen to us.

Another seemed to have a Christian fundamentalist slant:

Someone who doesn't see the Tekeze
Is very unlucky.
You will be born again
If you bathe in the Tekeze.

Yet for all the apparent friendliness wafting across the sandbar, these men had a hard time comprehending our mission. Over and over, they asked Daniel the three basic questions we would hear all the way down the river: Where did you come from? Where are you going? Why are you doing this?

They were aghast that we had chosen to sleep on the sandbar. Why don't you come stay in our village, they asked Daniel. It turned out, however, that their village was a seven-hour walk away. The warriors had hiked all night to intercept us.

In the withering heat of midday, our stationary plight began to feel oppressive. Though the natives showed not the slightest inclination to take anything of ours, we began to taste the strain of simply being stared at for hour after hour by strangers with whom we could not exchange a word. All of us itched to get back in the boats, and when we found that George's temperature had dropped to ninety-nine degrees, we decided to depart.

There was something Conradian about our dilemma. This tropical wilderness into which we had plunged had its aching beauty—savage basalt precipices swallowed in relentless green, tributary waterfalls threading and spilling toward the river—but it was too alien for us truly to absorb. Our sanity depended on staying in motion, achieving the journey that gave logic to our trespass.

AS A MAJOR TRIBUTARY OF THE NILE, the Tekeze, one might think, should loom large in history and myth. Yet as I had researched the region before heading to Ethiopia, the river seemed to disappear into a blank on the map. The only Ethiopian road that crosses the river is a highway from Axum to Gondar built by the Italians in the 1930s. I could find no hint of any journey either by natives or Europeans along the 250 miles that separate this road from the Tekeze's headwaters. We began to wonder, as the expedition gathered steam, whether the wilderness into which we were about to plunge had had laid upon it the dark curse of an immemorial badlands, a place to be shunned by traveler and native alike.

Having assembled in Addis Ababa, our entourage of twenty-two chartered a creaky Korean War-vintage Buffalo and flew, with our tons of cargo, to Lalibela. This genial town of some 10,000 souls, perched at 8,500 feet on a green slope beneath stern mesas, is one of the most astounding holy cities in the world, thanks to its eleven rock-hewn churches.

By a process still little understood, Christianity came to Abyssinia (northern Ethiopia) in the fourth century A.D. There it took root, spreading across the country through the Middle Ages but losing all contact with the mother church in Rome. A bizarre and indigenous Christianity flourished in the land, woven about the Monophysite heresy, the doctrine that

Christ had only a divine, not a human nature. We spent two rapt days touring the churches of Lalibela, which, carved in the twelfth century out of basalt bedrock with chisel and hammer, stand as the eeriest cynosures in Ethiopia of that obscure faith.

On our last evening in Lalibela, I had a drink with a local guide and the hotel manager. After a couple of beers, the guide said gravely, "Every year, if it rains too much, someone dies in the Tekeze."

We ordered another beer. "Do the people here understand why we want to go down the river?" I asked. The manager smiled quizzically and said, "I don't think so. I don't even understand myself."

On September 8, with a mob of hired porters, we hiked thirteen miles west from Lalibela to the rim of the Tekeze gorge. Here, on his reconnaissance the year before, after many false leads, Richard had found the only reasonable put-in on the whole river. We skirted fields of corn and young green *tef*, the staple grain of Ethiopians. The hills blazed with patches of the yellow daisy called maskal.

At the rim, sheer basalt cliffs shelved into fierce tangles of thorn and brush. On a clever path, we wound 1,100 feet down through the precipices to a vast gravel bar on the river. As we started down, herders on the rim hooted wild birdcalls that were answered by calls from the river. Even our mob of porters was unequal to the task of hauling all our baggage to the put-in. By late afternoon, a huge Russian MI-8 helicopter had made three landings on the gravel bar, delivering the heaviest and most delicate gear, including six sturdy eighteen-foot yellow rafts.

John Yost, cofounder of Sobek, who would prove to be the group's resident curmudgeon, surveyed our 8,000-pound mound of gear with dismay. "On the Baro, we only had five black bags," he commented. "Maybe one percent of what we've got here.

"It's not just overkill," Yost nattered on. "It's a serious safety issue. When a boat's overloaded, in high water it's very hard to navigate. Your momentum builds up, and it's hard to change direction. And if we have to portage, forget it! We'd have to hire a whole village as porters."

High water had been the guides' chief worry, after news had come of record rains elsewhere in Ethiopia. To our shock, however, the Tekeze—though its chocolate flood surged hard through the gorge—was alarmingly low. In Ethiopia, during the dry season (mid-September through May), the big rivers dwindle to trickles; some, like the Awash, peter out in desert sands. During the rainy season, the rivers are too high to run and impossible to approach. Our party's trick had been to nail the transition from rainy season to dry just right. Now, looking at the shallow river, the guides worried about hitting rocks and bottoming out. "I wouldn't want to be here a week later," muttered "the General," Jim Slade, Sobek's senior guide and the official expedition leader.

The next day we climbed into our boats and set off. Everybody hollered and cheered, for indeed, that moment of launching on an unknown river is pure cathartic release. But ours was a bad start: unaccustomed to the new boats, the rowers banged a few walls in the first mile and broke two oars.

One reason to expect big rapids was the simple gradient of the Tekeze, which averages twelve feet a mile over the 220 miles between our put-in and the take-out bridge. This is fifty percent steeper than the gradient of the Colorado in the Grand Canyon, with its famous rapids such as Lava Falls and Hermit.

But for three days we glided through nothing bigger than Class II—child's play for the experts manning our oars. And though the river dropped each day as the remorseless sun drained its flood, each tiny tributary we passed added current, until we realized we had more than enough water to make our run.

A classic first descent—think of John Wesley Powell's plunge down the Colorado in 1869—unfolds in a series of hair-breadth escapes, fatal rapids brilliantly outfoxed, with starvation threatening at every bend. Our descent of the Tekeze seemed instead to go like clockwork.

Then we ran into the crocodiles.

Though George Fuller had predicted that, thanks to the river's nearly evaporating at the end of the dry season, there would be not a single crocodile on the Tekeze, we saw our first reptilian monster in a shallow eddy near the right bank. Each day thereafter, the crocs got bigger, more numerous, and more aggressive. It took me a while to get the knack of spotting them, as they lurked a few feet off shore, only bug eyes and scaley upper head above water, but Jim Slade, in our lead boat, routinely racked up counts of thirty a day—more than any of the Sobek veterans had ever seen on a river.

On other Ethiopian streams, the guides had had boats bitten by crocs. Sure enough, by our fifth day, the occasional croc was charging a boat. Our response was to throw baseball-sized rocks (which we loaded up every morning) at the beasts. A week down the river, Bart Henderson drily mentioned that his boat had just dealt with our first "four-rock croc."

Beguiled by the nomenclature, I asked, "Is that some kind of subjective measure of the—"

"No," Bart interrupted. "It took four rocks to scare the bugger off."

The next day, I saw John Yost suddenly stand in the bow of his boat and swing an oar viciously overhead, slamming the water just in front of an overcurious croc. Later, another feisty reptile swam straight at Richard's boat, unfazed by the stones plunking near him, and surfaced with a thump under Richard's feet, before reappearing on the other side of the boat. Toward the end of our journey, with a herky-jerky delivery reminiscent of Luis Tiant's, Yost scored a bull's eye on a croc head from fifty feet—a Sobek first.

Despite these cheap thrills, no boat suffered a croc bite. Filmmakers John Armstrong and Eric Magneson, however, got badly spooked paddling their kayaks, and chose to pull out and ride atop rafts through the more suspect channels.

Each night in camp, the five of us reporting online set up our high-tech caravanserai under a huge tarp columned on boat oars: folding card tables and stools, five laptops, a satellite phone, power strips and cords galore, the whole thing run by a gasoline-powered generator. Jonathan Chester, an Aussie who had once climbed 8,000-meter Broad Peak in the Karakoram, downloaded dozens of digital photos he had shot during the day on extravagantly valuable cameras. Steve Lee turned audio tapes (of, say, a native playing a bamboo flute) and video snippets (of a boat bouncing through whitewater) into bytes. Richard Bangs and I typed away, turning the day's events into you-are-there prose. And Kevin Twidle, the techno-whiz from London, put all our "files" into .TXT and JPEG, set up a bizarre radioactive contraption with which he fixed a geosynchronous satellite hovering over the Indian Ocean, pushed the requisite buttons, and sent the whole mess at the speed of light to the Microsoft office in Redmond, Washington.

Thanks to the sat phone, we could call up our editors in Redmond and bitch about how they had mangled our prose or cropped our photos. And we sent and received a nightly flurry of e-mail messages. It was amusing to watch how outback-hardened Sobek guides, used to disappearing from the known world for a month at a time, lined up outside our tent to plead for 'puter time so they could peck out their "Honey, I'm doing fine" missives to wives and girlfriends.

Meanwhile, the film crew did their own thing. The team of eight, led by director Bill Anderson, were no BBC wimps: every one an experienced outdoorsman ecstatic at floating a virgin river, they went about their footage-mongering with slick professionalism. Yet making a movie is always a tedious business. Again and again we had to loll about while Bill set up some snippet of filmic narrative: a raft crashing through the biggest water we could find as we tried to make the rapids look hairier than they were, Richard hunkered by the shore as he "spontaneously" reminisced about the Omo and the Awash.

For the five veterans, all in their forties or early fifties, the Tekeze was not only a reunion but also a comeback—one last first descent to tuck under the expanding belts of their encroaching middle age. And Bill Anderson had scripted his film around this heartwarming "story." So he spent long hours crafting buddy-reunion vignettes: the guys passing a bottle of rum as they sat by a gratuitous bonfire in the eighty-degree dusk, all five poring over the map as they pretended to wonder where we were.

The only trouble was, you could hardly have found five old pals less sentimental about hooking up together once more. Richard Bangs and John Yost had worked in the same Sobek office for so long that each was weary to the bone of the other's foibles. Yost, a purist so ascetic he doesn't allow his kids to watch TV, was appalled by the largess and artificiality of our *voyage médiatique*. He was so uninterested in being part of the film that the only time the cameras could trap him was while he baked bread in huge pots over the fire.

Only Richard and Jim Slade had the knack of performing on camera, and both were so comfortable with that role, you would have thought they were actors hired to impersonate themselves. Bart Henderson, son of Mormon pioneers from Utah, had the chiseled good looks and stoic calm of his forebears, but also, unfortunately, their laconic reluctance to utter more than a wry monosyllable here and there. And George Fuller—even a healthy George Fuller—was an unfilmable eccentric, given to puttering about the beach looking for exotic bugs while he mumbled to himself. Bill Anderson strove time and again to capture some arcane pronouncement from his lips, but it became clear that any movie footage of our reclusive doctor would require subtitles.

So we careened down the Tekeze, filming by day and sending reports to the Web by night. It was hard work not only running a river but also recording every deed and mishap as we went, and there was no getting around the fact that this documentary extravaganza profoundly altered our adventure. I brooded on the pros and cons of what we were doing for days, and when my maunderings grew too claustrophobic, cornered Richard (the only other person on the trip reflective enough to be accused of being an intellectual) to thrash out my qualms.

It was all too easy to pinpoint what we lost by hitching our star to the cinema and the Internet. We began in a sense to live at secondhand: the filmmakers, for instance, got more excited about viewing the day's video-taped croc footage than viewing the crocs themselves. I found myself composing paragraphs in my head within minutes after some startling event had smacked me silly. On Alaskan mountaineering expeditions in my youth, an absolute separation of "in" from "out" had cast its spell on me and my cronies: for forty-two days on the Tokositna Glacier, the rest of the world had ceased to exist, and the four of us became a colony of monks dedicated to the rites of piton and ice axe.

Here on the Tekeze, we were never fully "in," not with the guides wringing their calloused hands over their loved ones' neglecting a day of e-mail murmurings, not with our sat-phone queries to techies in Redmond about which program to use to condense our digital snapshots. Being connected to the outside world also provided a huge, though not always comfortable, safety net, offering us the option, when his temperature rose above 105 degrees, of helicoptering George Fuller out. On an old-fashioned expedition, George's plight might have wrecked the trip, posing a genuine dilemma of life-and-death.

Richard, however, was eloquent in defense of our high-tech voyaging. "I think," he said one morning as we sat on a rock slab above camp, "that in the future we're going to see more and more vicarious exploration. There'll be communities of armchair travelers who care passionately about a river in Ethiopia without ever hoping to come here. Do you know about the Franklin River in Tasmania?"

I shook my head.

"One guy named Bob Brown launched a crusade to save it from the usual mad dam-builders. He got thrown in jail for lying in front of the bulldozers, then he got elected to the Australian parliament on the Green Party ticket the day after he got out of jail. What made it all gather steam was this single idyllic photo Brown used in ads and slide shows. That photo saved the river." Richard tossed a stone idly. "You know that an Italian company has already offered to build a dam on the Tekeze?

"In a curious way," he went on, "I think sharing our expedition with all the people who call up Mungo Park on the Web or watch the Turner film next July is less selfish than just making the first descent of the Tekeze for ourselves. Yes, the kind of writing that you and I are doing can be a little raw, but it has an honesty and immediacy that an article you write after you get back home never does."

I found myself growing irritated with my old friend's clever rationalizations. Count on a postmodern explorer to come up with a postmodern apologia that would have brought a chuckle to the gullet of Eco or Derrida. In weak moments on the Tekeze, I even found myself wondering whether Richard might be right.

Every day locals came to stare at us, gradually getting up the nerve to approach and talk with Daniel Mehari. Yet not once did we see a single thatched *tukul* along the banks. At first we assumed it was the crocodiles that scared the natives away. Indeed, we heard many a dolorous tale of croc death, such as the one related in a matter-of-fact tone by a young man whose brother had recently perished when he crossed the Tekeze to fetch his fiancée from her family's village. Said another informant, "When a crocodile eats you, he eats every part except the soles of the feet."

But it was George Fuller who, lying on his Victorian bier across the gunwales of his raft, lapsed out of his fever long enough to nail the right explanation. "Malaria," he croaked. "It's malaria."

Sure enough, the next day a native explained that his people could live with the crocodiles, but had learned that to inhabit the banks of the Tekeze was to invite certain death from the shaking sickness. I found that revelation astounding, as I imagined the generations of plague and sorrow that had taught the people so dire a lesson. As we pushed farther north, we talked to many locals whose villages, perched on high mesas, were waterless for seven months each year during the dry season. Every day women with large jars on their heads hiked as much as 2,000 feet down to the Tekeze and back just to fetch the life-sustaining water.

On the fifth day, we passed out of the gloomy basalt, glided through several quick eons of limestone, and emerged in a grandiose defile of sandstone. All the guides swore the landscape reminded them of the Grand Canyon. The lip of the Simien plateau, out of sight beyond nearer buttes and fins, was 7,000 feet above us. We had entered the deepest canyon in Africa.

And for the first time we were in Agow country. The difference was manifest: these staring villagers lacked the aquiline profiles of the Amhara, their skin was darker, their hair curlier. Perhaps half of them spoke a rudimentary Amharic, so Daniel, who knew no Agow, could comprehend their discourse.

Impoverished herders of goats, sheep, and cattle, these pastoralists are sneered at by the proud and haughty Amhara who live on the healthful Simien plateau far above the river. Their existence in the Tekeze gorge is so marginal that not only are the Agow smaller of stature than the Amhara, but so are their oxen.

Given the linguistic and cultural gulfs between these men and Daniel (let alone the rest of us), only the most hard-won glimmerings emerged from our brief conversations. Like the Amhara upriver, the Agow were stunned to see us, and afraid at first that we meant harm. Reassured that we came in peace, they found our exploit unfathomable. A recurrent misunderstanding fascinated me: again and again the locals thought we had brought our yellow boats to cross the river, not to float down it. In general, they had little knowledge of the Tekeze very far up- or downstream. One sympathetic young man named Teklat Kebede had hiked two hours to confirm the rumor of our passage; certain that we must be starving, he offered to find a friend who could sell us a goat to slaughter. (We gave him a salami-and-cheese sandwich, which he ate with polite suspicion.) Teklat had lived his whole life between the first small tributary upstream and the first down-stream, a range of perhaps seven miles.

Gradually we realized we were seeing a people on the very edge of survival, for here, where the Tekeze swung east toward Tigre, not a drop of rain had fallen during this year's rainy season. Twice we saw men furrowing the river bank with crude plows dragged by yoked oxen, in a desperate attempt to plant corn or sorghum in sand sprinkled with run-off alluvium from the highlands many miles away, where it had rained. Once several unmarried young men asked if they could climb aboard our boats and go with us—anywhere, out of the hopeless lives they led here on the margin of famine.

Yet for three days we drifted through a landscape of paradise. Scores of side canyons beckoned on either side—slots, V-shaped chutes, broad tributary gorges, twisted and polished with all the witchery sandstone concocts. We took a few hours away from our downriver march to hike three of these hidden corridors, dazzled by the scenic prodigies we were the first westerners ever to see.

We finally scared up some Class III rapids, which the filmmakers milked for every splash and wallow they could. George's fever waned, until he was once again puttering and mumbling like his old self. Though our freeze-dried glops were as bland and boring as camp food gets, there was never any risk we'd run out.

If there was one ongoing disappointment for me, it was the scarcity of solitude on the Tekeze. Some of my happiest moments came during rare lulls when I fled the group and hiked alone up side valleys, rousting a furious mob of baboons here, topping a ridge there to gaze across the limitless badlands stretching toward Tigre.

Day by day, the film crew grew increasingly anxious as no killer rapids impeded our progress. One night they held an earnest pow-wow about how to save the movie if the Tekeze turned into a nautical piece of cake. There was talk of trucking our four tons of gear from the take-out hundreds of miles down to the Awash, just to bounce through some good rapids the veterans had first conquered twenty-three years ago—not as fake Tekeze footage, but as a further reuniting of the old gang.

Some of the younger, fitter Sobek guides on our trip were also disappointed at the lack of whitewater challenge. An oddly Puritan mood hovered over our team, as if we were somehow cheating to run a river bereft of waterfalls and keepers. As a novice boater, I was quite content not to ride a raft in danger of turning over. I was heartened by a remark from Bart Henderson, who runs a rafting company in Alaska and who had survived his share of flips and flounders: "For me nowadays, a big rapid is just an obstacle." Bart went on to characterize a certain kind of client who feels gypped if he doesn't taste near-death: "'Scare me till I cum, but don't let me get hurt.'"

As each day unfurled, and the trip acquired the momentum of a genuine voyage, it began to dawn on me what a remarkable wilderness we had stumbled into. The sheer variety of birdlife was one measure of it: vultures wheeling on tall thermals, Egyptian geese cruising the shallows, a Goliath heron sawing the air above our boats. Though the heat and the bugs made us frantic, there were cool, misty mornings and sudden drenching downpours to alleviate the scene. Gigantic pinnacles of sandstone, never touched by human hand, burst into view as we rounded bends on the river. The crocodiles eyed us in beady appraisal.

And we found, here in the sandstone canyon, all kinds of signs of vanished human visitors, though how old these vestiges were, we had no way of guessing. One horizontal panel of carved petroglyphs abounded in parallelograms, stars, and what looked like a Maltese cross. A circle of stones with names engraved inside spoke perhaps of the magic of the harvest. Near a rare spring seeping from the canyon wall, we found many dwellings made of dry-laid slabs of slate: the largest, some locals told us, was a Christian chancel to which the *tabot*—the replica of the Ark of the Covenant, the box that once held Moses's tablets—was brought each year at Easter from a church many miles away. High above this wayside shrine, scrambling alone, I found a chilling panel of thin-lined petroglyphs scratched on orange slate: humans hung upside down, crisscrossed torsos surmounted by upside-down heads, fierce visages caught in the O-mouthed terror of mid-scream.

Only once during our whole expedition did we visit a village. It was named Meda, we learned—"the flat place," to distinguish it from the crags and peaks surrounding. Two thousand feet above one of the most barren stretches of the Tekeze, five miles to the west, it showed as a tiny circle on our satellite-surveyed map.

We took a layover day to hike to Meda. A shepherd in a distant field, agog and nervous as we walked up, dropped his chores to guide us past cornfields and pepper gardens to the town of some 100 *tukuls*. A wild buzz of gossip preceded the advent of these strange *faranji*. We were not the first whites these remote villagers had seen—AID workers had contacted them during the terrible famine of the 1980s—but we were the first whites ever to walk through Meda.

For four hours we strode the lanes, admiring conical *tukuls* topped with straw "penthouses," unlike any dwellings the Sobek veterans had seen elsewhere in Ethiopia. Richard teasingly offered the village priest a million birr to see the *tabot*, but the cleric disdainfully refused. We were invited into a house to eat roasted corn and drink coffee served in filthy cups. Never had I been treated more hospitably by strangers, all of whom seemed overjoyed by our visit.

Yet within an hour of our arrival, a very sick man of about forty—a hero of the recent civil war—died, and only three hours after that, he was buried. Somehow the pleasure our arrival brought the people could coexist with the procession of grief and mourning that now ensued—and which, to his great surprise, Bill Anderson was allowed to film.

Of all the things we saw on the Tekeze, to my mind the most stunning was a hermitage the Agow told us was called Hassena. Mike Speaks, our eagle-eyed naturalist and crackerjack guide from Alabama, spotted it high on the right-bank cliff. We hiked up to the haunting site.

Hassena amounted to a small collection of cliff dwellings fronted with thatch screens. Homely domestic furnishings—a stool, a gourd full of grain, a flywhisk—lay about the dirt floors. But on the cave walls, charcoal inscriptions spoke of some higher truth. Daniel recognized the words as Ge'ez—the ancient ecclesiastical language that only priests in Ethiopia can read today. One inscription stood beside a winged, Byzantine-looking cherub sketched in charcoal. After the expedition, I sent photos of the writing to one of the few scholars in the United States who can read Ge'ez. He told me the walls were full of names, presumably of pilgrims who had come to Hassena. But there was also a kind of poem:

> *Peace be to you, Debre Abay,*
> *Peace be to you,*
> *The place where the righteous go to pray.*

Debre means church, and Abay is the name of the Blue Nile. What the verse means to the initiated lies beyond my grasp.

Some of the structures at Hassena looked like walled-up tombs, and we found one skeleton laid in a niche in the cliff. Back down on the river, two Agow youths told us that the dead were indeed pilgrims who had come to the hermitage to be healed, but who had perished in this holy spot. And they told us that all during our visit the monk who lived there, invisible to us, had watched our doings.

The days drifted past with the river. We floated out of the sandstone, into a somber canyon of purple and gray granite. From one high walk, we gazed at the panorama of the eastern edge of the magnificent Simien Mountains, studded with pinnacles and buttes no westerner had ever approached. There lay a landscape of ambition, tempting us to another journey.

On our eighteenth morning, only a few miles from the take-out bridge, we packed the rafts for the last time. Worn out by the sheer toil of the trip, all of us looked forward to the expedition's end. Yet as I put on my life jacket, I felt a pang of loss.

The first time I had ever trod a place on the earth's surface where no one had been before had come at age twenty, on Mount McKinley. What luck it was, more than three decades later, to be able to boat a river no one had ever before run. The 220-mile voyage we were about to complete was the longest I had ever made unaided by a motor vehicle.

The Tekeze had been easier than any of the Sobek veterans had expected, but I could see in their smiles of contentment that last morning just how gratifying it had been for George, Bart, John, Jim, and Richard to get behind the oars once more and head downstream into the unknown. They had waited twenty-three years for their crack at the Tekeze.

As for my qualms about our postmodern media circus, well. . . . A few days after I got home from Ethiopia, I went to the neighborhood cyber cafe and called up Mungo Park. For the first time I saw my own stories on the Web. I clicked on a short video Steve Lee had shot. The boat floats past a big croc on shore, who looks asleep. Suddenly the reptile spies the boat and charges toward the camera, running like a tailback across the stones, plunging into the water, and swimming hard for Steve's offending lens.

I grabbed the sleeve of the cyber clerk loitering beside my PC. "Look at this!" I babbled. "We were there!"

LECHUGUILLA
A New Mexico Marvel

During my ninth hour underground, as I scrambled up a slanting tunnel through the powdered gypsum, Rick Bridges turned to me and said, "You know, this whole area was just discovered Tuesday."

Slow-brained with fatigue, I mumbled an acknowledgment. It was only later, as I kneaded my aching thighs during a rest stop, that Bridges' remark struck home. My God, I thought, how often does anyone have such an experience? In an age when every square foot of the Earth's surface has been mapped and photographed, how incredible to walk through a place no one knew existed before last Tuesday!

I was 1,000 feet deep inside Lechuguilla Cave in southern New Mexico, a neophyte privileged to join some of America's best cavers as they explored the most exciting underground labyrinth currently being "pushed" anywhere in the United States. I felt dog tired, apprehensive, ready to turn around and head for the entrance—yet caught up in the drama of pioneering.

Caving in this country remains an unappreciated, misunderstood sport. On the eve of my trip to Lechuguilla I told a number of friends, some of them avid outdoorsmen, what I was about to do. At best, they feigned interest; several could not suppress a shuddering repugnance for a sport that seemed to them little more than crawling through mud in the dark.

The National Speleological Society has recently grown to an all-time high of more than 7,500 members. According to Rick Bridges, however, there are only one thousand to two thousand "hard-core" cavers in this country. Yet caving worldwide is now in its golden age, an era of limitless discovery and innovation analogous to the 1950s in Himalayan mountaineering, when all the highest peaks in the world, from Annapurna to Everest to K2, were conquered.

Lechuguilla Cave lies only a few miles from Carlsbad Cavern, still within Carlsbad National Park. Lechuguilla Cave has been known since at least 1914, when three locals mined it for bat guano, which they sold as fertilizer. The entrance to Carlsbad Cavern is a huge amphitheater set in a natural hollow. Lechuguilla, however, begins with a narrow, dirty shaft set in a drab hillside swathed in cacti, yucca, and the lechuguilla plant—an agave whose sharp spines are the bane of the unwary hiker. Below the ninety-foot entrance shaft, early visitors found a humdrum passage that shot off at an angle, then ended in a pile of fallen rock rubble. As late as 1971 a park naturalist concluded that the "cave is very small and somewhat disappointing."

What serious cavers live for, however, is "virgin passage," and a single fact kept bringing them back to Lechuguilla: air was continually blowing through the rubble. At other sites, such a breeze had been a reliable harbinger of a big cave below. From the 1970s on, a series of teams plied the rock pile in hard-work, no-glory digging expeditions. They had no guarantee of success—the dirt and debris could end in intransigent (if porous) bedrock, and since there were several different spots where the wind blew hard, the diggers could be working in entirely the wrong place.

On May 25, 1986, however, a trio of grubbers made the breakthrough. Rick Bridges, my guide in Lechuguilla, was one of them. The team pushed onward, finding spectacular rooms and passages, and came to a frightening vertical shaft that was clearly deep. There followed a yearlong hiatus while National Park Service (NPS) officials pondered how to manage the exploration of what had quickly become the "hottest cave in the country." Only in July 1987—a mere nine months before my visit—did the serious passage-pushing begin.

Before Lechuguilla I had ventured only into the more accessible parts of just a handful of caverns, and I had done no technical caving. One of my fears was of being "sandbagged"—dragged in over my head by seemingly nonchalant veterans who thereby let you know how tough their sport is. Over the phone Bridges had said, "Since it's your first time, we'll do a short trip, maybe twelve to sixteen hours." I allowed as how maybe ten to twelve, or even eight or six hours should be plenty for me. Bridges didn't seem to hear.

My guide turned out to be a stocky, bearded thirty-five-year-old from Boulder, Colorado. A manic energy issuing in nonstop conversation is one of Bridges' stamps. He earns his living from oil exploration work but, like most of his underground colleagues, breathes, eats, and sleeps only to get through the boring periods between cave trips.

With two young men named Scott Adams and Randy Brooks—good, solid cavers, but not in Bridges' class—my guide and I formed a four-man team. Since Scott and Randy were gung ho to see some of the deeper wonders of Lechuguilla, I sensed the sandbag swaying overhead even as we approached the entrance.

Thanks to Bridges' continuous narration, our nine-hour trip into the side passage above Manifest Destiny—the part of Lechuguilla that had been discovered only Tuesday—served as a vivid firsthand résumé of the exploratory history of the cave. Less than an hour in, we came to Boulder Falls, in a sense the "crux" of the whole cave. It is a 150-foot vertical shaft named for the tendency of cavers to dislodge large chunks of rock and send them bouncing into the void. Potentially it is a dangerous place.

As a climber, I was not perturbed at rappelling into the pit, even though for seventy feet one pirouettes in space, touching no walls. It was the climb up the rope on the way out that worried me. On rock climbs, I had jumared up ropes with the aid of a pair of mechanical devices that slide upward along a cord but grip it under a downward pull. On anything like vertical terrain, however, jumaring with a pack is exhausting. Bridges assured me he had a better system, but the last thing I wanted to do was to hit Boulder Falls on the way out and find myself too tired to haul myself up the long, fixed rope.

As we passed each quaintly named territory on my way into the bowels of Lechuguilla, I had an inkling of the effort it had taken to get there the first time, and to survey and mark the place. The names thus commanded respect: Liberty Bell, Boulder Falls, Glacier Bay, Sugarlands, the Great White Way, Deep Secrets, the Fortress of Chaos, the Western Borehole and so on.

At the end of July 1987, Lechuguilla had threatened to peter out in a nasty, narrow fissure called the Rift. The only hope for continuation lay in a ninety-foot wall that looked all but unscalable. Cavers are not usually expert rock climbers as well, but in this case two men from Colorado Springs, Art Wiggins and Don Doucette, made a brilliant and risky ascent of what they called Captain Hook's Ladder. It was the key to the puzzle;

from the top of the wall, the cave went on and on. On the second trip through, another team discovered the Overpass, a hidden shortcut by which the Lower Rift and Captain Hook's Ladder could be eliminated. Its traversal, however, nearly occasioned Lechuguilla's first fatality. Unroped above a seventy-foot drop, expedition coleader Roy Glaser slid gingerly around a huge block of rock that seemed solidly attached to the wall. As he embraced the block with both arms, hands clutching its edges, the whole thing slid a few inches—then stopped. The spot, on which a fixed rope now hangs, is aptly named Freak-Out Traverse.

At a temperature that remains in the upper sixties, Lechuguilla is a warm cave. In higher, wetter, or more northerly caves, explorers often wear wet suits. Here the outfit of choice is T-shirt, old jeans, and lightweight boots. At Bridges' urging, I also wore knee and elbow pads, and leather gloves. Every caver uses a helmet with headlamp and carries two backup sources of all-important light. In our packs we hauled food, water, and technical gear.

At times in Lechuguilla, you could walk comfortably. Much of the going, however, required scrambling, unroped climbing, chimneying, crawling, and even slithering. The intensity of the sport lies partly in the fact that you must always be on guard: stable-looking piles of fallen boulders, because they have never been weathered by the elements, are as teetery as pick-up-sticks; that small, dark shadow just beyond your next step may be a shaft plunging to unseen depths.

One of the marvels of the route in Lechuguilla is how often the whole system narrows to an unlikely hole, through which one barely fits; then the cave expands once more into vast stretches of complex passageways. During the initial exploration, teams pushing the route feared again and again that the whole thing had come to an end. At one such impasse, as a team surveyed the Deep Sea Room, convinced it was a dead end, a relatively inexperienced caver named Louise Whitehead started up a steep slope, murmuring, "Where does this go?"

"Nowhere, as far as I know," said the project coleader, turning back to his survey notes.

Whitehead clambered on. A few minutes later, she discovered a stunning chamber full of conical mounds of calcite flakes. White Christmas Tree Room, as it came to be known, was the portal to miles of passage in the Western Borehole, whose termination cavers have still not reached.

Many big caves have drab interior landscapes, but Lechuguilla, like Carlsbad, is exceptionally well "decorated." On our trip in, we passed so many prodigies of slow-forming carbonates that my mind teemed with exotic images. Along with an uncountable variety of stalactites and stalagmites, we saw odd corkscrew helictites; "soda straws" hanging in breathtaking delicacy from the ceiling, one perhaps eighteen feet long; gypsum threads, some fifteen feet long and nearly invisible, as fine as angel's hair; tiny hydromagnesite balloons, found in only four other caves in the United States; smooth pebbles called cave pearls; generous terraces of gleaming flowstone; shelves of bulbous stuff known as popcorn; bespangled crystal networks, called aragonite bushes, that look like dwarf evergreens shagged with rime; gypsum flowers and chandeliers; and a dozen other exotic mineral formations.

To all but experienced speleophiles, caves tend, I suspect, to be profoundly disturbing places. In Greek myth, mountains are bland, official landscapes, the residence of Zeus and the Muses. The underworld, however, is enigmatic, a domain of longing and terror, the haunt of Charon and Cerberus. During rest stops in Lechuguilla, I tried to analyze the feeling of utter alienness that enveloped me. The darkness is paramount. A standard exercise that old hands like to inflict on subterranean novices is to have everyone sit down and turn off his light. A few always gasp or shriek with the shock of total lightlessness.

The silence, too, is unprecedented, and I should think it would be unsettling even for experts to go into caves alone. Nor have most people stood anywhere on earth where there is a complete lack of living things— the condition of most caves beyond the entrance regions. To operate for hours without a natural horizon—something that almost never occurs above ground—can be dizzying. And marvelous and novel though the formations in caves can seem, they are so unfamiliar that they, too, add to the strangeness. (It is an unconscious defense against this phenomenon, I would guess, that leads commercial cave developers to assign such cutesy, Disneyish names to the features.)

The other overpowering sensation I had as we crept deeper into Lechuguilla was of how infinitely complicated the labyrinth is. Without the identifying scraps of red tape and Bridges' knowledge of the place, I would have been lost twenty times. Lechuguilla is unusual in that some ninety percent of its known passageways lie more than halfway down. Below the Rift, where Doucette and Wiggins made their vital climb of Captain Hook's Ladder, the cave branches into three subsystems of chambers and passages, none yet explored to the end.

Manifest Destiny is a large oval chamber about halfway down the Western Borehole. Explorers on their way through had noticed a possible lead high in the ceiling, and only four days before my trip, Steve Davis, a caver from Georgia, had made a bold solo climb up an overhanging ramp to reach the unexplored lead. Then he had tied a rope around a block in the ceiling and dangled it till it reached the floor, establishing a vertical thoroughfare for future pushers of passage.

By the time we came to that rope, which snaked through space six stories up to the arcane regions, I was pretty beat. So were Scott and Randy, but they wanted to see what lay beyond. Rick Bridges' sandbag was subtly delivered. "You want to come up the rope with us," he asked me, "or wait here?"

Bridges' "ropewalker" system consists of one rope-ascending device attached to the right foot; another next to the left knee, with a bungee cord to keep it from drooping; and a roller strapped high on the chest to keep the caver upright. Using more adrenaline than technique, I bashed my way up the free-hanging rope. Soon the procedure started to come to me. To my astonishment, just as Bridges had claimed, you could actually climb a rope in such a rig without using your hands.

The passages that issued from the dark gap in the ceiling were some of the most beautiful in Lechuguilla. We slogged through dry snowdrifts of pure white gypsum; even Bridges had never seen the like. Within an hour we came to the farthest reach of Steve Davis' push the previous Tuesday.

We were in what cavers call boneyard—rock honeycombed with short, twisting passages. The impression is of being inside a gigantic Swiss cheese of stone. Four days before, Davis' team had taken a long rest in a big room here before heading back. Still psyched up by his discovery, Davis announced he was just going to check out one of the many boneyard tunnels. Without even picking up his pack, he popped into the passage. It seemed to curve futilely back on itself, making a semicircular loop. Within minutes, Davis stepped back into the room and muttered, "It doesn't go anywhere."

No one answered him. Confused, Davis looked around. It was not the same room that he had left. He turned back to find the tunnel from which he had just emerged. A dozen dark holes mocked him; he had no idea which one he had just come out of.

At first, Davis later confessed, he "lost it," running from hole to hole in a panic. Then he forced himself to sit down and take stock. Meanwhile, his companions, growing worried, had started shouting and looking for him, to no avail. After about two hours of searching, they sent another pair of cavers all the way to the surface to launch a full-scale rescue.

Davis later admitted he had never been so frightened in his life. He had no food or water, but he remembered that he had a roll of plastic surveyor's tape in his pocket. Methodically, he taped each passage in the boneyard as he checked it for the way back. After five and a half hours lost and alone, he emerged in the original big room—but on a balcony thirty feet above the floor. His relieved companions threw him a rope and he rappelled down.

Now, on our own trip, Bridges at last relented, saying he just wanted to do a little surveying and to look at a deep pit another team had found before we would turn back. Then he said, "If you want to check out that right-hand lead a little ways, go ahead. Nobody's been down there." I pulled myself to my feet and started off with a roll of tape. Tired as I was, the specialness of the deed entranced me. I stared at my feet as they printed tracks in the gypsum. I was in a place where, through millions of geologic years, no living being had ever trod. I pushed only about fifty feet, but in that distance I had to climb across a pit, crawl into subtunnels in the endlessly branching boneyard, and tape my path. I went out of sight and earshot of the others, and for a few moments, the romance of caving caught me utterly.

For hard-core cavers, the supreme reward is to explore big caves: size is a higher criterion even than beauty. There are different scales by which the giants are gauged. Perhaps foremost is depth. Right now the deepest cave in the world is France's Reseau Jean Bernard, with 5,036 feet of relief between its highest and lowest points. The most extensive cave system, by far, is Mammoth-Flint Ridge in Kentucky, whose combined passages add up to 350 miles or so. The largest single chamber, discovered only eight years ago, is a room, in a cave deep in the jungle of Borneo, with a volume of 530 million cubic feet. This is roughly fifty times that of the Washington Cathedral.

In early August 1987, the depth of Lechuguilla reached 1,058 feet, thereby exceeding by 20 feet its famous neighbor, Carlsbad Cavern. Subsequent expeditions pushed the depth another 150 feet. During the several days I hung out at the project headquarters a year later, a series of teams extended the depth record from 1,207 to 1,415 feet, vaulting Lechuguilla to the rank of second deepest in the United States. Only Columbine Crawl, in Wyoming—"a death hole, a horrible cave," according to Bridges—is deeper, at 1,550 feet.*

The exploration of a big cave requires not so much brilliant individual effort as the smooth coordination of survey and reconnaissance teams. Park Service policy allows no more than twenty people to be in Lechuguilla at any given time and requires that all visits contribute to the exploration. Project coleaders Roy Glaser, John Patterson, and Bridges announce, at regular intervals, ten-day or two-week exploration periods, welcoming pretty much any experienced cavers who want to come, and trying to sort them into effective three- and four-person teams. Accustomed to the internecine rivalry of rock climbing areas, I was delighted to witness a

---

*Since 1988, Lechuguilla has been pushed to deepest cave in the United States.

rendezvous of about sixty cavers, who had come from as far as California, New York, and even Switzerland, united in a common purpose. The rampant euphoria could have launched giant balloons—for each of these zealots sensed that he was unlikely in the rest of his life to get a chance to push a better cave than Lechuguilla.

Park Service officials have been extraordinarily cooperative. Ron Kerbo, the only cave specialist in the NPS system and an innovative caver himself, had drafted the thoughtful, go-slow policy for the development of Lechuguilla. Park superintendent Rick Smith called the new cave "the most exciting thing that's happened in my career."

Local citizens, seeing a commercial bonanza in another cave the size of Carlsbad, are agitating to "open it up," decrying the "elitism" of saving it for experts. As remote and serious as pristine caves are, no wilderness can be trivialized more easily. For many cavers, the nightmare is an elevator shaft blasted from the cactus-and-yucca-studded surface down to the middle of the Western Borehole.

It had taken five pushes over three months to reach the 750-foot level in Lechuguilla. The elevator in Carlsbad takes you to that depth in fifty-seven seconds. To Jim White, the rancher who pioneered Carlsbad at the turn of the century with cowboy boots, baling wire, and lantern, Carlsbad had been even more of an adventure than Lechuguilla was for Rick Bridges. Today, in the deep chamber White risked his life to find, you can eat sandwiches and buy souvenir T-shirts.

Carlsbad is accessible to nearly everyone. Twenty-eight million people have entered the cave since it opened as a national monument in 1923 (it became a park seven years later). I was perhaps the 300th person in Lechuguilla. Kerbo estimates that in Carlsbad 18,000 irreplaceable cave decorations have been broken or stolen. Caves are so sensitive that Carlsbad workers regularly clean the formations of lint, hair, and flakes of human skin that encourage the growth of mold and algae. (The depredations of mere human presence have forced the closing of Lascaux Cave in France, with its famous prehistoric paintings.) After my own visit to Carlsbad—one of the best-run "developed" caves in the world—I could not help wondering what visitors missed by not seeing this awesome place in anything like its wildness. As we got out of the elevator, the operator asked a group how they had liked the cavern. A young boy blurted out, "It wasn't scary!" The loss, I thought, was his.

Most of the Lechuguilla cavers were too poor to rent motel rooms; during the expedition they crowded into a pair of rustic cabins near the park headquarters, each paying $2 a night—meals they cooked themselves. The floors conjured up some college crash pad, with battered helmets, dirty clothes, and old sleeping bags strewn everywhere. I found myself drawn to the ingrown society of these cave fanatics. They reminded me of the homey, oddball ranks of climbers I had joined in the late 1950s, when I had first taken up mountaineering—an all but vanished breed today, now that climbing has become a trendy sport whose stars wear Day-Glo Lycra and make good money endorsing everything from tents to lipstick.

American cavers pore over home-printed journals full of rapturous narratives of virgin passage. They're still pleased to meet another caver— while climbers bemoan the waiting lines that form below popular routes. Cavers put bumper stickers on their cars that read, "Think Mud"; they wear T-shirts with the logo "Murcielagos Necesitan Amigos" (Spanish for "Bats Need Friends").

Most of them, like Rick Bridges, nurse desultory careers, free from nine-to-five demands, simply to support their caving habit. A case in point is the bearded, soft-spoken Donald Davis, who turned fifty during his latest trip to Lechuguilla. Davis scratches out a meager income selling his home-raised honey at Colorado flea markets; he lives for caving. Despite his age, he was one of the strongest pushers at Lechuguilla.

Davis is also a caving innovator. Before a trip to Spanish Cave in Colorado, he had been wondering whether that well-known system connected with a higher hole called Frank's Pit. In wet areas like Kentucky, cavers have done dye tracing in streams to demonstrate linkages before the actual connecting passage was found. The only thing flowing in Spanish Cave, however, was wind. Davis spotted a road-killed skunk, and an idea came to him. He stopped his car, milked the skunk scent into a half-pint jar, then later soaked a rag in the powerful stuff and had a friend place it at the mouth of Frank's Pit while he and other cavers hiked to the entrance of Spanish Cave. "After a while," he recalls, "it hit us like a bomb."

In Lechuguilla, after eleven hours underground, Bridges led Scott, Randy, and me back along the endless uphill trail toward the entrance. So convoluted is the place that Randy and Scott had trouble naming the major rooms as we passed through them on our return trip. In the White Christmas Tree Room we lay in the calcite flakes to take a ninety-minute nap. Bridges was snoring peacefully within thirty seconds, but, weary though I was, I felt too nervous to fall asleep.

When we came to Boulder Falls, with its 150-foot rope climb, Bridges went tandem with me, hanging 20 feet above to coach as we ascended the rope together. I had learned a lot from the rope climb in Manifest Destiny, and to my gratification I got up Boulder Falls in reasonable time and style.

At 8:15 A.M. on the morning of a new day, I emerged from Lechuguilla after a push of eighteen hours. As the sun touched my head and shoulders,

I breathed in the smell of earth, and saw the green of grass and the blue of the sky, and I could not help whooping out loud—wordless cries of self-congratulation at my successful rebirth into the world.

My legs and arms were sore for days, and I felt a persistent, leaden ennui. The night after my long trip, I had obsessive textural dreams—of miles of gray tunnel, mountains of rubble, speleothems spilling through my hands. I woke at 5:00 A.M. and drove to the top of Carlsbad mesa, where I stood facing east, waiting for the sun to rise. I craved sun for a week after my adventure.

And yet, one evening I found myself wondering what lay beyond that last bend of boneyard in the right-hand passage I had pushed above Manifest Destiny. Wouldn't it be great, I thought, to go back down there and give it another shot?

RAMBLING THROUGH
THE WINDS

We had managed to lose the trail in scratchy evergreen forest, and Cope Red was balking. The obstacle in his path was a mere three-foot-wide rivulet running through the underbrush. I pulled hard on his lead rope, but Cope declined to budge. Behind him, linked to his saddle by a short lead, Hot Shot munched grass in stolid bemusement.

"Balking, lying down, or spitting are signs of an ill-trained and possibly spoiled llama," it had said in my primer. A quick skim of Stanlynn Daugherty's *Packing with Llamas,* as well as a two-hour lesson from Scott Woodruff, the guide based in Lander, Wyoming, who had rented us his llamas, amounted to the sum of our experience with these remarkable animals.

"Come on, Cope, damn it," I muttered, hoping to coax him across the water. But my heart wasn't in my hectoring. How could I blame a llama for refusing to bushwhack with eighty-five pounds in his saddlebags and some idiot yanking on his head? Then suddenly he launched himself across the brook, pack and all; I had to scramble to escape his landing. The rope from Cope's saddle jerked Hot Shot away from his grazing, and in lumbering chain-reaction our second llama leapt the stream too, his 105-pound load snapping branches as it came.

Jon Krakauer and I were on our way to Stough Creek, a high basin in Wyoming's Wind River Range, our favorite mountains in the contiguous United States. We had each been in the Wind Rivers four times before. Twenty-two years earlier, I had groaned under eighty pounds myself as a friend and I hauled niggardly quantities of freeze-dried cardboard pork chops along with our climbing gear to the Cirque of the Towers. But in 1968 at the end of June we had had the Cirque to ourselves for eight days, as you could never hope to today, any more than you could drink the waters of Lonesome Lake untreated or put in a new route almost anywhere you aimed.

Jon had horsepacked a few times in his youth; I had never before allowed dumb creatures to aid my access to the mountains. But with the creeping infirmities of what could no longer be euphemistically called anything less than middle age, it seemed time. As Stanlynn had gently put it in her how-to book, "Many llama owners today are former backpackers, some of whom are no longer able to carry as much." Though Jon and I had heard all about llama trekking with guides, we chose to hire a pair of the fuzzy ruminants and blunder our way guideless to timberline as we made our own discovery of llama lore.

Before the trip, everyone I had talked to had a llama tip to offer. "You know what you're supposed to do if llamas are being really difficult?" an editor had confided to me over lunch in a chic Boston restaurant. "Get up very close and breathe on them. They love that." She had sipped her Evian and sighed, "Don't we all?"

Now I realized that my friend had had it backward. On the trail, Cope Red and Hot Shot gamboled along. I gave Cope's lead to Jon and took Hot Shot myself. In his eagerness, Hot Shot threatened to tread on my heels. Daugherty had several paragraphs on what to do when tailgated by a llama, but I had forgotten their gist. If I so much as hesitated in my steps, Hot Shot laid his muzzle on my shoulder and breathed moistly, encouraging me onward.

IT WAS A KODACHROME DAY IN LATE JULY with a stiff breeze from the west and nineteenth-century visibility. The Wind River peaks are the antithesis of the nearby Tetons, rising from the surrounding plains not in one melodramatic postcard thrust, but in a subtle matrix of plateaus and grassy winding valleys. It is remarkably difficult, in fact, to divine the range's inner secrets as you drive the lonely, straight highways parallel to the mountains that crease the sagebrush prairie. Yet every hike into the Wind Rivers is arcadian, thanks to the granite that informs the foothills—giant boulders adrift in the woods, huge level slabs underfoot, stained with darting black water streaks. Some of the best rock east of

DAVID ROBERTS

Yosemite builds sharp, steep headwalls here. In untroubled sleep, full of green ambition, climbers dream of such places.

No mountains in North America more abound in lakes. Upper Stough Creek, where Jon and I were headed, is a brachiated seven-square-mile basin packed with forty-seven lakes full of blue water and flitting trout. The Wind Rivers are a large range—110 miles long from Togwotee Pass in the northwest to South Pass in the southeast, and as much as 30 miles wide—far bigger than the Tetons to the northwest. There are still cirques here that go years without visitors and many a tower that has yet to be climbed.

Some of the trails follow old Indian paths. Before the white men came, the Shoshone claimed the territory west of the range, while the Crow dominated to the east. The Indians most familiar with the mountains, however, were little-known Sheepeaters, who hunted elk and bighorn sheep in the alpine meadows, using dogs and travois rather than horses. Pacifists by nature, they may have headed for the mountains to escape their warlike neighbors. Togwotee Pass, the gap that separates the Wind Rivers from the Absaroka Range to the north, memorializes the last Sheepeater chief.

Mountain men knew the Wind Rivers. John Colter, the blithe loner who has been credited with "discovering" Yellowstone, may have been the first white man to see them. Two of the highest peaks (scholars quibble about just which ones) were ascended early, one by the shadowy army-man-turned-fur-trader Benjamin Bonneville in 1833, the other by the well-documented John C. Frémont in 1842. Yet the range was bypassed during the main thrusts of exploration and commerce. So it remains today: a wilderness that, given its beauty, is strikingly undervisited.

Blissful though Jon and I found our surroundings, and however congenial our woolly companions (as Stanlynn likes to call them), we had had a hard time getting out of the town of Lander. The night before our journey, in search of the kind of send-off that sailors crave on the eve of an arctic voyage, we had cruised past the empty-looking Stockgrowers Bar to alight in the One-Shot Lounge, where a clutch of citizens was watching TV over pitchers of beer. I asked the bartender about NOLS, the National Outdoor Leadership School, which is based in town. "Some of the locals leave when they come in," she told me grimly. "They're diffurnt. We're western."

That is Wyoming in a nutshell. In the late sixties, on their way into the Wind Rivers, some of my climbing friends, hippie types from the East, had been pinned to the ground by cowboys, who clipped their hair with sheep shears.

In 1963, as a college kid fresh off Mount McKinley, I had landed a job

56

teaching for Outward Bound in Colorado. One fellow instructor, Paul Petzoldt, was a hero of mine, for he had led the first ascent of the north face of Grand Teton way back in 1936 and two years later had spearheaded the first American attempt on K2, which got within 2,000 feet of the summit. Petzoldt had vanished for a decade—some said the bottle was his hideout—but had resurfaced at Outward Bound clean and raring to go, his bushy white eyebrows arched and his burly physique trimmed down. This preppy academy in the Elk Mountains, however, was not his cup of tea: Petzoldt was Wyoming cowboy to the core. Around the campfire that summer, he would shake his head and say, "Now, I know a place up in Wyoming where you could run a real wilderness school."

Petzoldt launched NOLS in 1965 and for a long time people agreed that it was the best school of its kind in America. But his own board of directors kicked him out, and by 1990 his former Lander neighbors were turning up their noses at the "NOLSies." How were they diffurnt? Sometimes, the locals said, they came in from a month in the wilds without taking a bath. The girls often didn't shave their legs. As far as the citizens of Lander could tell, the students were all spoiled, rich eastern kids. The instructors periodically took over the One-Shot with their whooping and slam dancing. For the locals, it was either leave or fight.

After the One-Shot, on the way back to our motel, Jon and I stopped in for a last drink at Nemo's Longbranch Saloon. Here it was "Ladies Night," and the only word to describe it was wild. The women were clearly in charge, orchestrating the mayhem with a rowdiness that truck drivers might envy. Female barkeeps and customers alike were tossing back shots of butterscotch schnapps between beers or mixing up vile mélanges of Kahlúa, vodka, schnapps, and Grand Marnier. A brawny fellow wore a T-shirt that read, "Alcohol is a disease—get your shots here—Nemo's." One very drunk woman stood up every half hour or so, whistled with fingers and front teeth, and delivered, in the cadence of a champion hog caller, an extended boast about what the girls from Powder River like to do. Another woman, celebrating her birthday a night early, was outlining the details of her upcoming bachelorette party, which would star several homegrown male strippers. I had a shouted conversation with a man from the Wind River Indian Reservation whose mother was Shoshone, father Arapaho. "Sure," he said of the tribal mix, "we fight it out all the time."

The dancing was enlivened by a choreographic fillip I had never seen before, best described in the local vernacular: "Yeah, ____'s flashin' her tits again." As new boys in town, Jon and I received a generous reception, especially once we had established that we were not NOLSies. By last call, the world was a warm, lascivious blur, at least for me, though Jon would later sanctimoniously claim that he had switched to club soda at around 1:30 A.M.. At dawn, the thought of a hike, even abetted by llamas, was obscene. I agreed to confront the trailhead only after a transfusion at Daylight Donuts and the usual vow never to touch the hard stuff again.

BY LATE MORNING I FELT ALL RIGHT. After the snafu in the underbrush, our llamas had trooped like troupers. Hot Shot was a 340-pound, four-year-old piebald that Woodruff had raised himself. Cope Red was an oldster of nine, smaller and calmer than his accomplice; "Cope" came from the one-glance town on the eastern Colorado plains where he had been raised, "Red" from his auburn coat. On the trail, Hot Shot was faster than his friend, so in the time-honored tradition of Himalayan expeditions we put Cope in the lead, opting for seasoned maturity over impetuous youth. Oddly, Cope was the more squeamish llama: he would step daintily around puddles, or even leap across them, while Hot Shot plodded on through.

We ran into a few other groups on the trail, some including kids who were dazzled to giddiness at the sight of our llamas. All over Colorado, Washington, Oregon, and California, the llama-trekking business is booming, but in Wyoming it's still considered by the locals to be a mite weird. Woodruff tells many a tale of edgy encounters with old-time horsepackers who find the presence of these Peruvian freaks in the backcountry a bad joke. He makes it a point to stop and answer idle questions from onlookers, and he trucks around Lander in a pickup with his animals prominently displayed.

Cute though they were, our llamas did not much like to be touched, especially on the neck or head. When miffed, they would lay their long ears flat. At inexplicable intervals, one or both of them would start to hum. A high-pitched mew full of question marks, it was a very strange sound, especially coming from so large a beast. "It sounds like the Wookie in *Star Wars*," said Jon. The hum, writes Stanlynn, "may indicate a variety of feelings such as anxiety, curiosity, or discomfort." Our llamas had hummed steadily through the inadvertent bushwhack; they would hum again as we coaxed them to ford the Wind Rivers' rocky streams or bash through the krummholz. Yet at other times they would hum for no apparent reason, swiveling their heads alertly and giving us that very cinematic expression: we know something you don't.

Llama guides—though not Woodruff—have been known to wax smug over their creatures' ecological superiority to horses on the trail, and with good reason. A horse's hooves will mash a wet path into an ungodly mess; a llama's soft-padded feet leave less of a print than a Vibram sole does.

Instead of steaming piles of equine dump, llamas leave behind discreet mounds of dry, hard pellets that could pass for deer's. They need only a modicum of carried feed, a barley-oats-molasses gorp they'll take from your hand. Most of their food comes from the vegetation along the trail, and, as Stanlynn notes, "They rarely kill the plants they eat, preferring to nibble a morsel here and a bite there." Llamas can go days without water, will start when disturbed but will seldom bolt, and will pass a night tethered to a picket stake without a peep.

The virtues of these stoic beasts had, in short, won me over. I haven't owned a dog or a cat since I was eight; I don't really like animals, except for dinner. But on the trail I fell into the pet lover's gooey solicitude, talking baby talk to a llama: "Whassa matter, Cope? What is it, old boy?"

WE CAMPED THE FIRST NIGHT in a clearing with a picture-window view across a big nameless lake. Dinner was smoked oysters, steak, and a surprising zinfandel. The next day Jon found us an idyllic base camp in a grove of bristlecone pines right at timberline, around 10,700 feet. To camp even this far in was to outdistance virtually any other overnight visitors to the relatively popular Stough Creek Lakes; as far as we could tell, no one else had ever pitched a tent in our grove. Around this camp was a superb collection of rocks: nicely spaced boot- and sock-drying slabs, a cooking rock flat as a picnic table, and a massive cube we called The Throne, on which the noncook could sit to supervise the pancake flipper. Yes, we had pancakes for breakfast, and sometimes for lunch.

For a whole day we hiked in and out of one cirque after another, appraising possible routes, stopping to boulder on crags as well designed as artificial climbing walls. In the afternoon I started fishing. Despite four decades' practice, I would not call myself a devoted or particularly talented angler. I've gone as long as five years without taking out a rod. Each time I start again, I am smitten by the absurdity of the sport. There is something like golf about it—all that gear and know-how and men-will-be-boys folderol about an essentially inane pursuit. And then, lulled by the rhythm of casting into eddies and retrieving across wind ripples, by the dance of the fly above the darting silver shapes, I fall into a trance as complete as comes over me when climbing. Never does time pass so unobserved, never does one so forget the sorrows and duties of humdrum life.

I caught eight trout in an hour and a half, and put four back. My keepers were of three different kinds: brook, cutthroat, and golden, the last of which I had never caught before. Back in camp, we feasted on asparagus soup, shrimp risotto, trout fried in butter, and a young French burgundy.

That the Wind Rivers are an angler's paradise is chiefly owing to their most famous old codger, Finis Mitchell, who as a boy in 1906 settled on the fringe of the wilderness. During the Depression, desperate for gainful employment, Finis and his wife, Emma, concocted Mitchell's Fishing Camp at Big Sandy Opening on the southeastern tip of the range. The only problem was, no more than five lakes in the whole range appeared to have trout in them.

Undaunted, Mitchell packed 2.5 million trout into 314 different lakes over the next seven years, hauling them from a state hatchery in milk cans that he covered with burlap, slung from horseback, and jostled at regular intervals to oxygenate the water. Within a short time Mitchell was catching what he called "monsters," the offspring of his own transplants. One such specimen, he wrote, "looked like you had blowed him up with a pump he was so fat."

All this hiking, fishing, and bouldering took its toll, and I was glad I had included another novelty in our supplies; one of those hinged ensolite-and-nylon camp chairs I had eyed suspiciously in climbing stores. Now I found myself spending an inordinate amount of time seated in the contraption, using it even inside the tent, where it made reading by headlamp almost a pleasure.

One evening just before dinner, as I sat in my camp chair atop The Throne while Jon puttered away on the cooking rock, I lapsed into a pensive, nostalgic mood. Was I really happier, I wondered, eating steak and sipping wine in a dry grove at timberline than I had been in my Spartan heyday, huddled over a Primus stove on a storm-lashed glacier in Alaska, turning snow into water and oatmeal into mush? Could I feel as good strolling packless into the Wind Rivers with hired llamas bent beneath crushing loads as I had when I righteously humped my own impedimenta up to Lonesome Lake at age twenty-five? Was basking in a camp chair really better than hunkering in an igloo? Were ease, comfort, and luxury the true ingredients for fun in the mountains?

The answer was "yes."

I snapped back to reality. "Pass the frogs' legs, Jon," I bellowed without getting up.

JOE KELSEY'S GUIDE TO THE RANGE, *Climbing and Hiking in the Wind River Mountains*, lists only one climb, an easy one, on record in Stough Creek Basin. Jon and I saw plenty of routes to do all around us, but those that were not trivial looked hard and dangerous. Eight years before, we had climbed together out of Deep Lake, several valleys to the northwest, where the granite walls of Haystack and East Temple and Steeple Peak are riven with clean cracks affording some of the great classic climbs in the range. Here in Stough Creek, however, the rock is mostly quartz diorite, a gray, plated stuff seamed with white horizontal dikes—beautiful to look at, but lousy for protection.

We had nonetheless scouted a few prospective lines when a typical July weather pattern moved in: splendid, clear mornings followed by hail and lightning every afternoon. On the first such day, we sat in the tent, snug and dry, while ball-bearing-size stones drummed on the roof and rang the cooking pots. Jon opened a can of cashews.

"I feel guilty about the llamas," I said, scooping up a pawful of nuts.

"I'll go check on them," he offered.

"I'll do it," I bluffed, "if I can get out of this camp chair."

He was back in a minute, hail in his beard. "They're fine," he said. "Like Scott says, they've been around the block."

A bird singing in a tree could set Cope Red humming, but lightning and hail fazed him not at all. When the storm passed, we were amazed to find our llamas with inch-thick rugs of ice on their backs. So well insulated were they that it took several hours for the hail to melt.

On another stormy afternoon, I thumbed through the index of Kelsey's book, where those who first climbed the range's routes are listed. Although some of America's finest mountaineers—Yvon Chouinard, Fred Beckey, Royal Robbins, and Layton Kor, among others—put up bold new routes in the Wind Rivers, the range has not become an invidious, competitive scene like Yosemite, the Bugaboos, or the Diamond of Longs Peak. Indeed, as Chris Jones mentions in an aside in his book *Climbing in North America,* "The Wind Rivers have . . . contributed little to the development of North American climbing." The range's single finest mountaineering deed was the four-day ascent of the north face of Mount Hooker in 1964 by Robbins, Dick McCracken, and Charlie Raymond. Theirs was a line so pure that to see it even from a great distance sets the heart soaring.

Perusing the names in the back of Kelsey's book, I felt yet another nostalgic glow creep over me. Until the last decade, the list reminded me, climbers in America had still been members of a community. In the fine print, I counted forty-four men and women who were my friends or good acquaintances, and each triggered a little jolt of memory. Some had been pioneers, legends whom I considered it a privilege to meet: Robert and Miriam Underhill, Ken Henderson, Hans Kraus, Henry Hall, Paul Petzoldt himself. Others, my nearer coevals, had been the cronies of many a happy lark. With this one I had picked blueberries in the Brooks Range; with that, played blackjack in Reno. With X, I had kayaked on a spring morning in New England; with Y, drunk beer at Emil's after a hard day at the Gunks; with Z, broiled hamburgers on a patio in Aspen. I had listened to yet another play

Couperin on his home-built harpsichord and had cruised the topless bars of Anchorage with another. With yet another, I had even put up new routes in the Wind Rivers.

So the days passed. Seizing the morning hours before the storms rolled in, Jon and I hiked and scrambled up several nameless 12,000-foot peaks, gazing from their summits at sylvan holes that Colter and Frémont had been the first white men to see. We admired slick walls and savage towers that the next generation might climb. We took the llamas on day hikes and bouldered like burglars on the take. When the storms let up, we walked through hailstruck meadows, marveling at the flowers peeping through: paintbrush and aster, lupine and elephantela among the grass; pale columbine and Parry's primrose in rocky nooks; up high, tiny dianthus and forget-me-not. We sent coneys and marmots scurrying. At night we lay on our backs and counted satellites and meteors.

I continued to fish. At one point Jon shocked me by confessing to what he knew was an outdoor heresy: he wasn't crazy about the taste of trout. I switched to barbless hooks and played to shore a sixteen-inch cutthroat, then made a lot of noise that night about how good it tasted.

And we talked. Is there any better talk than that of old friends in the mountains? We weighed the upstart virtues of the Mariners against the vintage skills of the Red Sox. We relived hoary climbs. We speculated as to what makes llamas tick. We convinced ourselves that the disasters of youth had by now sublimed into gilded anecdotes. We anatomized most of our friends and some of our enemies. We wondered aloud about women as we never dared to in civilization.

Then one morning it was time to hike out. With regret, we fetched Cope Red and Hot Shot and saddled them up. Foolishly we had promised others that we would emerge from the Wind Rivers on a certain date. Back home, responsibilities lurked like tax collectors. We had drunk our last bottle of pinot noir. And besides, in one more day it would be Ladies' Night at Nemo's again.

THE RACE DIABOLIQUE

As the raft approached the rapid, nicknamed
The Steps by local river guides, something went wrong. It was the end of
the day, and everyone in the boat was on the verge of exhaustion. Later the
team could not reconstruct the setup error that led to the catastrophe: too
slow a paddle toward the first drop, causing the craft to strike at an angle?
Suddenly the rubber raft stood on its front end, hovered for an agonizing
moment, then flipped forward. All five team members and their local guide
were hurled into the crashing water.

Christine Claude, a thirty-two-year-old customs collector and cross-
country ski champion from northern France, had been uneasy about
whitewater in the first place. Now, trapped and tossed in a "keeper," she
swallowed water as she gasped for breath, knowing she was going to die.
The image of her two young sons, about to become orphans, flashed through
the panic of her mind.

Somewhere else in the maelstrom, Fabienne Mathey felt her helmet snag
on a tree branch dangling into the river. Locked in place with her head un-
derwater, her chinstrap cutting into her throat, she too anticipated death.
Then the branch broke, and Mathey was flushed downstream.

With a canny effort, the local guide swam to Christine Claude in the keeper, seized her life jacket, and pulled her out of the recycling wave toward the bank. One by one, the members of Team Objectif Raid made it to shore. They recovered their raft, but not all the paddles. Mathey and Claude clung to each other, shivering with shock and cold. There was no choice but to stop at once and camp.

It was the fourth day of the Raid Gauloises, the 250-mile race that pits more than forty crack teams from several countries against each other as it unfurls across some spectacular Third World wilderness. In December 1995, the course wound through the mountains, lakes, rivers, and pampas of Argentine Patagonia.

Until the moment when their raft flipped, Objectif Raid's gutsy effort looked like the best story to emerge from the seventh annual running of the Raid. The rules of the race require teams of five, one of whom must be a woman, to paddle, climb, hike, horseback ride, orienteer, and rappel together through the grueling course. If one member drops out, the whole team is disqualified. Because so much of the Raid rewards brute strength—hauling wet boats across a portage through a bamboo forest, or lugging heavy packs up a 4,000-foot climb on a glacier—nearly all the teams are composed of four men and one woman. But Objectif Raid was four women and a single man. And at the moment of the capsize, they stood in fourth place, leaving forty-four other teams panting in their wake as they pushed on, well within hailing distance of the three teams ahead of them.

Four days earlier, at 10:00 A.M. on December 4, as Raid organizer Gérard Fusil shot off a starter's pistol, the forty-eight teams from nine countries had sprinted toward the beach on the shore of Lago Nahuel Huapi, jumped into kayaks, and paddled away across the lake. The Raid, which in previous years has been run in such exotic locales as Borneo, Madagascar, and Oman, has always been dominated by French teams. In 1995, twenty-eight of the forty-eight teams were French. In France, the innovative race has become a well-known *spectacle sportif* in a country famed for all things *sportif*. Within the last few years, however, Americans have begun to take the Raid seriously. In Argentina, seven of the teams were American, including two or three given an outside chance of winning. The best an American team has ever finished was ninth in Madagascar in 1993. Like the leading French outfits, the American teams have learned that they must train vigorously as a group for at least seven months to have any chance of doing well. For the *conquérants*, as the French dub the competitors, the Raid approximates a full-time job. Even so, the race is so tough that something like half the teams fail to finish the course.

I had come to Patagonia a skeptic. The *éclat* of the Raid's novel approach to long-distance racing (in Japan the event is dubbed "the human Paris-Dakar") has generated considerable controversy. The previous May, in southeastern Utah, the Eco-Challenge, an imitation of the Raid Gauloises organized by a disaffected former partner of Gérard Fusil, outraged environmentalists.

It was not ecological desecration that raised my hackles so much as the whiff of neocolonialism that wafted from the Raid's press releases. Like the Paris-Dakar road race, the Raid seemed to use the Third World countries through which it careened as mere picturesque backdrops.

And in my first few days around San Carlos de Bariloche, an Argentine resort near the Chilean border best known as a college-kids ski area, I saw evidence to justify my qualms. Press, support staff, and *conquérants*—600 of us, all told—were lodged in a series of posh hotels twenty miles west of the ethnically complex town of San Carlos (pop. 90,000); we formed an aloof colony unto ourselves. On my trips into town, I learned that few of the locals seemed to have heard of the Raid Gauloises. Nor, as the race unfolded, did crowds of native citizens assemble to watch.

The French seemed oblivious to what was going on in Patagonia. From a young woman hitchhiker, I learned that Argentina was seized with a dire economic crisis, unemployment was twenty percent, and after a bad winter some of the poorer people in the hill towns were literally starving. When I ate lunch at sidewalk cafés in San Carlos, shy Indian kids—the indigenous Mapuches and the all-but-extinct Tehuelches—begged pesos.

In a pious gesture of rapprochement, Fusil had announced that HQ4—one of the five key transition camps and staffing centers along the route—would be lodged in an Indian school. At the pre-race briefing, Fusil had described the Indians as "very poor, but very nice people." Some of the *conquérants,* he went on, were carrying toys and games to give to the children.

Unfortunately, by the time the Raid hit HQ4, the kids were out on school vacation. The Raid officials, spouting communiqués into their walkie-talkies, took over the schoolhouse and sat down to hot meals served by several Indian women, whom the French treated like servants.

Yet I felt my skepticism wash away late on December 4, the first day of the race, as I intercepted the lead teams finishing their thirty-mile paddle across Lago Nahuel Huapi and started with them up the north ridge of a rugged mountain called Cerro Lopez.

For the fourth day in a row, the skies were cloudless. We wound on a sketchy trail through a forest of sixty-foot pines and cypresses. In the clearings, swaths of yellow broom blazed the hillsides. I hiked for an hour with Coflexip, a team from the Lyon area that counted two world champion kayakers among their number. The whole team seemed friendly and easy-going, but Laurent Maubré, a thirty-year-old manager for a Brazilian company, was particularly outgoing. Switching between French and a passable English, he chatted breezily with me as he trudged up the ridge. "Do you think there will be a restaurant on top?" he joked.

We burst above treeline to emerge on black slabs of broken granite. In the late sun, the Brazo de la Tristeza (the Arm of Sadness, a bay of Lago Nahuel Huapi) stretched west toward the magnificent Tronador, a glacier-hung 11,000-foot peak, highest in this part of the Andes and a pivot point for the competitors. A thirty-mile-per-hour wind blew from the west, but the day was so warm I climbed in shorts and a T-shirt.

Fifteen hundred feet above the lake, Coflexip was caught by their arch-rivals, Intersport, a pre-race favorite whose members also hail from the Lyon area. Not quite the equal of Coflexip on water, Intersport would prove a little stronger in the mountains. They seemed the temperamental opposite of the happy-go-lucky Maubré: intense, withdrawn, efficient. I hiked for a hundred yards with Béatrice Piollat, a twenty-four-year-old cross-country ski champion. Attempting small talk, I asked how heavy her pack was: "Combien de kilos?"

She didn't answer. "Beaucoup?" I prodded.

"Ouais," she muttered, then strode away.

Only eight hours into the race, these two teams had put some distance between themselves and the forty-six others in the field. I sat down on an outcrop and let the leaders surge on. It was 6:00 P.M., with the early-summer sun still high in the west. From my perch, I saw 2,000 feet below me the purple slivers of the slower kayaks still far from reaching shore on their paddle across the lake.

I realized abruptly that, for the first time in five days, I was alone. I had been so caught up in the pre-race bustle that I had forgotten that mountains had always promised me solitude and calm. In the contentment of that moment, another qualm about the Raid, having nothing to do with ecology or neocolonialism, rose to the surface. This part of Patagonia, I recognized, was one of the most beautiful places I had ever been. But for the *conquérants*, it seemed only a race course, a gauntlet of problems and obstacles. With their uniforms, their staccato equipment-list recitations at the checkpoints, the athletes conjured up some military campaign, not the carefree vagabondage of the hills.

My reflective moment was shattered by the thunder of a helicopter, carrying cameramen effortlessly up Cerro Lopez to shoot the leaders from the air.

Sportscasters claim that the hardest of all contests to televise is a marathon. The Raid was a marathon with a vengeance. For the fifty or sixty of us journalists trying to keep up with the race as it unfolded over the next week, simply getting into position to witness its drama posed an almost insuperable challenge. For a writer from Japan, a filmmaker from Germany, the chore was relatively easy: their whole interest lay in a single team or, in the German case, in a single competitor. But I set myself an impossible agenda: to be with the leaders as the race took shape, to take an inside look at the seven American teams, and to pick up the piquant and absurd events that befell other teams along the way.

I had rented a car in San Carlos, and for ten days I made crazy dashes on bad dirt roads as I tried to hopscotch among my priorities. Virtually the whole course plunges through roadless wilderness, so I also had to hike and scramble to find teams in the backcountry. By the fifth day, some eighty miles separated the leaders from the stragglers. In the stupor of my sleep-deprived jaunts, an analogy came to me. The length of the Raid course was about that between Washington, D. C., and New Haven. My frantic *reportage* was like careening daily between Delaware and Connecticut—with gravel roads instead of interstates and mountain ranges and forests corrugating the Eastern Seaboard.

The three Raid helicopters were ostensibly reserved for officials and the crew making the authorized film of the race, but it soon became clear that certain privileged journalists (chiefly those who had covered many previous Raids) got some air time. A pathetic begging contest among the other writers and photographers ensued. I decided early on not to take a single chopper ride, and the mountaineer in me took a dark pride in beating the lazier reporters to some choice location by reading the maps carefully and setting out on some obscure trail before dawn. Thus I got caught up in a Raid of my own, obsessed with catching Intersport at dawn at Checkpoint Twenty-two on the shore of a Lago Steffen, then barreling back to HQ2 to interview a despondent American who had dropped out.

And once again, the Raid was proving to be a debacle for the Americans. On the first night, as they bivouacked 2,500 feet up the north ridge of Cerro Lopez, Team Odyssey had to throw in the towel. That afternoon, Mike Sawyer, a fit young banker from Chicago, had watched as a rock dislodged by a teammate smashed the back of his hand, shattering it in a compound fracture. He tried to make it through the night, but blood loss began to pose a threat to his life. The team set off flares and their emergency beacon, and a nervy chopper pilot plucked Sawyer off his ledge in the dark. Odyssey became the first team to drop out of the running.

That same night, Susan Hemond-Dent, the woman member of potentially strong Team Dockers-North Face, began vomiting from dehydration. She spent a sleepless night, then gamely staggered on through the next day, with teammates carrying her load, before she had to give up. A member of the American team that had finished ninth in Madagascar, Hemond-Dent was devastated by her failure. Helicoptered out, she sat in a grassy field at HQ2 recounting her ordeal, bursting now and then into tears.

The next day another American outfit, Team Chart House, met disaster when they lost their "passport," the official card that must be stamped at each of thirty-five checkpoints along the course. They spent more than a day retracing their steps, searching frantically in the brush, asking other teams to keep an eye out for the lost treasure. Soon thereafter, Team Special Forces bailed when one of its strongest members collapsed from exhaustion. His friends guessed that he simply had too much weight in his pack—as much as sixty pounds, compared to the lightest loads of thirty pounds carried by some French *conquérants*.

In the end, only two of the seven American teams would finish the course. Teams Thorlo Xtreme and Endeavour ended up in a spirited head-to-head race for thirteenth place, actually jogging parts of the last rugged trail through the mountains after nine days of all-out effort. Thorlo Xtreme edged out Endeavour by a mere ten minutes, but their vivid minidrama failed to pique much interest beyond the American press.

Once again, it was French teams that dominated the Raid Gauloises: nine of the top ten eventual finishers would be French (the Austrian Red Bull team tying for ninth place). There were theories, some of them cynical, about the French preeminence. Even more than stamina, the race rewards shrewd route-finding. Supplementing the detailed maps is the Raid Book, a loose-leaf binder filled with step-by-step directions to the often obscure course. The Book comes only in French and English versions, and the English is often rendered less than felicitously. I found myself puzzling over a typical entry: "Descend from the summit towards the west in the direction of a large clearing of stones situated at the start of a brow sloping down toward the west." Clearing of stones? Start of a brow?

Even the best teams lost precious hours floundering around, sometimes in the dark, trying to find an arcane checkpoint manned by a *controlleur* in a one-man tent. But for, say, the Austrian or Swedish or Japanese team the task of reading the Raid Book was doubly hard, depending on their members' luck in untangling the sentences of a knotty English that was already not their first language.

Yet it took more than syntax to explain the French excellence—or, more to the point, seven years of dashed American hopes. By now, the Americans train just as hard as the French, maybe harder. Teams Special

Forces and Dockers-North Face, both early casualties, had looked at the start as fit as anyone on the course.

Jean-Pierre Dufour, a veteran reporter of the Raid for Agence France-Presse, thought the answer was simple: the Americans always carry too much weight, and they are not as good as the French at navigating. Another French reporter, Jacques Leleu, offered, "The Americans need to be more open-minded. They'll say, 'We're going to walk eight hours, then sleep at 7:00 P.M.' You can't have this clock. You must adapt to the conditions."

From the north ridge of Cerro Lopez, where I had left Intersport and Coflexip in the lead late on the first afternoon, the course plunged up and down steep mountain arêtes, crossed high passes, and finally tackled the glacier on the Tronador. Here was the ruggedest stretch of the whole circuit: all told, the *conquérants* would gain and lose more than 29,000 feet of altitude—the equivalent of Everest from sea level—and the bulk of those ups and downs came in this Andean ramble.

It was two days before I saw the leaders again. Meanwhile I installed myself at HQ2 at Pampa Linda (the Beautiful Field), a green clearing where two valleys come together near the head of the Rio Manso, perhaps the loveliest of all way-stations on the course.

On December 6, I set off up the Rio Alerce to intercept the leaders near Checkpoint Thirteen, where their course dipped low into the forest before surging up the Tronador. A bad trail led through thickets of fiendish, spiny bamboo, where for the first time I tasted the horrors of Patagonian bushwhacking. The rock in the gloomy valley had turned from the solid granite of Cerro Lopez to a mottled, greasy limestone. Thin waterfalls spilled from canyon rims lost in mist above.

Just before noon, I heard a noise in the jungle, then saw the maroon jerseys of Intersport. The *conquérants* had gone more than a day without having to deal with press: one Intersport member was so surprised he shook my hand.

"I heard you lost CP 12," I said. Radio bulletins through the night had revealed that all the leading teams had spent hours circling in the brush to get a bead on this most elusive of checkpoints.

The Intersport racer cursed vividly. "It is the fault of the Raid Book," he swore. "There is a bad mistake in the Book. We spent the night crashing and falling."

Five minutes later, I heard more noises in the forest, then saw flitting patches of white jersey. It was not Coflexip, however, but Objectif Raid, the team of four women and one man. By going lighter than any other team, they had performed brilliantly on the stretch that could well have been

69

their nemesis. After the race, Fabienne Daumas would explain: "We didn't take any sleeping bags. We slept five in the [obligatory] tent, head-to-foot, warm in our Gore-Tex. It was so tight, we had to turn over all five at a time! The other teams had enormous loads—we were shocked when we saw the size of their avalanche shovels. Ours was tiny."

Close on Objectif's heels was Proner Comatel, a team of guides from the Chamonix region who were expected to make their best showing in the mountains. The free-spirited Coflexip had slipped to fourth, almost two hours behind.

The next day I climbed 1,600 feet to a shoulder of the Tronador, to catch the leaders as they dashed down a set of fixed ropes culminating in an eighty-foot rappel. I had awakened to booming thunderclaps; at last, a week of perfect weather seemed about to end. But when I looked out of my tent, the sky was as blue as ever. The Tronador—the Thunderer—was doing its thing: the sounds came from giant séracs calving off thousand-foot cliffs.

Alone beneath the rappel, I recognized that here was one of the most dangerous spots on the course, for chunks of broken basalt came loose in the hands, and the risk of falling rock was extreme. Admiring an 800-foot waterfall, I heard cries above. Five athletes came in sight at the top of the rappel: it was Proner Comatel, in green. The mountain guides had climbed the 4,000 feet to a high saddle on the Tronador and descended faster than anyone else. The strain of the effort showed: in mid-rappel, one Proner racer started screaming at his partner that he hadn't screwed down the gate on his locking carabiner.

Intersport in maroon was only minutes behind. Unbeknownst to me, or even to Intersport, a contretemps involving their team and Proner Comatel had taken place in the mountains—a seemingly trivial deviation that would work itself out days later, with devastating consequences.

Half an hour later, Objectif Raid came in view. To minimize the hazard of dislodging rocks, they rappelled side-by-side on five parallel ropes. But as soon as the team reached level ridge and started hiking on, I realized they were in trouble. Tall, thin Fabienne Mathey kept doubling over with the dry heaves. She looked pallid and utterly spent, yet still she carried her own pack. Later team captain Michel Denaix would say, "Yes, Fabienne was weakest in the mountains, although in paddling she had been the strongest. Now she wanted only to stop and throw up. Fabienne had a great fear of slowing down the group. But it was never a question of giving up. Instead we tried to find the right words to give her psychological comfort. That's the way we worked."

Now I saw that effort in action, though at the time I misconstrued it as callousness. Even as Mathey bent and gagged, one of the other women paused to gaze north, then murmur like a tourist to her teammate, "Christine, look at the beautiful waterfall." Moments later, she surveyed the cliff of the fixed ropes and rappel and exclaimed, "I can't believe we just descended that."

From the Tronador, the teams hurried down to HQ2 at Pampa Linda. Each of the four HQs before the finish line was also a "transition" depot, where the *conquérants* met their support teams and, in this case, dumped all their mountain gear—crampons, plastic snowshoes, ropes, packs, and the like—and donned wet suits, packed new rations, and set out down the Rio Manso in inflatable canoes. If Intersport had one pronounced edge over all the other teams in the Raid, it was their efficiency at transitions. Now, by taking only thirty-four minutes at HQ2 to Proner Comatel's hour, they seized the lead once more.

A lot was at stake. Ostensibly for safety, but also to add strategic spice to the Raid, Gérard Fusil had imposed a number of "windows"—periods after which further progress was forbidden for hours at a stretch. One such window now loomed for the leaders, twenty miles downstream: no one would be allowed to paddle on the Manso during the night, from 8:00 P.M. to 7:00 A.M. At the moment, it looked as though only the four leading teams had a chance to beat the deadline.

The river was a straightforward canoe run, except for the stretch on the lower Manso, punctuated by three nasty rapids, where each team dropped its canoes and gear to be shuttled downstream, jumped into a rubber raft with a local guide, and bounced through the waves.

Coming first into The Steps, the nastiest of the three technical drops, Intersport lined up wrong and flipped. One of their team got trapped in a keeper, but burst loose. With remarkable aplomb, Intersport got themselves back aboard with a delay of only twenty-five minutes. Proner Comatel shot through the rapids without capsizing, as did Coflexip, whose champion paddlers brought them surging back out of fourth place. Passing two teams, they took out at the end of the Manso only five minutes behind Intersport.

Then Objectif Raid flipped in The Steps, and Christine Claude and Fabienne Mathey nearly drowned. All but unhinged by the ordeal, too demoralized to attempt to catch the window, they set up camp on the bank of the Manso just below the last rapid, built a fire, and tried to regroup. By missing the deadline, they had given away eleven hours to the three teams ahead of them.

By this point, on the fourth day of the race, my qualms had all but dissolved: I was immersed in the drama of the Raid. What saved it from becoming the patently artificial, arrogant spectacle I had anticipated was the courage and integrity of the *conquérants*. Time and again I was moved to admiration and even awe by their gutsy perseverance.

No one could keep running for seven or eight days without sleep. Much of the skill of the leaders depended on figuring where and when to stop for three-hour bivouacs, and how to get the most recuperative value out of those furtive naps.

Through the night of December 7–8, the three lead teams stumbled on, portaging their deflated canoes through a bamboo forest, on what Gérard Fusil had called "a veritable Vietnamese trail." This old Indian route had fallen into disuse, until a Raid reconnaissance team had reopened it with machetes. As a result, the ground was festooned with blade-sharp stumps of bamboo. "It is more dangerous than the glacier," testified a French reporter who went halfway with the team he was covering. "If you fall on one of these sticks—two minutes, and you are empty of blood."

And here, in the bamboo, Intersport's superior endurance began to show. In a sense, Proner Comatel had shot their wad in the mountains and on the river: forced to take a longer rest than they had hoped, by midday on December 8 the Chamoniards had fallen seven hours behind.

Coflexip kept things close, but checkpoint by checkpoint, the gap between themselves and Intersport widened: from a thirty-four-minute lag at Checkpoint Nineteen to a daunting two hours and twenty minutes at Checkpoint Twenty-two. Later Jean-Yves Paillier, the stoic navigator for Coflexip, would say that the worst moment of the whole Raid came in the wee hours on the morning of December 8. The team had forced their way over the bamboo portage without sleep. Now, as they paddled across Lago Steffen, none of them could stay awake. A racer would bolt upright, take two or three strokes to correct the boat's course, then doze off again. Finally Coflexip called a halt, sleeping on shore for an hour, tormented by the image of iron-willed Intersport paddling farther into the lead.

Back on the Manso, Objectif Raid spent a healing night by the campfire. But in the morning, the team was still spooked by their capsize: along the relatively easy last few river miles, back in their inflatable canoes, the team portaged one rapid that everybody else would run without trouble. Across the bamboo portage, Objectif trudged at a listless pace. It was as if the traumatic dousing had taken all the heart out of the once-blithe team. By Checkpoint Twenty-two, they had slipped all the way to sixth place.

Shortly after noon on December 8, Intersport left HQ3 on horseback. At this dusty roadside camp, the course departed from the mountains and lakes for good to circle east through a dry, scrubby pampas, classic gaucho country (the Raid hired real gauchos as wranglers). Everyone was bemused by the coming fifty-mile *équitation* stage. To forestall the possibility of mistreating beloved Argentine horses, Fusil imposed mandatory two-hour rests and minimum times between checkpoints. There would be no galloping—only a long route-finding puzzle through the chaparral.

The race, then, most observers thought, would go on two-day hold. All the best teams would nail the minimum times to the minute, and the Raid would proceed like an auto race under the caution flag, with teams unable to gain or lose position. Only at HQ4 (the Indian school) would the all-out dash to the finish line begin.

So Intersport, with its two-and-a-half-hour lead over Coflexip, had positioned itself perfectly to win the seventh Raid Gauloises. Then the bombshell hit. Its repercussions began as an angry and excited murmur among press and support crews around the bulletin board at HQ3.

Days before, high in the mountains, Intersport, in the lead, had crossed a pass and started down the other side. The trail descended a loose scree slope paralleled by a snow couloir. For fifty yards, Intersport had taken the couloir, until they saw cairns marking the path on the scree. Technically, they had gone off-route for fifty yards.

It was a minimal indiscretion: over 250 miles of wilderness, many teams had lost the route briefly and found it again. But Proner Comatel, coming along shortly after Intersport, had seen their predecessors' footprints in the snow. According to Intersport captain Hervé Dubuis, Proner had gone ahead to the next checkpoint and asked, with feigned innocence, whether it was allowed to descend the snow couloir. The checkpoint *controlleur* had radioed in the transgression. "They shot us in the legs," said Béatrice Piollat later, bitter about the Chamoniards' duplicity.

Now the Raid jury announced a two-hour penalty assessed against Intersport. Gérard Fusil himself was outraged, and lobbied against his own jury, but succeeded only in reducing the penalty to an hour and a half.

Riding off up the broad valley of the Rio Villegas, confident in their lead, Intersport still knew nothing of the penalty. They would not learn until they reached Checkpoint Twenty-six, almost two days later. Meanwhile, another piece of bad luck was about to afflict the team. As Béatrice Piollat later recounted it, "A Raid organizer told us it was easy to go from Checkpoint Twenty-two to Twenty-three in four hours [the minimum time], walking the horses. But after six hours, we hadn't found the checkpoint. We stopped for five minutes, then started back on our path, thinking we'd missed the checkpoint. We were wasted—we'd gone forty-two hours without sleep. And then we crossed paths with Coflexip."

The upshot of their blunder on the Villegas was that Intersport lost three hours to their arch rivals. By the time they pulled themselves together and trotted despondently after Coflexip's cloud of dust, they were twenty-five minutes behind. For the next day and a half, the gap between the two teams stayed exactly at twenty-five minutes.

Then, at Checkpoint Twenty-six, Intersport learned of their one-and-a-half-hour penalty.

By driving faint back roads, I caught up with Intersport and Coflexip at Checkpoint Twenty-six, as, only yards apart in the shade of tall cottonwoods, they waited out their mandatory two-hour rest together. Intersport looked glum and agonized; Pascal Bahaud, a silver medalist in rowing at the Seoul Olympics, paced in circles, cursing out loud: "Fifty meters! A matter of fifty meters! Nobody told us anything!" The penalty would not be served until Checkpoint Thirty-three, at the put-in for the last short canoe jaunt down the Rio Limay. Later the quieter Hervé Dubuis would admit, "The penalty hung over our heads like a sword of Damocles."

In contrast, Coflexip radiated a dawning joy. With his blue eyes ablaze and his black hair in tangles, Laurent Maubré entertained the kids at the local *estancia*, as he had everyone on the course. He gave them sweets, then rubbed his fingers, saying to the parents, "Mucho asucar." Pulling a scarf over his dust-coated face, he mimed, "Bandito! Pistolero!" The kids screamed their delight.

At four checkpoints in a row, the two teams of rivals had been forced to endure a one-hour-thirty-five-minute layover together. The teams maintained an aloof separation; yet late one night, as they finished a hasty dinner, Coflexip silently offered the remnants of their meal to Intersport, who silently accepted.

The Raid had turned into a two-team race. Yet something interesting was transpiring back down the course. Having seemed on the verge of collapse, Objectif Raid was making an astounding surge. From sixth place, they climbed steadily, passing three teams to regain third place. And somehow, despite the caution-flag plod of the *équitation* laps, they had made up six of the eleven hours they had given away to the leaders by missing the window on the lower Manso. At Checkpoint Twenty-six, the plucky women and single man were only five hours behind Coflexip.

At HQ4, I watched as Intersport pulled off yet another dazzling transition. Hervé Dubuis barked off a checklist to his teammates, who answered together, "Ouais!" An assistant asked, "Karim—a zero-three or a zero-four?" then tossed the competitor a prepackaged food bag.

A few yards away, Coflexip looked positively disorganized, rummaging through trunks in search of candy bars and fruit sticks. Laurent Maubré kibitzed with bystanders as he wearily changed clothes.

The sun was setting over a badlands of stubbled cattle pastures and grotesque sandstone towers. Suddenly Intersport set off. One minute behind them, Coflexip grabbed their packs and hurried after, like kids about to miss their school bus. In one last brilliant transition, Intersport had stolen back twenty-six minutes from Coflexip, and the lead—or at least the apparent lead, given the one-and-a-half-hour penalty lurking in their future. The gambit had a stunning psychological impact.

From HQ4, the course wound back up through a labyrinth of craggy spires and brushy gulches. This section had been crafted as a test of the teams' orienteering skills, with four checkpoints scattered high on arcane ridges. But nobody had anticipated that the battle for victory would unwind here through a pitch-dark night, witnessed by no one but the ten *conquérants* themselves.

Laurent Maubré spoke for the others when he said later that this blind stagger through the night brought the race to its psychological pitch. "C'était un coup chasseur, un coup chassé," he put it in his aphoristic way: "It was first hunter, then hunted. When you were behind, you had the gun. When you were ahead, the other team had the gun."

A virtually fail-safe strategy occurred to Coflexip. They could simply walk on Intersport's heels, guaranteeing an arrival together at CP 33, the put-in on the Limay. Then, as Intersport sat out its penalty, Coflexip would have an hour-and-a-half head start on the home stretch.

But the gallant *conquérants* disdained such a ploy. Coflexip had an ace up its sleeve: Jean-Yves Paillier, one of the finest navigators the Raid has ever seen. Through the dark labyrinth, Paillier chose his team's route, winding among ravines and ridges on old goat paths his headlamp found in the brush. Later Cathy Lefèvre-Isambourg spoke in wonderment: "Jean-Yves would read the map without ever losing his sangfroid, always in control of the situation. We followed him like the sheep of Panurge."

The modest Paillier was at a loss to explain his gift. "I take my time," he said blandly, after the race, "I look around me. I stay concentrated all the time. If I have any doubt, I stop. Maybe there was also a bit of luck!"

The performance of Lefèvre-Isambourg was a remarkable story in its own right. A twenty-five-year-old champion speed sailor, she joined the team only a week before the Raid, when Paillier's sister dropped out with a back injury. She met her teammates only at the airport, departing France. Amazingly, she had never before worn crampons and was a novice equestrienne.

As darkness fell on the rugged sandstone ridges, Intersport realized that to stand any chance of winning, they had to pull out all the stops. They parted ways with Coflexip as, ignoring the valleys with their goat paths, they took azimuth and compass readings on distant silhouettes and tried to bash overland on a beeline to the next checkpoint.

It was a desperate strategy, but a bold one. As Béatrice Piollat put it,

"Ça passe ou ça casse!" ("It works or it falls apart!") As the team blundered over steep ridges, trying to keep to their heading, they kept running into blank cliffs and impenetrable tangles of thorns. Yet in the dark, anything might happen: the other team could lose a checkpoint altogether, have to wait till dawn to regain its bearings.

Later Hervé Dubuis recounted the moment of truth: "We walked all night. Then, suddenly, we saw Coflexip's headlamps far ahead of us. We were completely demoralized. We said to ourselves, it's all over."

In the end, Intersport lost two more hours to Coflexip in the labyrinth. By the time they got into their canoes on the Limay, they were nearly four hours behind. Unless one of the Coflexip team collapsed, the race was over.

On the morning of December 11, I climbed 2,000 feet up crags and slopes in the Valle Encantado (Enchanted Valley) to meet Coflexip. After the easy paddle on the Limay, the course wound high again along rocky ridges, some fixed with ropes, before plunging to a 200-foot overhanging rappel just minutes from the finish line.

At Checkpoint Thirty-four, the last checkpoint, the *controlleur* and I waited for the leaders. They came in sight just after 11:00 A.M., trudging steadily across a hillside swaying with head-high grasses. It was our eleventh straight day of perfect weather. An audience of two, we clapped and cheered as Coflexip came in and threw down their packs.

"Forty-two hours, no sleep, running, running," Maubré said to me in English. "But it is good for the health."

How had they found the obscure checkpoints in the dark, I wondered. Cathy Lefèvre-Isambourg nodded at Paillier: "This man is a genius."

I hiked down the mountain with Coflexip. The exhausted *conquérants* moved with the worn-out stumble of old men. Now and then each would stop, bend over, plant a palm on a knee, and try to suck a little more energy out of his ravaged body.

The racers stopped at the top of the rappel. Suddenly Maubré pulled out a cardboard throwaway camera and handed it to the *controlleur*, who shot a souvenir portrait of the victors arm-in-arm. Surprisingly, I was still the only journalist in attendance. But then, as Coflexip got on rappel, they came in sight of the finish line a quarter-mile away, and a great cheer rang through the Valle Encantado.

Several days later, the whole Raid Gauloises entourage met at a racing ground near San Carlos de Bariloche for the outdoor victory celebration. Wine, beer, champagne, and bonhomie flowed freely. Each team among the top ten strode to a makeshift podium and offered a few remarks. Intersport, which had come in four hours after Coflexip, had been moved to find their rivals waiting to greet them at the finish. Now Hervé Dubuis was gracious in the extreme: "Coflexip was always very fair," he said. "The course was very, very fine. We saw so many beautiful things."

Objectif Raid had finished third, rapping the 200-foot cliff in the dark at 2:00 A.M., thirteen hours after Coflexip. Once all hope of catching the leaders had vanished, the team had coasted, still comfortably ahead of any challengers for third place. Now captain Michel Denaix dead-panned: "It is not easy to go with four women. They were always gossiping among themselves." The crowd heartily razzed Denaix, not least because all four women grinning at him on the podium were beauties.

Once again, Coflexip stole the show. They had composed a gypsy ballad in honor of the race, which they sang, with Maubré strumming a mean guitar:

> CP maso, CP maso
> Je cherche dans les roseaux
> Où vas-tu mon enfant? Où vas-tu mon enfant?
> Livrer mon paquet cadeau.

(Essentially untranslatable, but something like: "Checkpoint maso[chistic], CP maso / I search among the bamboo / Where are you going, my child? / To deliver my gift-wrapped present.")

The ceremony turned into an all-night party. Booze and noise and sheer relief that the ordeal was over turned the world into a happy blur. I found myself hugging *conquérants* I had never spoken to. Back home, in the cool light of reassessment, perhaps my qualms would edge again toward the surface. But at the moment, in the heart of Patagonia, we were all comrades, and the Raid Gauloises seemed, as Gérard Fusil at his most fulsome had vowed, a celebration of the joy of being alive.

BLEAU

I am no lover of forests. The birch mazes of the seeping Adirondacks; the incestuous conifers tangling the White Mountains; the hideous ravines of the Cascades, choked with clinging brush; the gauntlet of squat taiga that enfilades the Alaska Highway—such woods have always seemed to me landscapes of gloom, brewed up by Darwin's mutative riot at its most careless. Even the open lodgepole and ponderosa stands of my boyhood Colorado served only as glades of passage, gateways to the bursting promise that timberline laid bare.

But Fontainebleau—there is a forest I can love. Only thirty miles southeast of Paris, bisected by roaring A6 (the Autoroute du Soleil), Bleau—as the climbers call it—should not be confused with wilderness. From the 1130s on, the forest was the royal hunting grounds for the kings of France. The palace of Fontainebleau, exceeded in magnificence only by Versailles, served for centuries as the swankiest hunting lodge in the world. The 62,000 acres of surrounding woods are thus crisscrossed with ancient, hand-cobbled carriage roads that meet in puzzling *carrefours* in the middle of nowhere.

Despite its name—an antique contraction of *fontaine de belle eau*—the forest is all but waterless, a desert of sand out of which pines and oaks and beeches and wild cherry trees somehow contrive to spring. The eons glued the sand into rock, then flooded the plain with limestone; millennial rains wore this softer stuff away, leaving the woods strewn with grotesque and dramatic sandstone erratics up to fifty feet high. The homely taxonomy of English calls such an assemblage of rocks a "boulder pile"; in French, it forms a *chaos*.

During the last hundred years, many of the best mountaineers in the world, from Pierre Allain to Guido Magnone to Catherine Destivelle, found in Bleau both a nursery for their youth and a Sorbonne of their maturity. Parisian office workers today routinely shut off their word processors at 5:30 P.M. and careen down the *autoroute* for an evening's sport at Bleau. No major city in the world has a more genial rock garden so close at hand.

On my fifth visit to Fontainebleau, I discovered the ideal way to apprehend the place. Shunning the thronged cafes that edge toward the palace, I alighted in the one-street town of Barbizon, at the Hôtellerie du Bas-Bréau. The very same inn, known then as the Hôtel Siron, sheltered the salon of a lively gang of nineteenth-century painters who trooped daily into the forest, armed with canvas and easel.

No group of artists has fallen into a moldier neglect than the Barbizon School: Corot, Millet, Théodore Rousseau, and their lesser-known cronies. Often they are damned with the faint praise of serving as "precursors to the Impressionists." To my mind, however, the savage woodland epiphanies of Corot are far more powerful than Seurat's picnics. Sleeping at the Bas-Bréau, visiting the small museums housed in the *ateliers* of Millet and Rousseau, venturing each day into the forest, I began to see Fontainebleau through the painters' eyes, and to recover the wild revolutionary fervor with which their landscapes teem.

For these were the first European painters who dared to paint nature for its own sake, rather than as a backdrop for mythology or history. Trees, rocks, light, and shade—these made as noble a subject as the martyrdoms of saints, declared Rousseau. The gleaners and sowers celebrated by Millet, so innocuous to the modern eye, adumbrated a radical socialism, a "workers of the world, unite" uttered in pigment no less searing than Karl Marx's cry.

The bold paintings of the Barbizon School seize upon the disorder of nature: even a restful clearing brims with fathomless mysteries. The ancient oak trees of Fontainebleau are bent and tortured; the painters believed they had been rendered thus by the twisting agonies of arboreal thirst. So dark are their canvases that the artists' detractors accused them of painting with prune juice.

Yet what a raucous, hedonistic band the Barbizon School was! Their number included Lazare Bruandet, gentle as a lamb while he painted, but a great brawler when drunk, accosting strangers at the Siron and once throwing his wife out the window; Alexandre Decamps, who died in the forest, victim of a runaway horse; the visionary one-legged mystic, Narcisse Diaz; and the eccentric military hero, Stamati Bulgari, who held a parasol in one hand while he painted and wiped his brush on his linen shirt. My favorite was the nervous insomniac, Rousseau, whose passion for the forest amounted to a private religion. King Louis-Philippe had ordered 15 million pines, not native to Fontainebleau, planted in regimental rows. To Rousseau the magnificent oaks of the forest bespoke the divine, and he so hated the king's trees that he organized expeditions into the woods to tear young pines up by the roots.

The Barbizon School had its groupies. Coyly, the painters posted a sign in the salon dining room declaring, "Under pain of fine, visitors are forbidden to excite the artists." Yet by moonlight, they marched with their admirers into the forest to the tread of trumpets, built campfires in caves where brigands had once lurked, drank flagons of wine, and made love all night.

To the Hôtel Siron one day in 1875 came the twenty-four-year-old Robert Louis Stevenson, still unknown to the world, but already wandering in search of relief from his tubercular ailment. At once he ensconced himself in the painters' salon. As I sat in the Bas-Bréau garden, shaded by a giant copper beech, I read Stevenson's pair of little-known essays celebrating that sojourn, "Fontainebleau" and "Forest Notes."

"Theoretically, the house was open to all comers," Stevenson noted. "Practically, it was a kind of club." The Sirons went to bed early, but left their wine cellar open to the thirsty painters, who paid on the honor system. Pigeons roosted in the bedrooms. For once, Stevenson was too happy to write. "We returned from long stations in the fortifying air," he later recalled, "our blood renewed by the sunshine, our spirits refreshed by the silence of the forest; the Babel of loud voices sounded good; we fell to eat and play like the natural man; and in the high inn chamber, panelled with indifferent pictures and lit by candles guttering in the night air, the talk and laughter sounded far into the night."

On an outing to the nearby village of Grez-sur-Loing, Stevenson met and was struck dumb by Fanny Osbourne, a married American woman with two children, ten years the writer's elder, who became the love of his life and eventually his wife. The wooing of this sophisticated world traveler and great beauty, at first impervious to the writer's flatteries, cost Stevenson many a sleepless night, but only deepened the enchantment of Fontainebleau.

Steeped in these nineteenth-century glimmerings, I set out into the woods each day on my own excursions. In my pack I stuffed a loaf of the hearty peasant bread called *pain seigle*, a local cheese, a *saucisson*, some fruit, and a bottle of wine. For many a lazy hour I followed the blue dots that designate the old Denecourt trails. Claude-François Denecourt was an ex-soldier under Napoleon who settled near Fontainebleau in 1832. Astonished to find only a single trail penetrating the deeper wilds of the forest, he set out to handcraft *sentiers* that eschewed the rectangular logic of the king's roads in favor of winding tours of Fontainebleau's hidden wonders.

Denecourt's paths, which seek out every *chaos* in the forest, are like nobody else's. The man's fondness for lairs and nooks made him route his ways so that they deliberately scuttle through natural tunnels, or corkscrew around a handsome boulder, or linger on a ledge with a view of acres and acres of sand. Coming upon the numerous masonry-improved caves in which, as late as the eighteenth century, outlaws and hermits and society's castoffs had lived, I recaptured the old fear of the forest as a dangerous, alien place. The words of an earlier traveler who had crossed Fontainebleau to reach the king's great hunting lodge murmured in my mind: "We had to go four leagues with nothing to eat or drink, and to console us we had nothing before our eyes but frightening and horrible mountains full of gross rocks, piled one on top of another."

And every day I chose a bouldering circuit, the specialty of Bleau. Each circuit is a numbered sequence of boulder problems, as many as seventy or eighty, that weaves in and out of a particular *chaos*. The rocks are neatly painted with tiny arrows, numbers, and parenthesized dots (the last indicating a jump). Color-coordinated by difficulty, the circuits range from the yellow *peu difficile* to the fiendish black *extrêmement difficile*. In the United States, eco-vigilantes would have squelched such desecration of the scenery before it got started; at Fontainebleau, the circuits integrate the human and the natural, just as do the formal gardens of the palace.

I had lost for good, I thought, the urge to boulder: at stateside crags, the scene reeks for me of chalk dust and ego and painful calisthenics. But Bleau reawakened my sense of play. On a warm, windy day, with no one else in sight, I puttered through the seventy-one-numbered blue (*difficile*) circuit at Manoury. Every single problem has a fanciful name: I tackled The Mustard Pot and The Camembert Traverse, was stumped by The Drunkard's Arête and The Subway Handle, but managed Toto's Slide.

Then I lounged on a sandstone table and opened my bottle of wine.

Rousseau's gnarled oaks swayed in the breeze, and Corot's umbrageous glooms flickered on the periphery of thought. As the beaujolais worked its charm, I lapsed into wistfulness, rueing—as Stevenson had, because Millet had died a few months before he came to Fontainebleau—the eternal injustice of having been born too late. But the leaves danced my regret away, and joy washed in: for an hour longer, the ancient forest would be mine.

WANDERGOLF
IN THE TIROL

Call him Edwood. The man had in fact been growing grim about the mouth, and though it was June, a damp drizzly November had settled over his soul. The insular city of the Manahattoes held him captive. Friends and colleagues prescribed flight.

Not easily, however, could Edwood be detached from his desk in the office of a certain magazine, where he put in many a long day ungarbling wayward paragraphs and flagellating writers by fax. One day a scribe whom Edwood had kept on a short leash in the past poured a honeyed proposal into his ear.

Edwood deliberated for weeks, while the honey seeped inward, clogging his puritan heart. At last he seized the telephone. "Roberts," he blurted into the mouthpiece, "let's do it. Everybody says I'd be crazy if I didn't go."

So writer and editor betook themselves to the sybaritic village of Kitzbühel, Austria, for eight days of Wandergolf in the Tirol. On the masthead, as in life, the editor had always gone under the name of Atwood. But the magic of the telex turned him into Edwood on the register of the Sporthotel Reisch.

Quintessential Edwood he became during certain moments in Austria—as when he pounded his three-wood upon the offending patch of fairway that had somehow caused his shot to veer into uncharted forest, or while downing shots of Jägermeister with Rock Steady Eddy at the Londoner Pub.

Wandergolf was Roberts's idea: Indeed, he had coined the term, in honor of the German language's penchant for hooking words end-to-end to create a monster noun that was more than the sum of its parts. Wandergolf—"wandern" meaning "to hike"—also served as a specimen of that modern bastardization of the tongue that might be called Germglish (by analogy with Franglais: "le weekend," "le pique-nique"). On the Golfplätze of the Tirol, after tuning up on the Drivingrange, Edwood sauntered down the fairway, consulting his Birdiekarte to learn how many meters yawned between his unplayable lie and the invisible green.

In his prime, Roberts had been a mountaineer of some repute; doddering along at fifty-one, he still enjoyed a challenging scramble, and the Tirolean Alps were one of his favorite ranges in the world. During the last three years, he had succumbed to the lure of golf, trudging his way around enough public courses in eastern Massachusetts to qualify as a bonafide weekend hacker. But he had never played golf in German.

Edwood, on the other hand, had a video swing and a fourteen handicap (during a year off between magazines, he had lowered that number to nine). Yet he had done little hiking among any real mountains, and though he was, at thirty-eight, remarkably fit for an editor, he arrived in the Tirol with new boots and a blithe alpine innocence.

Prior to the trip, Edwood and Roberts had only once gone out for a beer together. Each nursed a private fear that, during a solid week of close companionship, the other would prove himself an impossible bore or an egregious egomaniac. Roberts, in particular, had noticed with mild vexation that the older he got, the harder it was to take people of any sort for more than about twenty minutes at a time.

Kitzbühel, Roberts had learned, was calling itself the Golfzentrum der Alpen, with three courses in town and ten others within a seventy-mile radius. An hour after their arrival, Hermann, their host, had Roberts and Edwood poking their jet-lagged way through the Schwarzsee course, owned by the very tourism office for which Hermann toiled. "It is," he explained, "the first course in Austria with nature parts. The Greens, they think it is okay. The grass is not fancy imported."

Edwood was not impressed. When Hermann wandered out of earshot, he muttered, "This could be a public course in New Jersey."

"With that kind of scenery?" Roberts gestured north toward the savage limestone fangs of the Kaisergebirge, south toward the Kitzbüheler Alpen rising toward the glaciers gleaming on the Italian border.

Edwood looked, letting his club slip to the ground. "Goddamn it, Roberts, you're right. We're in the Alps!"

That evening, in the hotel, a gimpy old guide named Franz, who knew every wrinkle of the nearby mountains, suggested itineraries. Franz was missing the last digits of two or three fingers, severed perhaps by some toppling boulder. His spectacles were cracked, probably in some more recent mishap. He pointed to Edwood, of the rugged physiognomy and Prince Valiant locks: "So this is the mountain climber?"

Edwood chuckled. Roberts raised a feeble hand. Franz continued to assess the younger American. "I thought his face would be right for the rocks."

The Sporthotel Reisch, at the center of the cozy village, made a splendid headquarters. The staff was solicitous and attentive. But the reason that Roberts and Edwood lingered over breakfast, sipping coffee like cops in a bad TV show, was Dominique. A young American relative of the owner, Dominique arrived on the Wandergolfers' second day, to work the morning shift in the hotel and learn German over the summer.

A generation of pulp romance writers had minted their clichés in homage to the Dominiques of the earth. Darting in and out of the kitchen, bearing platters of bread and flagons of orange juice, she was ineffably coltish, lithe, long-limbed, high-breasted, raven-tressed, sloe-eyed . . . and genuinely sweet to boot. The smitten travelers gazed upon her fleeting appearances with the longing of the dispossessed.

To their astonishment, Dominique at once befriended the two Americans old enough to be her father. But every garden has its toad. The Reisch's was one Frau Michael, a plump witch whose disingenuous smile camouflaged a heart black with rage against the beautiful. "I'm not supposed to talk to the guests," Dominique confessed with an anxious look over her shoulder as the swinging door to the kitchen creaked. The next morning, Dominique had spoken no more to our heroes than, "How was your golf?" when Frau Michael alighted at her elbow, scowling as she smiled, and spat out, "Get back in there and make sure the coffee is ready!"

This last, delivered in machine-gun German, was deciphered by Roberts as Dominique fled. Eons ago, in junior high, he had studied the language for six months; proceeded to forget all he learned; then, on his first trip to Austria a quarter-century later, found that glimmerings of the Teutonic tongue still coursed through his tangled circuitry. By now, after eight or nine trips to Germany and Austria, he could order dinner brilliantly, catch the gist of newspaper headlines, and even bluff his way, with the scattershot bravado endemic in the freelance writer, through pseudo-conversations with strangers met on trail or tee.

This slipshod grasp of German served him well at Schloss Kaps, a rolling nine-hole course just above town that Edwood found far more interesting than Schwarzsee/Jersey City. Here, the tee boxes were hung with long-winded signs that began with the alarming Achtung! One of them, Roberts sensed dimly in the midst of his backswing, urged golfers not to tee off when cars appeared on the paved road that bisected the fairway. He checked his swing and spared a trundling VW. Roberts puzzled out another sign while Edwood took four or five vicious divots prior to flogging his drive. "I think it says," Roberts informed him, "no practice shots on the tee."

Germglish was alive and well on the Austrian links. On the green, one made "putts" just as in English; in the fairway, yelled "Fore!" when endangering others. At Schloss Kaps, the Americans were paired with Volgar and Sabina from Munich, who spoke no English. "Schön abgeschlagen!" Volgar crowed when Roberts hit a rare clean shot: something like, "Well struck, old chap!" Then Edwood launched a titanic drive, and Volgar bellowed, "Zoo pair!" It dawned on Roberts that a Germglish superlative was Volgar's intent.

Tramping the hilly fairways had filled the golfers with wanderlust. On their third day in the Tirol, Roberts and Edwood assaulted the Gamshag, a handsome, straightforward peak looming 4,000 feet above the trailhead where they parked their Meat Wagon. (This last, Edwood's coinage, upon learning that a rental car was a Mietwagen.)

They began under towering firs, tracing a sinuous chasm out of the Brothers Grimm. Halfway up, they broke free of the trees and passed an antique dairy farm clinging to a dizzy alp, from the pigsty of which the antique proprietor glared. The trail wound on through a hanging valley, as the Wanderers worked off their hangovers, sweating the joy of the penitent.

While they hiked, Roberts regaled Edwood with tales of the atrocities various editors had wreaked upon his blameless prose. Edwood, in turn, offered doleful accounts of certain freelance writers, thought until recently to be reliable contributors, who, in the face of an important assignment, Had Failed to Come Through.

Four hours out and up, they traversed over the spiky Teufelssprung ("Devil's Leap"). Edwood seemed to be riding a euphoria no mere thirty-foot putt could give him. "Incredible!" he kept yammering. "Look at these mountains!"

In his day pack, along with cheese and chocolate and rolls filched from

Dominique's platter, Roberts carried his rusty three-iron. On the way up, other hikers crossing their paths had guffawed in Germglish at the unmistakable handle protruding like a flagpole above his head. It was Roberts's fancy to penetrate to the heart of Wandergolf by driving several golf balls off the summit of the Gamshag.

As they reached the top, Edwood turned to his colleague and delivered a stern admonition. "As your editor, I must tell you that the magazine in no way condones the folly you are about to perform. In fact, the magazine officially urges you to refrain from this desecration of the wilderness."

Roberts nodded contritely. Perhaps it was folly, or at least foolishness. . . .

"Now, where are those balls?" said Edwood as he limbered up his swing.

The alpine linksmen chose the precipitous north face off which to blast their rockets. Scanning the slopes below, they made sure no fellow Wanderers were trekking up the distant zigzag trail, no chamois browsing among the mosses. Roberts scrambled out to the end of a sharp fin that overhung both sides, as Edwood begged him to come back; then, in his overeagerness, mishit his first ball and pooped it pitifully off the cliff.

From the summit itself, Edwood hit two clean shots. Roberts tracked the second, marking on the map where the ball hit terra firma far below. The Wandergolfers had recalled the astronaut who had stroked a drive on the moon; in their memory, his ball had traveled a mile or more.

Later Roberts resurrected his high-school geometry to calculate his companion's best shot. The hypotenuse revealed that, with a three-iron and a nervous swing, Edwood had managed to hit a golf ball 572 yards *in the air*.

This still seemed a modest achievement compared to lunar golf, until, a few weeks later, Roberts came upon a news clipping commemorating the astronaut's deed on its twenty-third anniversary. Contrary to myth, Alan Shepard—who, like Edwood, had a fourteen handicap—flubbed his first shot with a jerry-rigged six-iron, dribbling it a mere 100 yards into a crater. Shepard hit his second shot clean, but the ball, even with its airless roll, traveled only 200 to 400 yards—no match for Edwood in the Tirol. On the other hand, Shepard wore a space suit so bulky he had to swing one-handed.

Back in Kitzbühel, determined to burn their candles at both ends, Roberts and Edwood set out in search of night life. They dined in one charming Stuberl after another. But at a later hour, the town's two discos—whose names, Take Five and T Five, testified to some inexplicable Dave Brubeck cult—were gloomy and deserted. Nor were the Austrian bars much to write home about, except for the Big Ben and the Londoner. The Anglophilia of the resort dates from the 1930s, when the glamorous abdicator the Duke of Windsor and Wallis Simpson made Kitzbühel the place to be seen.

The Londoner, actually an Australian pub, was the hottest place in town: after 10:00 P.M., the Kitzbüheler youth jammed the place, striking poses, chain-smoking, and downing grosse Biere by the keg load. This, too, seemed inexplicable to Roberts, who had seen facsimiles of the Londoner in down-at-the-heels towns in darkest Queensland, and to Edwood, who located the American equivalent in Daytona Beach.

The obligatory downing of Jägermeister shots had to be accomplished by holding the glass with thumb and little finger while the middle fingers curled into an effete fist. The bartenders wore (and sold) T-shirts emblazoned with the mottos by which they lived: "It's a Hard Life in the Mountains," and "Happiness is a Tight Pussy." They spoke Germglish so raw Roberts couldn't comprehend it. The featured singer, Rock Steady Eddy, was an abrasive crooner and guitarist who, defying a century's worth of jazz legend, only got worse as he got more drunk.

"Well," said Edwood, as Eddy expired after mangling "Satisfaction," "I guess it's better than 'Sylvia's Mother.'" This ditty, along with many another that had not been heard in the United States in two decades, was piped into the breakfast salon every morning at the Sporthotel.

Back on the Golfplätze, Roberts and Edwood played three superb courses in as many days. At Seefeld, the fairways swerved and pitched like ski runs among the larches, with stunning views of the fog-hung Karwendel mountains for backdrop. Quaint old hay sheds, some still in use, served as obstacles more daunting than bunkers, for at times one had to chip over them to approach the green.

Our heroes made a foursome with Hermann, their Kitzbühel host, and Walter, his Seefeld equivalent. Walter told them about Sepp, a Tirolean gremlin who inhabits the fairway-guarding woods, running out invisibly to steal golf balls. Roberts was suffering an extended bout of leaving putts short. In America, he had heard many a frustrated puttsman berate himself, "Hit it, Alice!" Now, however, he was startled when Hermann, eyeing yet another Roberts six-footer as it came to rest eight inches short, said, "I think that was a very homosexual putt."

On about the seventh hole, bewildered by the Stableford scoring system Walter had imposed, irked that no one would grant him even the easiest gimme putt, Roberts realized that he was playing in a tournament—the first of his life. Afterwards, downing beer in the clubhouse, he listened placidly as Walter announced the winners, with sly in-jokes about various members' foibles. Suddenly Walter was talking English. "And our third-place winner, from the Manhattan Ocean Club—" Cheers broke out;

Edwood stared wide-eyed, got to his feet, and had thrust into his hands a spiffy glass trophy.

After that he was insufferable. At Kössen the next day, under drizzly skies, the duo had to themselves what Roberts soon realized was the hardest course he had ever played. Every fairway seemed to warp in a double dogleg; not a single green could be seen from its tee; and woods, swamps, and ponds crowded hungrily in on every side. Sepp took it easy that day: rather than having to run out from his gremlin lair to snatch balls, he lay back and waited for Roberts to feed them to him. Before the day was over, he would lose eleven balls, a personal record, and shoot his highest score in three years.

On the twelfth tee, with Roberts's despair troughing out as he blasted his eighth lost ball into a jungle of cattails, he heard a small voice behind him. A twelve-year-old girl with braces on her teeth had biked down a nearby road. "Brauchen Sie Golfbälle?" she repeated—"Do you need golf balls?" The little angel/hustler's name was Manuela, she lived nearby, and she regularly appeared at this corner of the Golfplatz with her school satchel filled with used balls. Now she sold Roberts five balls with strange European labels for ten schillings (about ninety cents) apiece. For the next two holes, Roberts hit straight and true, before Manuela's spell wore off and he reverted to form.

That night, at 3:00 A.M., the seventh game of the NBA finals was broadcast live on Austrian TV. Edwood and Roberts struggled out of their Wandergolf nightmares to attend the event in Roberts's room at the Sporthotel. It was beguiling to listen to basketball in German, but the tension in the room was thickened by the fact that Edwood confessed himself a Knicks fan so blind that he could occasionally admire John Starks, while Roberts nursed a partiality for Hakeem Olajuwan.

As the close game unfolded, there was nothing for it but to ransack the mini-bar. Barely palatable Austrian snacks got washed down with Austrian pilsner; after halftime, our heroes started in on the airplane miniatures. Sam Casell hit a three-pointer, and the broadcaster sang, "Rookie-time!" Otis Thorpe checked in to the sobriquet, "Der Reboundkönig der Rockets!"

"Are we out of vodka?" Edwood moaned as his team fell seven points down.

"There's rum. Have a dollop."

It was Roberts's turn to become insufferable. Near the end, Starks threw up a three-point airball. "Ja, Starks," Roberts jeered, "zwei für achtzehn!" Two for eighteen! Edwood had passed out.

With an hour and a half of sleep, the golfers set out in the morning for

Zell-am-See, a valley bottom course made stylish by the cunning use of ponds and hay sheds. Not only had Edwood's team lost, but also he was off his game. Tired of being trounced, Roberts relentlessly needled his golf partner. "No glass trophy today!" he gloated as Edwood put one in the lake. The editor, morose and laconic, pounded the fairway in frustration. "It's entirely possible," Roberts pointed out on fifteen, "that you could lose to a weekend hacker."

At the end, Edwood added up the score. Roberts had won by a single stroke (the numbers need not be divulged). Said Edwood, handing over the card as he strode toward the Meat Wagon, "Frame this and mount it on your wall. It'll never happen again."

On the Gamshag, Edwood had proved himself a worthy mountain acolyte. As the climax of their trip to the Tirol, Roberts decided to drag his companion up a Klettersteig, even though, in the pedagogy of mountaineering, that was like leaping from first grade to junior high. Still an alpine innocent, Edwood declared himself all for it.

At the Sporthotel, the solicitous desk clerk asked Roberts and Edwood where they were off to that morning. "Something in the Kaisergebirge," Roberts answered.

Her face grew grave. "Oh, but be careful. There are many dangerous mountains."

"Yes, we know," smiled Roberts. "Ich bin ein Bergsteiger."

The Klettersteig to which Edwood soon found himself committed was a route that climbed a spectacularly steep limestone headwall by means of a series of cable handrails. The going was relatively easy, foot by foot, but the exposure was formidable, and at most points if one let go and slipped, one would indeed bounce to a quick but messy death.

Via a narrow ledge, the route traversed into a concave amphitheater between the Predigstuhl and the Fleischbank—soaring peaks that glowed in Roberts's ken with the names of many a legendary climber—then zigzagged 3,000 feet up crack systems and a snowfield toward a high col.

"The one thing to watch out for," Roberts counseled, "is climbers above kicking loose rocks." Sure enough, even before the pair had reached the amphitheater, Roberts heard a sound he knew in his guts—the whir of airborne stones. "Rock!" he yelled as he shrank into the nearby wall. Half a second later a basketball-sized chunk of limestone smashed a foot above his head and bounced over him.

The fusillade finished, Roberts looked up to see two young louts—Germans, he guessed—setting up a technical climb 150 feet above. It was they who had dislodged the missiles, not bothering to warn the mere pedestrians below. "Man muss etwas sagen!" Roberts screamed in fury, hoping that it conveyed, "You have to say something!" The louts shrugged, offering not even a muttered "sorry." "Assholes!" Roberts added in Germglish.

Once on the zigzags, Roberts regained his composure. Ever game, Edwood inched his way up the Klettersteig with baby steps. "Try not to lean against the wall like that," Roberts urged gently. "Try actually to stand on your two feet." Edwood tried. "Now look down," Roberts exhorted. Edwood's head swiveled slowly, like a robot's, the eyes goggling. "Now look up. Yes. But just because you're looking up doesn't mean you have to clutch the cable so hard." Edwood unclenched minimally. "It's like golf—all you have to do is relax."

Edwood's responses were at first confined to oaths and obscenities. Yet the editor crept inexorably upward. They passed the usual plaques to climbers who had died in the neighborhood. The unverglückte Josef Frank, age twenty-six, on the north wall of the Predigstuhl in 1978—it was always "unfortunate," death in the mountains. Some more recent youth, known only as Bernhard, his small wooden crucifix wrapped with a piece of nylon climber's cord.

About 1,500 vertical feet into his ordeal by terror, things began to click for Edwood. He stood on his two feet. He held the cable with only one hand. He looked up and down and around. He posed for a picture with a grin on his face.

"Roberts," he declared, as the duo kicked steps up the snowfield below the col, "this is amazing. I'm feeling emotions I've never felt before."

For Roberts, the extremity of Edwood's reaction was rejuvenating. Thirty-four years in the mountains had jaded him, allowing him to forget just what a primal place a precipice could be.

As he gained confidence, a dam of words broke in Edwood. "Roberts, what I want to know is, how is it that you have the nerve to climb the steepest cliffs in Alaska, and yet still leave all those four-foot putts short?" They lunched in sun at the col. On the way down, Edwood was positively nonchalant. "This is one of the greatest experiences of my life," he babbled.

On their last night in Kitzbühel, the Wandergolfers finessed a dinner date at one of the nicer restaurants with Anita, who had replaced Hermann as tourism host, and Dominique, liberated for the evening from the scowl of Frau Michael. A twenty-nine-year-old ex-model, Anita had guileless blue eyes, billowing blond hair, and a certain chilly reserve that Roberts had come to think of as a trait of Austrian women. As the wine flowed—Grüner Veltliner followed by Blaufränkisch—he lapsed into a manic mood. "What is it with these Austrian wines?" he asked Anita, who drank only Mineralwasser. "The white wine is called green, the red is called blue."

In a backhanded effort at flirtation, Roberts raised the question of whether a chilly reserve was a trait of Austrian women. "Some people say I am chilly and reserved," Anita allowed. "But I'm not, underneath."

Roberts blithered on in the same perverse mode, wondering out loud how many Tirolese had never heard of Sigmund Freud. On some kind of jag, he poured out much of what he thought and felt about Austria. Over his second Vogelbeerschnaps, made from an untranslatable local berry, he began to rhapsodize about the minor-major modulations in the late Lieder of Franz Schubert. Yawns were stifled.

Suddenly Edwood spoke. "While you two are settling Schubert's hash, Dominique's going to take me window-shopping. Catch you later." With that, the editor vanished, winsome maidservant in tow.

Around 2:00 A.M., Roberts woke to pounding on his door. It was Edwood, distraught and exhilarated. The mini-bar was raided one last time, while Edwood unveiled the poignant narrative of his stroll. The man was in pain.

"Twenty years ago she—!"

"Twenty years ago she wasn't born."

In the morning, in the Meat Wagon headed for Munich, the Wander-golfers licked their wounds. "You know," said Edwood, "they're not going to be very sympathetic at the magazine when I tell them I need a week off to recover from a week in the Tirol."

"Just don't let them know you had any fun," Roberts suggested.

On a country road, they were passing just south of the Kaisergebirge. Edwood looked out at the scene of his mountain conquest. "Fun? It was work from dawn till midnight."

PROFILES AND POLEMICS

A MOUNTAIN OF TROUBLE

Climbing hard all day, Jeff Lowe had forced an intensely complicated route through a wilderness of false leads and dead ends, but darkness caught him short of the ledge he had hoped to reach. He had no choice but to carve a makeshift cave in the steep fan of snow where he was stranded, then crawl inside. Stupefied with weariness, he fired up his balky stove and turned pot after pot of packed snow to water. *Hydrate, hydrate*, his brain cajoled his listless body.

In the middle of the night the storm came in. The wind was moderate, but a heavy snowfall poured out of the black sky. As the snow gathered, it set loose spindrift avalanches that filled Lowe's cave and threatened to smother him. All night he lay in his sleeping bag, pushing and pounding the walls of his bivouac tent to keep some space inside the cave.

A lifelong tendency toward claustrophobia compounded Lowe's distress. As he grew drowsy, he would be seized with panic; ripping open the door of his tent, he would gasp fresh air, allowing snow not only to spill inside the cave, but also to fill his bivouac sack and his sleeping bag, where it melted and soaked his clothes.

By morning, Lowe was in a perilous situation. It was Thursday,

February 28, 1991, his ninth day on the north face of the Eiger. He was 4,500 feet up, but in the 1,500 feet of frozen limestone that still hung above him, he was sure he would find the hardest passages of all. He was running out of food. He could not stay warm at night. And he was on the verge of exhaustion.

This, Lowe knew, was how climbers died on the Nordwand—as the most dangerous wall in the Alps had come to be named. In just such a way the brave Toni Kurz had come to grief, his rappel jammed on a knotted rope; or Stefano Longhi, abandoned by his partner to freeze to death after he had taken a bad fall; or Max Sedlmayer, climbing hopelessly toward the avalanche that would pluck him from his life.

From so high on the north face, in the midst of a storm, it would take a desperate effort simply to climb down. At the moment, Lowe could not escape his snow cave, because of the avalanches that thundered over the cliffs above and swept the fan of snow.

Hunkered inside his claustrophobic hole, alone in a gray universe of nothingness, Lowe brooded on his predicament. During the last few days, with the weather holding, he had climbed so well; at last he had felt in perfect form, as success had dared to whisper in his ears. Now the prospect of failure loomed larger with every hour of mindless snowfall. And if things got any worse, Lowe would face a battle for his very survival.

No, things were not going right—and the pattern was all too familiar. For a year now, things had been going wrong for Jeff Lowe. Major things, disastrously wrong. Bankruptcy. The failure of his marriage. Separation from his three-year-old daughter. He had scrambled to hold it all together, but his despair had peaked in late October, leaving him sleepless, his antic mind tormenting him with a parade of furious creditors and disappointed friends. Out of the nadir of that depression had come the idea of the Eiger. A new route on the north face—a clean, direct vector between the Czech and Japanese lines. Solo. In winter. Without bolts.

If he could pull it off, the climb would be the greatest achievement ever performed by an American in the Alps. And Lowe had just turned forty, a milestone after which virtually no mountaineer in history had performed his finest exploit. At a deeper, more personal level, the Eiger might somehow tame the internal voices howling of failure and loss. It would be a way for Lowe to return to his strength, to the thing he did best in the world, the thing he did better than all but a handful of his peers.

A little after noon on the twenty-eighth the snow let up. With a tight rope to his anchoring pitons, Lowe cautiously climbed out of his cave to survey his blizzard-struck surroundings. He peered into the void below his feet, still blank with clouds, as he remembered the nine days of agonizing work that had brought him to his stance three-quarters of the way up the Nordwand. Then he craned his neck to look upward, toward the ledge, plastered now with rime, that he had failed to reach the night before. Lowe kicked his right foot into the snow and stepped up. He kicked his left foot: another step.

Seven hours later, in darkness, Lowe settled once more into his soaked sleeping bag. He would have to spend another night in the hated snow cave. He got out his two-way radio and warmed the batteries. Rousing his support team at the hotel far below, Lowe spoke slowly, his voice seamed with fatigue. "I've got a decision to make. Whether to go up or down. It's a tough one."

There was a long pause. "I don't know how hard it would be to get down from here. I figure it'll take three days minimum to reach the summit if I go up. And that's only if the weather's good tomorrow and Saturday."

Another pause. "I guess tomorrow's going to tell. If I go for it, I'll have to pull out all the stops."

HAD JEFF LOWE BEEN BORN a Frenchman or a German, he would be a celebrity, sought after for product endorsements, asked to write his memoirs. But in the United States, great alpinists remain as obscure as chess champions.

Lowe, moreover, is a purist. He makes a wry distinction between "expeditions," which he disdains, and "trips with friends," on which, with from one to three cronies, he can attempt daring routes on unexplored mountains. From his only Everest expedition, a massively funded assault on an easy route involving fourteen climbers, Lowe came home disenchanted. But on some of Lowe's trips with friends, he has performed splendid deeds on such Himalayan mountains as Tawoche, Kwangde, and Nameless Tower; on his ascents of Pumori and Ama Dablam, the only friend was himself.

In his twenties, Lowe was the best ice climber in America, perhaps in the world. Names such as Bridal Veil Falls, Keystone Greensteps, and the Grand Central Couloir—extraordinary ice routes that Lowe was the first to master—can bring an awed hush over parties of cognoscenti.

In the last two decades, the cutting edge of mountaineering has become "good style"—and nobody's style has been cleaner, bolder, or more prophetic than Lowe's. Says Michael Kennedy, editor of *Climbing* and a frequent partner, "Beyond a shadow of a doubt, he's the most visionary American Himalayan climber who's ever lived."

One of eight children growing up in a close-knit family in Ogden, Utah, Lowe and his three brothers were pushed hard by their lawyer father to excel in sports. He started climbing at fourteen, quickly developed his skills, and managed to survive the usual near-disasters of adolescent ambition. After three years at unaccredited Tahoe Paradise College, Lowe scrounged a living from the kinds of marginal jobs most American climbing addicts resort to: pounding nails, teaching at Outward Bound, and tutoring beginners in the sport.

In 1972 Lowe's brothers Greg and Mike launched an outdoor equipment company called Lowe Alpine Systems, which quickly gained a cachet for its innovative packs. Thirteen years later, Lowe started his own company, Latok—named for his most memorable failure, an attempt on Latok I in Pakistan—which sold technical climbing gear, then branched into clothing. His first full-scale business venture, it began to fail after only two years. Lowe Alpine Systems bought out Latok, bailing Lowe out.

Looking back, he says, "I think part of my business problems stemmed from a feeling that I had to be more than a good climber, that I had to do something more 'meaningful.' And that may come from my father."

In 1982, Lowe married a woman he had met in Telluride. The couple settled down in Boulder, where Janie Lowe became her husband's full-time business partner. In 1987, they had a daughter, whom they named Sonja.

The next year, at Snowbird, Utah, Lowe joined with entrepreneur Dick Bass to run the first international climbing competition on American soil. Contests on artificial walls had become one of the hottest spectator sports in Europe; Lowe gambled that Americans would embrace the spectacle. Snowbird '88 was an aesthetic success, but far fewer people than anticipated were willing to fork over twenty dollars apiece to stare at the inch-by-inch progress of European stars whose names they had never heard of. Lowe fell far short of breaking even, and paid off the prize money only many months later.

Undaunted, he incorporated himself as Sport Climbing, Inc., attracted sponsors and investors, and laid plans for Snowbird '89. Thus began the downward spiral that in two years sucked Lowe into a whirlpool of failure. The second Snowbird competition also lost money, and Lowe began borrowing from future projects to pay off past ones. His third stab at an international competition took place at Berkeley in August 1990. Lowe persuaded The North Face to be title sponsor for the event.

Anxious to keep up his climbing, and in need of a quick infusion of cash just to pay his personal bills, Lowe concocted a trip with friends to Nameless Tower in Pakistan, to be filmed for ESPN. The big draw, in terms of European sponsors, would be a summit push pairing himself and Catherine Destivelle, a thirty-year-old Parisian who was the world's most famous woman climber.

Lowe left the United States, his business partners say, knowing that he couldn't come close to paying for Berkeley. The competition turned into another financial fiasco. Bart Lewis, a Vancouver promoter who marketed the competition, claims that The North Face, rather than suffer humiliation as title sponsor, forked over $78,000 that Sport Climbing, Inc., had agreed to pay. "Basically, in my view, Lowe blackmailed North Face," says Lewis. Lowe and Destivelle climbed a hard route on Nameless Tower. The film was broadcast on ESPN, but several European sponsors had backed out at the last minute. Lowe came home from Pakistan deeper than ever in debt, unable to pay even climbing friends who had worked as his support party.

On Nameless Tower, Lowe was deeply impressed by Destivelle's performance. As their teamwork evolved, Lowe realized that with only one or two men had he ever felt so confident climbing in the great ranges. At some point, they began an affair. Because her private life is intensely scrutinized in France, Destivelle urged Lowe to be discreet about their relationship.

In September 1990, Lowe returned from Nameless Tower. "When he got home," says Janie Lowe, "he seemed very angry and distant. It was as if he wanted nothing to do with me. I asked him if he was having an affair with Catherine. 'No, no, no.' Finally, it came out. I asked him, 'Why did you lie to me?' That hurt me so bad. He said, 'I'd promised Catherine.' I said, 'After twelve years, you tell me your loyalty to Catherine is greater than your loyalty to me?'"

On September 13, Lowe turned forty. He was deep in the whirlpool, clutching for flotsam. At the end of October, Lowe declared bankruptcy. As his business partner, Janie took an equal brunt of the bankruptcy, and their relationship grew more troubled. As she tells it, "Jeff would come home and go straight into his study and close the door. Sonja would say, 'Mommy, why doesn't Daddy want to talk to me?'" In mid-December Janie kicked her husband out of the house, and they began divorce proceedings.

"I fell apart," Jeff says. "I felt hopeless. All I knew was that I couldn't stand it after a couple of weeks. I had to start dealing with things one by one."

By early February, Lowe was in Switzerland, standing at the base of the Eiger.

BEGUILED BY THE SHAPE of this unfolding drama, Jon Krakauer and I had come to Switzerland as well, to serve as Lowe's support team. Lowe's business woes were common knowledge in the climbing community, and word of his Eiger project had spread far and fast. More than one observer suggested that Lowe might be headed on a suicide mission. Boulder climber and writer Jeff Long, a loyal friend of Lowe's, later admitted, "With all the pressure he had on him, I was afraid he was going to use the Eiger as some kind of exit."

Suicidal or not, the scheme—a new route, solo, in winter, without bolts, on the most notorious face in the Alps—seemed wildly improbable to most climbers. Destivelle later told Lowe that her French friends were of a single mind: "He'll never do it. It's too cold in winter, and too hard."

Jeff Lowe does not look like a climber: an accountant, you might guess on meeting him, or maybe a viola player. He stands five-foot-ten, weighs about 150; his slender physique seems more wiry than muscular. Clean-shaven, he has an open face, on which alertness struggles against a natural placidity. He wears the wire-rim glasses of a professor. The long, straight blond hair conjures up the hippie he once thought himself. Though his hairline is receding, he combs his locks straight back, as if daring them to retreat further. When he smiles, his eyes crinkle shut, and incipient jowls shadow his jaw. To call his low, cadenced speech a drawl is to suggest a regional twang it does not possess: his voice is rather that of a tape recorder whose batteries are running low.

When he had married, Lowe said, he had promised Janie that he would scale down his climbing ambitions and would take her along on trips to Europe instead of heading off to the Himalaya. Now he grimaced: "You know, I was in love when I told her that bullshit."

Janie had told me, "For the first five years, we were extremely happy. I think our problems had a lot to do with having a daughter. When Sonja came along, things changed for us."

Now Lowe commented obliquely on marriage and business. "It's a lack of freedom. I'm trying to get my freedom back. I'm trying to go back to where my path turned about ten years ago.

"I could have saved my marriage if I had chosen to. But when I was forced to take a new look, I realized, 'Hey, it's not what I really want.' If I do what I really want—it's a weird thing, but climbing is still at the center."

Lowe paused. "The Eiger—even if I succeed—isn't going to make all the other shit go away. I don't expect this climb to make everything right." The crinkly, slow-dawning grin broke upon his face: "It'll just feel real good."

The hotel at Kleine Scheidegg is a rambling Victorian masterpiece, festooned with tiny rooms supplied by elegant if quirky plumbing, with cloth wallpaper and wood paneling, with cozy reading nooks, eighteenth-century engravings, and wooden floors that creak and undulate like a glacier. For fifty-six years the hotel has been the headquarters for

Eiger-watching. As he prepared for his ascent, it became Lowe's base camp.

The hotel is owned and run by the legendary Frau von Almen. She is a good-looking woman of seventy with an imperious manner and a constant frown of disapproval on her brow. Checking in for the three of us, I told her about Lowe's plans. The frown deepened. "This is insane," she pronounced. "It is more than insane—it is mad." She turned and walked away. "I do not like the accidents," she nattered. "Because they are so unnecessary."

To stay in the hotel is to put up with Frau von Almen's tyrannical regime. There was a lengthy codex of unwritten rules, a good portion of which we managed to break. I wore my climbing boots upstairs; Krakauer and Lowe brought sandwiches from outside and ate them in her cafe; all three of us dared to order only drinks in the cafe during lunch hour; I foolishly asked her to unlock the front door of the hotel before 8:00 A.M.; Krakauer had the nerve to wonder if he might move and photograph a portrait of the pioneers who had made the first ascent of the Nordwand in 1938.

There was no way to get on her good side. After dinner one night, I complimented her fulsomely on the four-course repast. "And did your friend enjoy the dinner, too?" she asked ominously.

"Oh, yes," I answered.

"Because he will not eat like this up on the mountain."

Only Frau von Almen's longtime guests—those who had come every winter for more than a decade and skied innocuously each afternoon—seemed to bask in her approbation. The truth was that she was down on climbers. And this was sad, because her husband, Fritz, who died in 1974, had been the climbers' best friend, watching them for hours in his telescope, exchanging flashlight signals with their bivouacs each night. The frau still had the telescope, but would unpack it, she said, "only for emergency." An old-timer told us that a few years ago some climbers accidentally knocked over the telescope and broke it, then ran away.

On February 11, Catherine Destivelle arrived from Chamonix. A very pretty woman five feet four inches tall, with curly brown hair, a conquering smile, and formidable muscles, she is a superstar in France; yet fame has left her relatively unaffected. Though they could hardly disguise the fact that they were staying in the same room, at first Lowe and Destivelle maintained a demure propriety. Gradually the handclasps became less furtive, the kisses semipublic.

Throughout her career, Destivelle has been accustomed to being the center of attention, the star over whom others fussed. It was thus strange for her, on the eve of Lowe's climb, to become the aide and worrier. I had not guessed there was an ounce of maternal blood in Destivelle, but in the face of the boyish helplessness Lowe projected, she grew altogether motherly.

For a first-rate climber, Lowe seemed woefully disorganized. For days his gear was spread all over the floor of his hotel room, but as he inventoried it, he discovered that he was lacking essential items. From Krakauer he borrowed a headlamp, pitons, first aid supplies, and a crucial pair of jumars for ascending ropes; Destivelle brought him foodstuffs (she swore by powdered mashed potatoes) and a two-way radio.

Destivelle was scandalized by Lowe's preparations. "I can't believe," she told us again and again, "he is climbing with equipment he has never used before. I would never do this." Lowe pooh-poohed the problem, omitting to mention one of its causes: he was so broke he had had to sell much of his climbing gear, and now was dependent on the largess of European companies intrigued with his Eiger project.

On the evening of February 18, Destivelle joined Krakauer and me in the bar, where she chain-smoked half a pack of Marlboros. (Ordinarily, she goes months without a cigarette.) At breakfast the next morning, she said she had dreamed obsessively about an all-out war in which everybody was hunting Jeff. She had spent a fitful, miserable night, while beside her Lowe had slept soundly.

They rode the cog railway up to the Eigergletscher station and kissed goodbye. Lowe put on his skis and headed toward the base of the wall. At once Destivelle took the train down to the valley and drove back to Chamonix. The prospect of a multiday vigil in the hotel was too nerve-wracking for her.

ON FEBRUARY 19, HIS FIRST DAY on the Nordwand, Lowe cruised up 2,000 feet in only two hours. The going was easy but dangerous, a matter of planting the picks of his ice axes in a steady rhythm, of stabbing the crampon points strapped to the soles of his boots into brittle ice overlying steep rock. He soloed without a rope: if he slipped, he would die. But Lowe was in his element on this nerve-stretching ground. The speed and precision that had made his technique famous among a generation of American climbers spoke in every swing of his axes.

It was, however, still the heart of winter, and this was the Eiger. Over the last six decades, it was the easy start on the north face that had seduced so many alpinists: between fifty and sixty of the best climbers in the world had died here, in a variety of gruesome ways.

Eight of the first ten men who set out to climb the Nordwand were killed trying. The first man to attempt a solo ascent backed off prudently, only to die on a subsequent attack with a partner. The second, third, and tender blobs, and the nails had begun to crack away from the cuticles. Each morning, his fingers were so sore and puffy he had a hard time tying his shoelaces.

Worse, his sleeping bag, thin to begin with, was soaked like a dishrag: it gave almost no warmth at all. That night Lowe got not a wink of sleep. For fourteen hours he shivered, waiting for dawn, as the snow fell outside his cave.

In the morning it was still snowing. "Where I am," he radioed, "it's hard to even peek out of the bivy tent without dislodging everything. I'm going to sit here and hydrate." An acute dilemma hung over him. If he holed up and waited for the storm to end, he could run out of food and gas and succumb to hypothermia. But if he pushed upward prematurely, the storm itself could finish him.

By noon he had not moved. At 2:00 P.M., through a break in the clouds, we saw him climbing slowly above the Fly. As he started to climb, however, he grew deeply alarmed. Something was wrong. He felt weak all over, weaker than he should have from fatigue alone. He had been going on too little food; he had spent a sleepless night; despite the long hours, he had not gotten enough rest; and he had probably not drunk enough fluid. He resolved to do no more that day than advance two pitches and string the ropes. Then he would devote himself to resting and drinking and trying to get warm.

For this was how climbers died on the Eiger. This was too much like what had happened to Longhi and Kurz.

ONCE MORE, SLEEP WAS IMPOSSIBLE. Lowe shivered through his second night, even though he lit the stove and burned precious fuel in an effort to heat his frigid cavern. The weather had cleared in the late afternoon; now the sky was sewn with stars. There was an odd acoustic clarity: toward morning he could plainly hear dogs barking in Grindelwald, miles away and 10,000 feet below. And he thought he heard something else: a humming, crystalline, harmonic music in the air. Was it an aural hallucination? Was he beginning to lose his grip?

At 7:50 A.M. on Monday, March 4, we received Jeff's morning radio call. For us, the night had been filled with premonitions of disaster, and it was astounding to hear him say cheerily, "Right now I'm just watching some beautiful spindrift going by."

At 8:20 A.M. he started climbing. A perfect day had dawned, of which he would need every minute. Good weather had been forecast to last through the evening, but another storm was due on the morrow. We called

REGA, the government-run rescue service, and alerted them to a possible need for summit pickup. Then we watched Lowe climb. At 9:15 A.M., he turned a corner and disappeared into a couloir we could not see. Two hours later, there was still no sign of him, no murmur over the radio. Though we did not admit it to each other at the time, Krakauer and I both separately trained the telescope on the base of the wall, where we swept the lower slopes. In just such a way over the decades, the fate of a number of Eiger victims had been discovered.

Lowe had hoped that above the Fly the going got easier. But in icy chimneys broken by bands of brittle rock, he was forced to perform some of the hardest climbing yet. Normally he never let himself be rushed on a climb: it was one of the secrets of his sangfroid and his safety. Now, however, he kept looking at his watch, and his brain hectored, *Oh, no, hurry!* Ever so slightly, his technique lost some of the precision for which it was famous. He felt less weak than the day before, but the sense of struggling to meet a terrible deadline oppressed his efforts.

It was hard to place good protection anywhere. Lowe found himself hooking with front points and axe-picks on rounded rock wrinkles that he had to stab through the snow to locate. His balance was precarious, and then, just before it happened, he knew he was going to fall.

The picks scraped loose: he was in midair, turning. Twenty-five feet lower, he crashed back-first into the rock. The self-belay had held, but he was hurt. He felt as though someone had taken a baseball bat and slammed it into his kidneys.

Oddly, instead of panicking him, the long fall calmed him down. *Okay,* he said to himself, *you've done that. Don't do it again.*

He pulled himself together, started up again, and found a way through the dicey hooking sequences, despite the pain pounding in his back. At last he surmounted a buttress and reached a good ledge, only 400 feet below the summit.

But here he faced a problem. The warm sun had loosened the summit snowfields. Every chute and runnel became an avalanche track. One swept right over Lowe, filling his goggles with snow dust, buffeting his body as it tried to knock him from the wall.

He was moving faster now, as slides shot down all around him. For two hours he climbed doggedly on. During that time, three more avalanches engulfed him. One knocked his feet loose, but he hung on with his axes. At 3:20 P.M. he called.

"God, Jeff, those avalanches looked bad," I said.

"Yeah, they were pretty horrendous. I got really douched. I'm totally wet." His voice was ragged with strain. "Am I about a pitch from the west ridge?"

111

"A pitch and a half, maybe."

"I'm going to call for a pickup. I just want to get up this thing."

We signed off and called REGA. They were waiting in Grindelwald, ready to fly the moment Lowe emerged on the west ridge, a few feet below the top. But a stiff wind had begun to blow a steady plume off the summit. The wind could defeat the helicopter's maneuvers, or even cause it to crash.

To our dismay, Lowe disappeared once more into a couloir. The minutes ticked by. At 4:15 P.M. he emerged, fighting his way out of the top of the gully, spindrift hosing him at every step. He was only forty feet below the crest of the ridge.

We prepared to call REGA, then watched in distress as Lowe stopped at a mottled band of rock and snow, only twenty feet below the ridge. For ten minutes he thrashed in place; we saw him seizing stones and tossing them into the void below.

In the hidden couloir, Lowe had found it impossible to get good protection. He had dashed upward, aiming at the mottled band, but when he got there, he found only a skin of ice holding together rocks that were as loose as a pile of children's blocks. When he flung stones aside and dug beneath, he found only more of the same. He could get no protection in— neither piton, nut, nor ice screw.

Only twenty feet short of safety, he had run out of rope. His own anchor, 300 feet below, was imprisoning him. In despair, he realized that he would have to climb down at least 40 feet to the last previous band, try to get some kind of anchor there, rappel for his gear, and jumar back up. He was not sure he could make that downclimb without falling. What was more, he was running out of daylight.

Lowe got on the radio. Krakauer uttered what we were both thinking. "Jeff, if you just dropped your rope and went for it, could you solo the last twenty feet?"

"No problem," said Lowe. "But are you sure the helicopter can get me?"

If we urged Lowe to abandon his gear and the helicopter failed, he would be stranded near the summit without ropes, tent, food, stove, or even his parka. He was soaked to the skin. The wind was whipping hard, and the sky had grayed to the color of lead. Tuesday's storm was arriving early.

Krakauer said, "I'm almost positive they can pick you up."

"Let's do it," said Lowe.

He untied his rope and pinned the end behind a loose rock. He was abandoning all the gear that he had fought for nine days to haul up the 6,000-foot precipice, and with it, deserting his own last refuge.

We called REGA; the helicopter took off from Grindelwald. To be picked up on the summit was not a true rescue; more than one previous Eiger climber had resorted to flying from the top when he was far less strung out than Jeff was. It would, however, be a kind of asterisk attached to his great deed. It would not be the best style, and that would bother Lowe. But it was survival.

He seemed to sprint up the last twenty feet. All at once, Lowe had escaped the north face. He stood on a broad shelf of snow on the west ridge, just below the summit. Krakauer and I cheered wildly. All around us, the guests and skiers cheered, even though Lowe was too small to see with the naked eye. The helicopter spiraled upwards toward him.

Still talking to us on the radio, he couldn't keep the shivering out of his voice. Krakauer instructed him: the helicopter would lower a cable, which he was to clip in to his waist harness.

Now the chopper was just above him, hovering in the stiff wind. Suddenly it peeled off and flew away toward the Jungfraujoch. For the first time, Lowe seemed to lose it. He wailed, "What the hell's going on!"

The chopper, we later learned, was carrying three passengers—a copilot, a winch operator, and a doctor. Appraising the tricky situation, the pilot decided to deposit two of his colleagues at the Jungfraujoch, so he could fly as light as possible when he made the pickup.

"He's coming back, Jeff," I yelled into the radio.

The helicopter hovered again, its rotors straining against the wind. The steel cable dangled from its belly. We saw Lowe swipe for its lower end, miss once, then seize it. He clipped in, and the helicopter swept him into the sky. He was off the Eiger.

The cable wound upward, as he rode it toward the open door. The winch man reached out his hand. Lowe climbed through the door, and crawled back into the conundrum of his life.

OUTWARD BOUND
RECONSIDERED

The magazine ad displays a sketch of a figure rappelling off a cliff. Claims the headline, "It means so much more when you've done it yourself." The pitch, however, is not for some outdoor camp or wilderness school, but for an investment advisory newsletter. Nowhere does the ad copy draw an explicit connection between the challenge of rappelling and the adventure of playing the stock market. The icon seems self-explanatory.

Another ad, in the business section of the *New York Times*, above a wintry photo of jagged mountains, blazons a dare: "For $2,500, we'll throw you off a 300-foot cliff in the Bavarian Alps." What Luft Taucher, Inc., is hawking is "international rappelling tours."

> When was the last time you jumped off a mountain? Or, for that matter, did anything truly challenging? Without challenge, a mind can go soft, a spirit can weaken. Two ailments that can hinder a successful career.
>
> That's why Luft Taucher, Inc., is offering an exclusive series of rappelling tours for executives and professionals. . . .

The notion behind both ads is an intriguing and controversial one. In the course of the last quarter century in America, the idea has spawned an educational movement and a proliferation of small businesses. In a nutshell, Luft Taucher and hundreds of other companies and schools claim that courses in outdoor adventure can not only teach participants self-confidence, teamwork, leadership, and sensitivity to others, but also that the lessons readily and lastingly translate into skills to be used in "real life"— deployed against problems as disparate as kicking a drug habit or surviving a corporate merger.

The concept of nature as a moral classroom is an old one; in different guises, it animates the thinking of writers from Wordsworth and Kipling to Jack London and Hemingway. For that matter, Moses climbed a mountain to receive the tablets of God, and Christ hiked into the wilderness to resist the temptations of Satan. Less explicitly, our popular culture is steeped in homiletic metaphors of voyage and ascent: we congratulate ourselves for "getting to the top," for "peak experiences," for "crossing a new frontier" and "conquering the unknown."

In its focused, pedagogical form, however, the notion that carefully designed outdoor challenges can be directed toward lasting personal change derives mainly from the Outward Bound (OB) movement. The brainchild of Kurt Hahn, an Englishman of German birth, Outward Bound was concocted during World War II as an attempt to answer a question that was vexing the British Navy. As Allied ships were torpedoed by the Germans, it was often the case that among the lifeboat survivors, the youngest and fittest crewmen were the ones who gave up and died most easily. Hahn had been developing his ideas for more than a decade; in 1941 he started a school in Wales to teach young sailors that they had more control over their fate than they believed. After the war, Outward Bound became a training program aimed at turning British citizens into more productive workers.

In 1962, the movement came to the United States with the establishment of the first American Outward Bound School in the Elk Range of Colorado. As an OB instructor in Colorado's second year, I was well aware just how odd the school's program then seemed to most Americans, how much explaining it took to make its central premise plausible. But at the time, I wondered little about the validity of that premise. A passionate twenty-year-old mountaineer, I was astounded to get paid to go hiking and camping instead of having to pound nails or flip hamburgers.

The basic structure of the OB course was imported from Britain. The students were divided into twelve-man "patrols" named after American wilderness heroes like Boone, Crockett, Bridger, and Carson, each with

115

a pair of instructors. The course was twenty-six days long. Among its curricular linchpins were the "solo" (a three-day stationary bivouac out of sight of others), the "morning dip" (a daily run at dawn culminating in a dive into an icewater stream), top-rope rock climbing, a 200-foot rappel, ice-axe self-arrest practice on a steep snowfield, a six-mile "marathon" race, a simulated back-country rescue, and the "final expedition" (a five-day trek without leaders as a graduating test of competency). At the end, there was a banquet at which the boys received their diplomas.

This odd, tough version of summer camp caught on in a big way. In only twenty-five years in the United States, the OB philosophy has become one of the accepted ideas of our time.* Today, there are at least 200 outfits selling outdoor adventure as character improvement, under names like National Outdoor Leadership School, Wilderness Institute, Inner Quest, Visionquest, and Challenge/Discover. Although OB's original target population in America was boys from ages sixteen to twenty-two, the movement has expanded to embrace not only coed groups, but also corporate executives, inner-city minorities, "youth at risk," substance abusers, institutionalized criminals, the physically disabled, feminist and women's-only groups, and Christian fundamentalists. Some 300 colleges and schools have built "outdoor programs" into their curricula; most offer credit toward graduation.

OB got a huge boost toward credibility in the late 1960s from academic reformers and the human potential movement, with their emphasis on experiential education and interpersonal dynamics. And the school seemed willing to modify its objectives to suit the fashions of the times. At Colorado Outward Bound in 1963, we didn't talk much about empathy or sensitivity to others; instead we dwelt on toughness and competition (patrols even got points for tent inspection). Indeed, a 1964 *Life* article celebrating the Colorado school was titled "Marshmallow Becomes a Man" (the marshmallow being an overweight mama's boy who grew hard and able like his peers). Puzzled by the woeful dropout rate of lower-class black youths, OB went through a spasm of liberal guilt in the early 1970s that had its instructors being dumped in urban ghettos with a single dime in their pockets and the mandate to survive a weekend.

Yet the central idea of OB is by now so well accepted that articles and TV shows uncritically hail the breakthrough achievements of drug-dependent adolescents slogging across the desert, or of CEOs rejuvenated by a

---

* This was written in 1987.

whitewater rafting trip. For all the effort that has gone into adapting OB to special groups and needs, most of its basic exercises, from the "solo" to the "big rappel," have survived intact. The twelve-to-two ratio of students to instructors remains canonical. Largely for business reasons, though, the original twenty-six-day curriculum is now often whittled down to two-week, one-week, or even three-day courses.

In a commonsense way, it is obvious why some of the OB challenges are effective. If you have never rappelled before, to back off a vertical cliff with nothing but a rope to hold onto is terrifying. Yet rappelling takes virtually no skill, and when supervised properly it's as safe as watching television. To the client, however, it seems a piece of raw derring-do beyond his capabilities. Thus when he overcomes his fear, backs off the edge, dangles his way down the void, regains terra firma and unclips from the rope, he is seized with a powerful sense of accomplishment and mastery. Another favorite exercise requires a patrol to get all its members across a twelve-foot wooden wall, often against a running clock. The thing cannot be done each man for himself; thus to get the whole gang across requires the development of some form of teamwork.

The tricky question, however, is what the big rappel or the twelve-foot wall teaches that can be used in the boardroom or the job interview.

In the promotional material they send to prospective clients, the character-building programs assert results as if they were known facts. An OB flyer brags of

> A countless number of life-impacting experiences which have improved:
> - self-confidence
> - leadership
> - teamwork
> - friendship
> - community spirit
> - compassion
> - curiosity, and above all
> - spirit

The National Outdoor Leadership School (NOLS) says flatly, "A NOLS course increases self-confidence, responsibility, and motivation." A Denver-based outfit called Leadership Training Institute asserts, "The wilderness is our most powerful teacher. . . . The intimate contact with wild nature, coupled with the challenges of climbing, skiing, and rafting, creates an atmosphere of honesty and caring within the training group. . . . "

The Boulder (Utah) Outdoor Survival School (a tough course with the acronym BOSS) argues that

> Learning to survive with the land and to cope with the elements is one of the most challenging, strengthening and character building experiences to be found. *One learns not to fight nature. She is impartial, but unforgiving* [emphasis in original].

Pacific Crest Outward Bound's program for "youth at risk" claims to attack problems like "chronic lateness," "running away," "criminal mischievousness," and "substance abuse at a nonaddictive level." Colorado OB's executive courses promise that rappelling, climbing, and rafting will "help participants identify and overcome many of the barriers that stifle achievement in the workplace."

Christian Adventures, out of Grand Rapids, Michigan, announces, "We have observed in our study of Scripture that God used the Wilderness setting to develop the character of many of His men. We believe He still desires to do this today."

What proof of their efficacy do these schools and programs advance? In the early years, OB relied on the personal testimony of its graduates to back up its claims about personal growth. The school still sprinkles its brochures with quotations from alums: "The experience I encountered will last the rest of my life. I noticed a change in me. It was great. . . . "

As educational psychologists know, however, this sort of proof by self-report is a can of worms. When clients voluntarily choose to undertake any experience, pay money for it, and receive a diploma on finishing, they are highly likely to internalize the "party line." No matter how little they have actually learned, graduates of Harvard or Yale are all too willing to regard themselves as the best-educated twenty-one-year-olds in the country. Clients emerge from EST marathons or firewalking seminars convinced of immense new funds of willpower. Subscribers to the Great Books Program feel classically well-rounded.

Since the late 1960s, a minor industry in America's graduate schools of psychology and education has sprung up around the questions so provocatively posed by Kurt Hahn and his followers. Scores of studies and dissertations have attempted to put some rigor into the claims of personal growth through outdoor adventure. The findings are far from uniform; their implications, far from clear.

The most consistent change that these studies find in Outward Bound graduates is an improvement in what the testers call "self-concept." Using a standardized "test instrument" (usually a questionnaire called the Tennessee Self-Concept Scale), investigators prod subjects with a long series of questions about their self-perceptions. A majority of the studies show statistically significant improvement in self-concept from before a course to after, as measured against a control group who did not take the course.

Other studies, though far less uniformly, find positive change in group cohesiveness, self-confidence, empathy, and "locus of control." The prevalence of such results leads one researcher, Alan Ewert, to conclude, "A powerful suggestion is made that Outward Bound does something 'good' to or for the participant, but like electricity, we know it does something but we're not sure how it does it."

These findings are often vitiated, however, by methodological snags. The "instruments" used by the researchers, no matter how cleverly devised, still depend on self-reporting. Thus the tendency for OB grads to internalize the stated claims of the course and spew them back as test answers cannot be weeded out. One provocative study found that students claimed changes in self-concept that were (in testing terms) invisible to their instructors. If the changes were genuine, they did not readily translate into behavior; alternatively, the students believed they had changed far more than they actually had.

Another snag lies in the fact that those who go to Outward Bound may be, a priori, a self-selecting group; i.e., they may have already committed themselves to personal change before starting the course. Closely related is the Hawthorne effect, named after a famous 1927 study of Western Electric employees: it argues that *any* change in environmental conditions (including the removal of all previous changes!) will result in improved productivity and morale. Thus for OB students, simply leaving the normal routine of home and work may provoke the positive personal changes detected by researchers.

A further problem with the studies is that almost all of them rely on tests performed immediately after the wilderness course, or at most a few months later. Whether the changes reported in the short run tend to last over years remains a largely untested question.

It seems to be true, moreover, that many of the investigators want so badly to find evidence of personal growth that they unconsciously overstate their conclusions or remain oblivious to serious design flaws. In a 1981 overview of Outward Bound research, L. M. Burton found that

> In general, the results indicate that Outward Bound-type programs do have a positive impact upon self-perceptions such as self-concept, locus of control, self-assertion, and personality, but this impact is less significant among those studies selected as methodologically adequate. Actual behavior such as grade-point average,

observed behavior, school functioning and absenteeism does not undergo much significant change as a result of Outward Bound-type programs.

Some of the best-designed experiments have come up with skeptical results. Robert H. Stremba found an increase in self-concept among graduates of a twenty-three-day OB course, but no change in four other crucial parameters of self-esteem. A Colorado team studied sixty-five OB grads, of whom roughly half paid their way and half were on scholarship. They found no positive changes, but a decline among the subjects in terms of their acceptance of others. James H. Gillette also found virtually no attitudinal changes after a twenty-two-day OB ski course.

John C. Huie's study of a semester-long course at North Carolina Outward Bound School scrutinized one of the most extended wilderness programs in operation. One might expect the longest courses to produce the most dramatic results. Focusing on "locus of control," self-respect, and "ability to make meaning of their lives," Huie tested the participants ninety days before the course began, on the first day of the course, and on the last day. Although he hoped to demonstrate Outward Bound's usefulness, Huie was forced to conclude, "In all three areas of investigation, the statistical results showed minimal change." An interesting finding was that the students reported changes within themselves that were not independently borne out by such standardized tests as the Rokeach Value Survey. "The study concludes," wrote Huie, "that the [purported] effects of the Outward Bound course are not demonstrated by the statistical results."

In another careful study of North Carolina OB clients, L. Borstelman tested instructors as well as students. He detected a kind of self-fulfilling prophecy: the students whom the instructors perceived as getting most out of the course tended strongly to be those very souls whose values tested beforehand as closest to the instructors' own. In general, "the enthusiastic types seem to do best and the more abstract thinking types do not do so well." A disturbing corollary finding was that what effectiveness OB seemed to have in terms of bolstering self-confidence and self-determination "can be costly in other relevant goals, namely, goals such as affection, forgiveness, and compassion."

The jury of educational psychologists, then, is still out as to the lasting personal impact of Outward Bound. Long-term change of any sort, of course, is a perilously elusive thing to document. And self-reports tend to be glowing testimonials. Devotees of the wackiest religions claim that their faith has made them happier, kinder, better. Thus skepticism in this matter is all the more crucial, because of the universal human propensity to believe that the right program can invigorate our humdrum lives, improve our chequered characters.

The treatment of alcoholism may form a cautionary analogue. Largely on the basis of an overwhelming body of self-reported testimony over five decades, even doctors and psychiatrists have begun to think that the sort of treatment offered by Alcoholics Anonymous (AA) offers the best hope of long-term recovery from alcohol abuse. Yet, as Herbert Fingarette demonstrates in his rigorous survey, *Heavy Drinking*, research has consistently failed to show that AA is effective over the long haul for the general population. According to Fingarette, scores of careful studies argue that "Despite the ubiquitous good opinion of AA, there are no satisfactory data to justify the widespread confidence in it. . . . "

Another point can be made without resort to tests or statistics. All the various schools and programs spawned by the OB movement—with all their various agendas, from fostering feminism to rehabilitating criminals to enabling the handicapped—use similar exercises and techniques. The "solo" and the big rappel and the twelve-foot wall crop up again and again. Would it not be remarkable if the kind of personal growth that helps an ambitious businessman land a promotion were identical to the kind that helps an alienated woman forge a new identity? If the tools for kicking cocaine addiction worked just as well for deciphering God's hand in the wilderness? In its plethora of adaptations (often coexisting within a single school), the OB idea begins to look like a universal panacea—and thus to give off a whiff of snake oil.

There are, to my mind, very few snake-oil salesmen in the OB movement; the wages are low, the hours long, and idealism is rampant. Yet the very process by which Kurt Hahn's radical hypothesis has become a received idea may tell us something about our times. Every educational movement has its (perhaps hidden or unconscious) political platform. As Michael Rosenthal demonstrates in his brilliant book, *The Character Factory*, Baden-Powell's Boy Scout movement was in its very essence an effort to preserve class distinctions and to rationalize the British Empire. Although it is too soon to see what it may mean, the popularity of Outward Bound must have its own covert significance.

So what? one might reply. Something like ninety percent of the clients in outdoor adventure courses report that they had a good time, got their money's worth, and so on. A three-week OB course sailing off the coast of Maine or climbing in the Cascades costs only about $1,500—less than many people spend drinking piña coladas in the Caribbean. Even if graduates come back thinking they've changed more profoundly or lastingly than they really have, what's the harm?

121

The most obvious harm is that some people get killed in the name of personal growth. The American Outward Bound Schools have suffered fourteen fatalities since 1962. Spokesmen point out that, as of June 1987, 170,000 people had graduated from OB courses; the implication is that fourteen deaths is not so bad a record. Yet any death is one too many, and the scuttlebutt surrounding each OB accident has suggested to experienced observers that most, perhaps all, of the deaths were eminently avoidable. Outward Bound has been threatened with a number of lawsuits arising out of the fatalities, but has always settled out of court.

For the character-building industry as a whole, no statistics are available on accidental deaths. It is hard even to guess at the total number of casualties because programs and schools that suffer fatalities usually do their damnedest to keep them out of the newspapers. Since 1962, the number of deaths in Outward-Bound-style programs in this country is three or four score at the very minimum, perhaps as high as 200 at the worst. National Outdoor Leadership School, founded in 1965 by an OB defector whose idea was to focus more on leadership skills and less on transferable lessons, has had seven deaths in twenty-three years, while graduating some 25,000 students.

Both OB and NOLS have gone to great lengths in recent years to improve their safety procedures. Only one of OB's fourteen deaths has occurred in the last nine years: NOLS's last fatality was in 1978. It is probably true that relatively new schools and programs, those shortest on accumulated outdoor wisdom, are the most dangerous.

Clearly, the regimens at some outdoor-training schools verge on the criminally negligent. Yet even when superbly taught, activities like mountain climbing, whitewater rafting, and ocean kayaking are intrinsically dangerous; there is no way to rid them of risk. Moreover, the economic necessity of a twelve-to-two ratio of students to teachers adds extra hazards to activities that are ideally conducted one-to-one.

There is a considerable ethical burden in introducing beginners to high-risk sports which they have no way of assessing, especially when the promise held out is not simply, "Try it, it's fun," but "Try it, it's good for you." The burden is even greater in programs, like many of those run for criminals or delinquent teenagers, which are not entirely voluntary. A stint at Outward Bound has often been prescribed as an alternative to legal punishment.

Problems of decision-making in the field can be knotty enough by themselves. The institutional framework, with all its hidden payoffs, adds a host of complications that are as hard on the instructors as on the students. These include peer pressure, pressure to complete the curriculum, the prospect of financial loss when the students drop out, competitiveness among instructors, and the freight of everyone's tendency to believe in Kurt

Hahn's ideas. At Colorado Outward Bound in 1963, I was entrusted by the senior instructor of Boone Patrol to take our twelve students on a four-day circle tour. On the afternoon of the third day, we had to cross the high ridge between Capitol and Snowmass Peaks, a traverse that neither I nor my superior had ever done before. Descending the far side, we ran into a treacherous cliff full of loose rocks, requiring exposed scrambling.

What I should have done was to retreat at once to the near side and circle back the way we had come. But this would have meant returning to base camp two days late and disappointing my senior, who was something of a hero of mine. At twenty, I was an experienced mountaineer, having just come off a first ascent of a new route on Mount McKinley. But my youthful machismo easily won the day over caution. We headed down the cliff. At tricky places, I "spotted" each student, placing hands and feet on holds. (Using a rope would have only slowed us into benightment.) Sometimes I hung on with one hand and caught rocks the students kicked loose with the other. We made it down the cliff without incident, but today I shudder when I recall my folly. The mandates of Outward Bound—not messing up the schedule, following my supervisor's instructions, preserving face before my students—played havoc with my judgment.

In May 1986, in one of the worst mountaineering accidents in American history, seven students from the Oregon Episcopal School and two adults died in a snow cave on Mount Hood. Bad weather, uncertain leadership, the lethargy and inertia that mask the onset of hypothermia, and sheer bad luck all contributed to the disaster. So did the fact that an effort to reach the summit had been built into the school's curriculum as a requirement for graduation, and that there were no make-up dates left in the spring term. The official inquiry concluded that "One of the primary culprits in this accident was the need to try to adhere to a schedule. . . . Guiding young neophytes on climbs such as Mount Hood requires . . . a clear understanding of where *educational decisions must become secondary to safe mountaineering practices*" [emphasis in report].

In the wake of this tragedy, the public reaction was curiously forgiving. Here, one could argue, was a disaster at least as terrible as the *Challenger* Space Shuttle's blowing up—two more lives were lost—and at least as preventable. The *Challenger* debacle threatened NASA's whole space program, and public and Congress alike were quick to condemn. In the Mount Hood case, the relatively few expressions of outrage were swept under a tide of reaffirmations of faith in the school's program and of talk about students dying while they were doing what they believed in.

This sort of response, I think, amounts to a sentimentalization of risk. The unexamined notion that nine hikers died in a courageous effort to

123

improve themselves through daring and stress is one measure of how thoroughly Kurt Hahn's proposition has won the day.

In 1970 I was hired by Hampshire College in western Massachusetts to devise an "Outward Bound-style program," to be offered on a voluntary basis to all students in lieu of traditional sports and physical education. At the age of twenty-seven, I had been a serious mountaineer for ten years. But I had not liked everything I had seen at Outward Bound, nor was I convinced that the personal traits it took to become a top climber were the sort that should be cultivated by everyone.

During my nine years at Hampshire, students in the Outdoors Program made first ascents in Alaska's Brooks Range, climbed El Capitan in Yosemite, tackled 14,000-foot peaks in Colorado in winter, and kayaked on serious wilderness rivers. To my mind, however, the most important measure of those nine years was that we had not a single serious accident—nothing more than the occasional sprained ankle or rope burn. I did everything I could to encourage students to reflect morally and intellectually on their adventures; as an English professor, I devised courses like "The Literature of Great Expeditions." But in the field, I was at pains to hold out no promise of ulterior rewards for, say, getting to the top of a thirty-foot rock climb. If a student got scared and wanted to go down, it was fine with me. No one insisted it would make him or her a better person to persevere and reach the top.

In the summer of 1979, moonlighting for another school that gave college credit for outdoor learning, I led a hiking course in the Adirondacks. On our third day, a young woman who had never been stung before got several bee stings on the throat and immediately went into severe anaphylactic shock. (Several hundred Americans each year die from insect stings and bites.) Partly at my insistence, the program had for the first time that summer outfitted instructors with bee-sting kits. We had to give the young woman three shots of epinephrine over four hours, improvise a litter, and carry her four miles to the road. I took her to the nearest hospital.

By the next day, she was feeling better. To my astonishment, the program's safety director wanted to let her indulge in an understandable determination to finish the course; he urged that she be allowed to rejoin our group. It was bee season in the Adirondacks, and we were being stung daily. Only the most vehement opposition on my part kept her from heading back into the woods. She went home without her college credit.

In retrospect, I think the safety director's wish and the student's own passionate impulse to get back on the horse that had thrown her owed much to the sentimentalization of risk that schools like Outward Bound have convinced the public is acceptable. It may seem smug on my part, or even a double standard—but while I could decide that attacking unclimbed walls in Alaska was important enough to me to justify a serious chance of getting killed, I was prepared to decide for someone else that hiking in New York State to the end of gaining college course credit was not worth a similar risk.

There is another reason, having nothing to do with danger, for resisting the Outward Bound credo. In the long run the idea that outdoor challenges provoke beneficial personal change is simplistic, intellectually lazy. It betrays, moreover, a didactic moral bias that ultimately undercuts adventure as not sufficiently valuable in its own right. It is like the old maxim that the reason for studying Latin in school is to help one with etymology as an adult; or, for that matter, like the notion that sex is only justified for procreation.

The glory of rock climbing, sailing, or exploring is that such pursuits have meant so many different things to so many people. The wilderness fetches ascetics like Lawrence of Arabia and sensualists like Aleister Crowley; men of God like David Livingstone and agnostics like Vilhjalmur Stefansson; bluff optimists like Edmund Hillary and brooding melancholics like Robert Falcon Scott.

Anyone who has ever been deeply involved in outdoor challenge has pondered its effect upon his psyche. Herein lies the opportunity for a bold act of self-criticism, and the ponderer needs to be open to as many ways of seeing the question as possible. In particular, he must entertain the fancy that what he learns in the wilderness may *not* be applicable to "real life."

For fifteen years, mountaineering was the most important thing in the world to me. Like other "hard men" (as alpinists refer to fellow zealots), I had an alarmingly large number of friends who were killed climbing—four of them before my eyes. At my most dedicated, it became essential to steel myself against pity, compassion, and self-doubt in the face of such setbacks. Now that first ascents are no longer my goal in life, that process of cauterizing myself against tragedy and sorrow seems to me an especially poor model for normal existence. Serious climbing is, in one respect, something like war; but the qualities that make a good soldier do not guarantee a good citizen.

If Kurt Hahn's proposition is true, its results ought to be most evident in the lives of those who have taken outdoor challenge most seriously. Yet when one looks at the subsequent careers of great adventurers, one sees only ambiguity. The Norwegian Fridtjof Nansen, the finest arctic explorer of his day, made the first crossing of Greenland in 1888; seven years later, on skis, he reached a new farthest north of 86° 14'. His book, *Farthest North*, is one of the lyrical classics of the genre. Later Nansen became a High Commissioner of the League of Nations. His heroic work in repatriating

125

prisoners and refugees of World War I and in relieving Russian famine won him the 1923 Nobel Peace Prize. Nansen believed that the lessons he had learned on the polar icepack led directly to the making of the statesman and humanitarian.

A contemporary of Nansen's was Joshua Slocum, the Yankee skipper who was the first person to make a solo circumnavigation of the globe, in 1895–1898. His book, *Sailing Alone Around the World*, is every bit the equal of Nansen's, a classic of wit and spunky pragmatism. Slocum did not adjust well to dry land, however. He turned his marvelous boat *The Spray* into a kind of floating museum and lived like a down-at-the-heels Buffalo Bill, rehashing his exploits for any audience that would hear him. The boat grew filthy and decrepit. In 1906, Slocum was arrested for raping a twelve-year-old New Jersey girl who had come on board; he spent forty-two days in jail. (Probably Slocum's offense was exposing himself, not rape.) In 1909 he set out in the unrepaired *Spray* and was lost at sea.

The two Frenchmen who reached the summit of Annapurna in 1950 (the first 8,000-meter peak ever climbed) lost their fingers and toes to frostbite but became international heroes. Maurice Herzog found himself profoundly enriched by his sacrificial triumph, later writing, "I was saved and I had won my freedom. This freedom, which I shall never lose, has given me the assurance and serenity of a man who has fulfilled himself." Louis Lachenal, on the other hand, was tormented by his loss. In a futile quest to regain his legendary gracefulness, he turned to reckless skiing and automobile driving, and died in 1955 when he skied unroped into a crevasse on the Mer de Glace.

Like anything complex, nature is no mere school of character. The moral principles we try to derive from its challenges tend to be vague homilies. If nature has her lessons, she poses them as dark conundrums. To the stirring task of unraveling them, adventurers like Nansen and Lachenal gave the best part of their lives. A quest like theirs is not the sort of thing that can be accomplished in a twenty-six-day course.

ROMAN DIAL AND THE
ALASKA CRAZIES

One day near the end of his first full-fledged mountaineering expedition, in the Arrigetch Peaks of Alaska's Brooks Range, Roman Dial noticed that a big black bear was headed up-valley toward base camp. For three miles, Dial watched the bear slink from boulder to boulder, hiding as she stalked her prey. The uncomfortable feeling grew upon Dial and his three teammates that they were the prey.

His friends climbed atop their food-cache boulder and tried to make themselves invisible, but Dial unlimbered a 30.06. "I like to hunt," he says today. "Hunting's a really primal thing." At the time, however, Dial had never shot a big animal. He was only eighteen, and he was scared.

As the bear waded into the stream across from base camp, Dial fired a shot. Wounded in the leg, the huge animal took off running. Dial rejoined his friends. "Roman," one of them said, "we're not going to hike out with this wounded bear in the valley."

"OK," answered Dial. "I'll go get her."

Twelve years later, Dial recalls the chase. "I was running across tundra tussocks and boulders and I didn't even know they were there. It was like my body was on autopilot. At first I was trailing by drops of blood. Then I spotted her." After a two-mile pursuit, Dial crept close to the bear. "I could see where she was going to run between two rocks. I lay down, and she stepped right in there, about twelve feet away. Boom! I hit her right in the heart."

Most climbers would have left it at that: the shooting had come, after all, in self-defense. But Dial considered himself a meat hunter, not a sport hunter. For three days, he ate as much of the bear as he could, with only one of his three teammates helping out. Then he cached the rest of the bear's carcass in a snowbank. The four men hiked down to the Alatna River, where a plane picked them up and flew them to Bettles.

As his friends returned to their normal lives, Dial acted on impulse and hitched a plane ride back in to the Alatna. He had decided to hang around a while longer in the Arrigetch, camping alone and living off bear meat. He hiked back up to base camp. "When I got there," Dial says, "I discovered that a wolverine had pulled the carcass out and defecated on it. I couldn't eat it. I didn't really have much food now. I'd heard there was a lodge over on Walker Lake," forty miles away, across trailless hills, serious river crossings, and mazes of dwarf willows. "When I got to Walker Lake, I ran into a geology group, and hitched another plane ride out."

The story is pure Roman Dial. For the last dozen years, this thirty-year-old wild man has been the pivotal figure in a gang of about fifteen Alaskans who have turned conventional ideas of what to do in the wilderness upside down.* Some of the gang are first-rate mountaineers who have hung their lives out on unclimbed routes by going lighter and faster than their predecessors thought possible. Some are cross-country explorers, applying the same radical fast, light style to glaciers, rivers, and tundra wastes. Some are devotees of backcountry races in which, defying federal regulations and park rangers, they blitz their way across hundreds of miles of dangerous wilderness in head-to-head combat. And some are "hell bikers," using mountain bikes on game trails and glaciers to careen across terrain where wheels have never before rolled.

Only Roman Dial is all four of these things. And though his group of Alaska crazies is too anarchical to admit of a spokesman or leader, Dial, in the fevered and panegyrical prose of the narratives he writes, in the prickly iconoclasm always ready on his tongue, seems the resident theoretician and idealist of the gang.

He loves to tweak establishment noses, to espouse unpopular ideas. Here, for example, is his spiel on Sierra Clubbers: "They don't understand

*Written in 1991.

how the world works. They live down in California, where they don't see the impact of their consumer demands. They contribute to the throwaway society just by being in it, yet they never criticize themselves. It's like blaming the peasants in Brazil for burning the rain forest, rather than the people who invest in portfolios that include the World Bank."

Here is Dial's diatribe on guiding, tempered slightly by the fact that some of his best friends—including George Ripley, one of the certified crazies—are guides. "I don't dislike guides. I dislike guiding as an idea. Guides get down on me for using mountain bikes in the wilderness. 'You spoil our wilderness experience,' they say. Well, goddamn it, their whoring spoils my wilderness experience.

"It's just like prostitution. It's not paying for the physical act that's wrong—it's that you're buying somebody's emotions. To me, the wilderness is a very emotional, spiritual place. It's where I've found my strongest bonds with friends, even family. Why would I let somebody pay me to share that?"

To perpetuate their marathon dashes across some of the most difficult wilderness in the world, Dial and his fellow crazies have cut their margin of safety to a fingernail, counted on toughness and pluck to get them out of nasty fixes, and innovated against the grain of traditional wisdom. Yet in an important sense, these daredevils are throwbacks to the pioneer days in Alaska.

Consider Dial's climbing. Throughout the 1970s, Alaska drew top-notch alpinists from all over the world to its unclimbed walls. The "in" ranges were the Cathedral (Kichatna) Spires and the Great Gorge of the Ruth Glacier, where sheer granite faces up to 5,000 feet high abound. The outstanding deeds of the '70s were performed chiefly by non-Alaskans, who had learned their big-wall techniques in Yosemite and the West.

In the 1980s, however, the best Alaskan climbs were pulled off by men and women living in Alaska, with Dial and his friends in the vanguard. These alpinists turned away from the Kichatna Spires and the Ruth Gorge to seek out challenges in such neglected areas as the Hayes Range. For mountaineering and for ice climbing on waterfalls, Alaska is a paradise, but the state has virtually no handy rock-climbing areas of quality. Standards on pure rock in Alaska have consequently lagged well behind those in Colorado, California, or New England.

Dial quickly became a paramount ice climber, making the first solo ascent of the legendary Keystone Greensteps near Valdez. "On the crux pitch of Love's Way," says Jon Krakauer, who seconded Dial on this difficult waterfall climb in Valdez, "the ice was too rotten for protection. If he'd fallen, he would have cratered and died. He hesitated at first, but once he got psyched up, it was as if there was nothing he'd rather have been doing."

When Dial turned his eye to mountaineering, it was not big granite walls that appealed to him so much as long, tortuous ridges mixing snow, rock, and ice. "I like ridge climbing," he says, "because Foot Fangs, Friends, new ropes—none of that stuff helps. The Hummingbird Ridge is just as hard now as it was when Allen Steck first did it." The Hummingbird is an immense, fiendishly corniced ridge on the south side of Mount Logan in the Yukon. On its first ascent in 1965, Steck and his five teammates found that a snow shovel was their most valuable technical tool. Twenty-five years later, their route had not been repeated. In 1987, David Cheesmond and Catherine Freer were killed trying to climb the Hummingbird alpine-style. Cheesmond and Dial had originally planned the climb together.

The first outstanding ridge climb performed by Alaskans of Dial's generation was the east ridge of Mount Deborah. First attempted in 1964, the ridge had begun to acquire "last great problem" status when two teams (British and American) met on the mountain in 1977 and joined forces. Cheesmond and Carl Tobin, one of Dial's best friends, spearheaded the successful assault.

From 1979 through 1985, Dial himself pulled off a series of brilliant routes in the Hayes Range, including the southeast ridge of Hess, the east face of Peak 10,910, and the east face of Mount McGinnis. The latter was perhaps Dial's masterpiece, and it came close to costing him his life.

In top form, Dial led four rope-lengths of ice up what he called Cut-throat Couloir on McGinnis—"the hardest pitches of ice I've ever been on," he says. With partner Chuck Comstock, Dial bivouacked on the summit.

"We were cocky," he reflects. "We said, 'Let's go down the southeast ridge.' It had only been climbed once, and it was very hard. I was leading late the next day. We'd passed a possible camp site. I was thinking about the Hummingbird, which I was planning to do with Cheesmond. Suddenly I said to myself, I don't want to go. I just want to get off this ridge alive.

"I reeled Chuck in, and took it all out on him. 'Chuck, it's getting late. Why didn't you make us stop back there, at that camp site?' I ragged him out.

"He said, 'Well, goddamn it, Roman. You've got a shovel. I've got a shovel. You've got a cookpot, I've got a cookpot. You've got a stove, I've got a stove. Here, take your rope, give me mine, and we'll go our separate ways.'

"Here we were, 2,000 feet above the glacier on one of the most difficult ridges in Alaska, and he's untied from me. I said, 'Look, Chuck, please, man. I'm sorry. You were right. I was wrong. Please tie back in to the rope.'

"So he tied back in. I paid the rope out as he led, but my belay was worthless. He stopped and was probing with his ice axe. I thought, 'I should take a picture. No, it'll be more spectacular in a minute.' And then I watched Chuck disappear.

"I knew he had broken the cornice loose. I had only one option—to jump off the opposite side of the ridge. I pendulumed 200 feet before the ropes caught me. I was okay, but Chuck had gone down a rocky, eighty-five-degree gully, and the cornice had fallen on him like a freight train."

Dial jumared back up his rope and joined his bruised and shaken friend. A desperate retreat ensued—eleven consecutive rappels, using up all the pair's hardware, interrupted by a bivouac in the middle of the 2,000-foot precipice; then an arduous ski trip out of the Hayes Range.

When he got back to Fairbanks, Dial says, "I realized that the mountains were just too objectively hazardous. I'd climbed long enough. I'd been running with the big boys for six years. So I said to Peggy, 'Let's get married.'"

SIX YEARS LATER, IN 1991, Roman and Peggy have two children, a boy of four and a girl of two. She is a slim, pretty fellow adventurer and Alaskan; they met in Fairbanks in 1980. Recently turned thirty, Roman remains boyishly hyper and boyish-looking; clean-shaven, lean, with sandy brown hair, he talks a nonstop stream of improbable anecdotes and sharp analyses.

At the moment, however, both Roman and Peggy seem surprised to find themselves far south of Alaska—in Palo Alto, California, in fact, smack in the midst of the detested Sierra Clubbers. A graduate of the University of Alaska with a B.S. in math and biology, Dial has put his adventuring on temporary hold to pursue a Ph.D. at Stanford. His dissertation will have to do with the populations of various species in the rain forest. Fieldwork takes him for six months at a time to the Luquillo Experimental Forest in Puerto Rico—a wilderness about as different from Alaska's as you could find.

"My hypothesis is that anoles control the arthropod population," he says, then explains with the same zest with which he might recount a mountain-bike extravaganza. "Anoles are a genus of lizards. I have to climb into the tops of trees, noose the lizards off the leaves, keep them off, and see what happens to the insect and spider populations. It takes six months to be statistically significant." It sounds a bit sedentary for Dial, but getting into the trees is a challenge: he shoots a line over a high branch with a crossbow, hauls up a rope, and jumars to the treetop. There he hangs out on a Portaledge made for big-wall climbs. Last spring Dial managed to lure fellow crazy Carl Tobin to Puerto Rico to be his assistant.

Despite the extended distraction of graduate school, Dial's heart remains in Alaska. The Palo Alto condo where he and Peggy have landed feels like a garage they're camping in—bikes and gear strewn across the floors, un-packed boxes overwhelming the meager furniture. "My goal is to become a professor of biology in a university in Alaska and pay for my trips by selling stories," he says. Would he not prefer to convert his voyaging into a career, as certain climbers, rafters, and other outdoor enthusiasts have? "No. My wild trips are an adventure. I don't want to turn them into a job."

Roman makes, he estimates, about $10,000 a year selling pictures and articles. An excellent photographer, he's also a flamboyant writer who publishes accounts of his trips in such magazines as *Alaska, Climbing, Mountain Bike,* and *Northland News.* He likes to grab his readers' attention with hyperbolic titles, tongue only half in cheek, such as "Frozen Whiskey, Broken Skis, and the Taste of Death" (about a winter ski traverse in the Brooks Range). As he warms to his task, his prose hums with a lyric bravado reminiscent of Kerouac:

> As wild jocks establishing the boundaries of the possible, we realized that planning for every contingency meant staying home. As backcountry veterans with thirty years combined experience, we could get away with what the less savvy might consider foolish, and as Alaskans we feel comfortable with raw adventure.

This sounds like arrant boasting, but the more you get to know Dial, the more you read such passages in the spirit of the zany passion for adventure—a kind of naiveté, perhaps—that infused the trips they celebrate.

The article in which the lines quoted above appeared, called "Live to Ride, Ride to Die, Mountain Bikes from Hell!" provoked predictable outcries from the readers of *Mountain Bike:* "In our estimation, these weren't 'wild jocks establishing the boundaries of the possible,' but rather, reckless jocks ignoring basic wilderness courtesy and safety." Dial replied with an ironic apology "for not explaining Alaskan traditions":

> When I say "camped without shelter," I mean we bivouacked like alpinists, siwashed like Bob Marshall, and traveled in emulation of John Muir, who spent many Sierra nights with just a bag of bread crumbs and an overcoat. . . . The wilderness we pedal is bounded spiritually—not politically. It's guarded naturally by rivers, remoteness, and bears—not by rangers. It's labeled by the hearts of locals—not by an act of Congress. . . . It's a different world up there, believe me.

THE NON-ALASKANS WHO DID hard routes in the 1970s tended to fly into and out from remote ranges like the Kichatnas and the Ruth Gorge. Often they had little or no idea how to hike out to civilization if the bush pilot had failed to pick them up on the glacier. From the start, however, Dial and his fellow Alaskans combined overland travel with their mountaineering. Roman's first big Alaskan venture, at age sixteen, was a solo walk across the Alaska Range east of Mount McKinley. In this respect, the crazies of the 1980s harked back to the early days of Alaskan mountaineering, before it was transformed by glacier pilots: to the Sourdoughs on McKinley in 1910, or the sturdy team that hauled ten tons of supplies 140 miles in winter to approach Mount Logan in 1925. The pioneers relied on horses and mules, on ferried loads, on depots and well-stocked camps. Dial and his friends, in contrast, believe in pushing as fast and light as humanly possible.

It was natural, then, when at age twenty-four he quit expeditionary mountaineering after the close call on McGinnis, that Dial's interest in long backcountry journeys would only intensify. The idea for a wilderness race came at the end of an unsuccessful attempt on Peak 9448 in the Hayes Range in 1981. There had been serious frictions among the party of three, and Dial decided to ski out by himself. "I thought, 'I wonder which way is the fastest way out? Down the Black Rapids Glacier or out to the north? The only way to find out would be to have a race.'" Dial chose the latter route, and skied fifty-four miles in fifty-four hours without a map or a tent.

The next year Roman met George Ripley, who had his own pipe dream of a wilderness race on the Kenai Peninsula. Dial had been musing about an itinerary in the Alaska Range. "George said, 'Okay, Roman, you come down and do my race and then I'll do your race.'" Thus in 1982 was born the first Hope to Homer race, 150 miles across birch forest and swampy tundra, skirting the Harding Icefield. Ten contestants entered; only four finished.

One of them, Dick Griffith, was at fifty-five by far the oldest of the Alaska crazies. Years before, he had been the first non-Inuit to traverse the Brooks Range longitudinally, from east to west. "We came to the first stream and everybody balked," remembers Dial. "It was a big, cold glacial river—you'd have to swim it. Dick Griffith pulls out a vinyl raft, puts on a Viking cap with horns on it, says, 'Old age and treachery beat youth and skill every time,' and paddles across. We all swam the damned river. Dave Manzer almost drowned."

Five days later, the race shaped up as a dead heat among Dial, Ripley, and Manzer. His feet bloody from running in boots, Ripley trotted barefoot along the gravel bar of the Fox River. In the end, Dial crossed the finish line half an hour ahead of Manzer. "We had a kind of banquet afterwards," he says. "We all said, 'George, it's a great idea. But we're never going to do this ever again.' The next year, of course, we all showed up."

The race has been held every year since, along various routes in different ranges. Known nowadays as the Alaska Mountain Wilderness Classic, it has never drawn more than about twenty-five competitors. Dial, who organized the race for six years, won again in 1983 and 1988. "We never made any money off it," he says happily. "I got prizes donated, like a Sherpa raft. We'd put the prizes on a big table. The guy who finished first got first pick, and so on. There were always more prizes than finishers. It would spoil the spirit of the thing if money got into it."

So far, the races have seen no fatalities. "I always scared everybody away," says Dial. "I had a release that said, 'You can die on this. If you're in trouble, you get yourself out. If you think you might need a rescue, you arrange it beforehand.'"

Dial goes on ebulliently, "The neat thing was, we defied the feds. Every race we had, the Fish and Wildlife or the BLM tried to shut it down. They'd say 'Races are not appropriate in wilderness areas.' When we did a race in the Wrangell–St. Elias National Park, we sent a letter to the Superintendent: 'Dear Superintendent: We are going to have a race. We have no permit. We won't even accept a permit if you give us one.'"

Dial has also finished first or second in other Alaska endurance races: the Denali Dash (skis), the Hot Springs Sprint (foot and boat), the Iditabike (bikes on the Iditarod Trail). He analyzes the talent that makes him the best of the crazies at wilderness racing: "Dave Manzer is faster. Chuck Comstock is tougher. Carl Tobin is smarter. But—not to brag—I'm the best in Alaska at reading landscape."

Manzer amplifies: "Roman's definitely the best river swimmer I've ever seen. He has tremendous upper-body strength. When I first met him, I thought he was a little on the ripe side of impetuous. He is impetuous, but what a lot of people would consider half-assed, dangerous behavior is just status quo for Roman."

Hell biking evolved after Tobin, having broken both his legs getting avalanched off Peak 9448 in 1984, lent his mountain bike to Dial. Enamored of the contraption, Dial bought his own and took it caribou hunting. He carried a four-pound raft in his pack; when he came to a river, he inflated the raft and floated his bike and himself across, thereby adding a new wrinkle to Dick Griffith's invention of pack-rafting. "I said to myself, man, this is it. I can go anywhere I want." In 1986, Dial became the first person to take a mountain bike onto an Alaskan glacier.

With Carl Tobin as his usual partner, Roman launched a series of bold mountain-bike wilderness journeys: 180 miles north-to-south across the Wrangell–St. Elias Range, 200 miles across the Arctic National Wildlife

Refuge (ANWR), 250 miles traversing the Delta and Hayes Ranges east to west. Dial defines hell biking as "any backcountry bike trip where at least twenty percent of the distance is pushing, carrying, or floating the bike. If you ride more than eighty percent, it's just a bicycle tour. Kind of banal."

On such trips, Dial and Tobin reduce their loads to a mere thirty-five pounds. Taking neither sleeping bags nor a tent, they use a light rain fly for shelter and wrap themselves in bivouac sacks to sleep. They cook on wood fires, eating straight from their only pot with bike tools and sticks instead of utensils. Dial has discovered a Spartan rule of thumb: "For every extra pound on your back, you go one mile less per day."

He adds, "I think Carl and I are the only people in the world riding 100- to-200-mile trips on trailless terrain." In response to critics who would ban mountain bikes from the wilderness, Dial says, "You're actually more in tune with the terrain on a bike. You can hike through anything. With a bike, you're forced to think about where to go. People say bikes tear up the tundra. Bikes don't tear up the tundra. The guides who give me flak for riding across ANWR think it's perfectly okay to fly fifteen clients in by airplane and float down a river."

In 1989, with two cronies he would prefer to keep anonymous, Dial biked illegally from the north rim of the Grand Canyon down to the Colorado River, inflated a trio of pack rafts, floated forty-five miles over two days without a permit, then biked up to the south rim in the dark. "It was an outrageous trip. On the river we ran into a group of guides doing their own trip. 'You guys have a permit?' they asked. 'You bet we have a permit.' They thought it was hilarious. 'You better hurry,' they said, 'because the Park Service is a day behind you.' Because of that worry, it wasn't as much fun. We couldn't play in the rapids."

Ken Miller, head ranger for the Grand Canyon, says the Park Service was unaware of Dial's transgression, but, "These kinds of things go on. We catch most of the guys who do them. We take them to the U.S. magistrate in Flagstaff." Punishment, Miller indicates, ranges from forfeiture of equipment to stiff fines and even time in jail. "Mountain bikes are illegal below the rim," he says. "They're incompatible with the established uses already in place. And it's illegal to go on the Colorado without a permit. There are four to five thousand people waiting patiently for their own Colorado River trip.

"If Dial has flouted the rules of the park," continues Miller, "taken his own enjoyment at the expense of other visitors, and then you write an article glorifying this, you're doing a tremendous disservice to your readers."

To all of which, Dial might well utter a loud raspberry, followed by a passionate rationale for his style of confronting the wilderness. The history of exploration in Alaska is replete with canny innovators and their vocal critics. The Sourdoughs on McKinley were discredited by the mountaineering establishment, until a fourteen-foot spruce pole they had left on the north summit was rediscovered by Hudson Stuck. When Bradford Washburn began using the airplane to approach climbs in the 1930s, old-fashioned purists grumbled. For that matter, John Wesley Powell's first descent of the Colorado River, now hailed as an epochal journey, was widely regarded as a hare-brained and suicidal stunt in 1869.

In his fourteen years of Alaskan adventuring, Roman Dial has had his close calls: the cornice collapse on McGinnis; a fire that nearly destroyed his tent in the Brooks Range at sixty-five degrees below zero, 100 miles from the nearest road; a huge pillar on a Valdez ice climb that collapsed seconds after Chuck Comstock scurried off it, while Dial belayed; an ominous encounter on the Seward Peninsula between Dial on his bike and a mother grizzly and three cubs galloping after him ("I didn't even have a bike pump for a weapon").

None of which diminishes his enthusiasm for the creative ordeal. Few men or women have loved the Alaska wilderness as deeply or as originally as Dial does. Here is an explorer who finds even bushwhacking so interesting he has devised a seven-grade system to classify it. ("Class four: you need your body weight. Football brush, I call it. You can break an arm in Class four. . . . Class seven: New wave ice climbs near Valdez. They call them ice climbs, but it's really technical bushwhacking. Moss clouds—frozen moss on a rock wall. You belay from alders.")

"It frustrates me," says Dial, "when people look at me, shake their heads, and say, 'You're crazy, you're out on this macho trip.' It's not the case at all. I'm just enjoying myself."

THE MOAB TREEHOUSE

Fleeing the hordes of rafters, climbers, hikers, and mountain bikers around Moab, I drove south in a rental Jeep and pushed deep into an obscure valley on the outskirts of Canyonlands National Park. Where the road gave out, I parked, then hoisted a light pack and started hiking up one arm of the brachiate canyon.

It was a perfect Sunday in October, with a breeze nudging cumulus clouds across the azure sky, the cottonwood leaves trembling on the autumnal brink between green and yellow. For five hours as I walked I saw no one else. Not even an old footprint scarred the windswept sand of the canyon bottom stretching before me. The walls on either side soared 600 feet high, purple and gray sandstone coalescing in domes and fins and the occasional arch.

I turned a corner and came upon a startling scene. In an alcove in the canyon wall, people had camped, leaving abundant evidence of their visit. The party must have built a huge bonfire, for black soot smeared the stone at the back of the alcove. Rather than pack it out, the campers had simply tossed their trash on the slope below. I saw their dinner debris, scraps of what might have been a barbecue of chicken wings and corn-on-the-cob.

Somebody had smashed a jar and left the pieces on the ground. To add to the desecration, the campers had scrawled graffiti on the wall: cartoony stick figures documenting their "Kilroy was here" vaunts.

Staring at the campsite, I felt awe and delight creep over my spirit. For the assemblage of leavings was an Anasazi ruin, dating from between 1100 and 1300 A.D. In the dry air of the desert Southwest, nothing decays: the campfire soot looked as fresh as last month's work. The small corn cobs bespoke the staple food of the ancients; the gnawed bones were probably those of ground squirrels. The remnants of the jar were sherds of a gray corrugated cooking pot. The paintings were pictographs—mysterious humanoids resonating of gods and heroes whose names we will never know.

The ironies of my outing lie at the heart of the current fuss over what doomsayers call the ruination of Moab. And Moab epitomizes the quandaries of a debate over the future of wilderness and the West that grows fiercer and knottier each year.

Had the campsite I stumbled upon been the wreckage of some beer-guzzling gang of Anglos, I would indeed have felt dismay rather than delight. Last week's trash disgusts us; 700-year-old trash stirs us to archaeological wonder. During my eight October days in and around Moab, the most regrettable sight I beheld was a stunt attempted by a couple of bozos in a Jeep on the Moab Rim Trail. As I watched through binoculars from half a mile away, the Jeep tackled a thirty-five degree slickrock slab head-on. A hundred feet up, the vehicle shuddered to a halt: perched there, it looked as though it might do an "endo" flip backwards, like a kayak trashed in a keeper hole. Excruciatingly slowly, the Jeep slid backwards down the slab, brake pedal to the metal, leaving twin tracks of burnt black rubber on the slickrock.

Yet to escape the bozo Jeepers, I had rented a Jeep myself. To get away from hikers, I had hiked on my own, leaving the very footprints I was only too pleased to find none of.

During my stay in Moab, I heard much talk about Aspen, Telluride, and Santa Fe. These figured as cities of the damned, lost paradises that had succumbed to the gold fever of their own chic. Their names were muttered in cautionary tones: if the goddamned journalists kept writing their articles about what a great place Moab was, the best little unspoiled town in Utah might become another Aspen.

At Canyonlands National Park headquarters, I mentioned to the young ranger on morning duty that I was writing a piece about the area. "And you'll tell your readers not to come here," she snapped, with no apparent humor. The woman behind me in line sang out, "I remember going through

Moab in 1980, when there were only two dirt-bag motels and a ratty grocery store, and it was *great*."

Neither of these ideologues was a Utah native. The ranger was a seasonal in her first month at the park. The visitor was on vacation from her white-collar job in New York City. Their knee-jerk upset at the notion that Moab might be publicly eulogized, however, sprang from a tide of unexamined passion that floods the streets of the best little unspoiled hamlet in Utah.

I had conceived my own visit as an attempt to gauge that tide with the tried-and-true hydrographic instruments of reason and skeptical irony. Though I had spent most of my own thirty-five years in the outdoors trying to find wilderness that other people had yet to discover, and though on environmental issues I would still call myself a bleeding-heart liberal, the longer I listened to the complaints about Moab's ruination the more impatient I got.

At the moment, to be sure, a real crisis faces Utah's wildlands. It is essentially political in nature. A bill sponsored by Congressman Jim Hansen that would open 20 million Bureau of Land Management acres in Utah to mining, industry, and road-building recently* won approval by a House subcommittee. It is altogether likely that Congress will pass such a bill, which looms as the greatest threat in decades to wilderness in the continental United States.

But as I poked around Moab, I held the political fray at a distance. It was the personal, emotional debate that interested me. And gradually I discovered that beneath an apparently simple issue being nibbled to death all over the West—whether rampant progress is good or bad for places like Moab—lies a puzzle so complex that it calls into question the very acts of embracing the landscape and of coming to terms with oneself.

A GOOD WAY TO GET A HANDLE on the Moab debate is to pick up a copy of the *Canyon Country Zephyr*, southeastern Utah's *Village Voice*. Its editor is Jim Stiles, designated prophet of doom for the best little outback in the West. In a recent issue, Stiles narrates his own pilgrimage—with a bottle of Kulmbacher beer left in his refrigerator in 1987 by Edward Abbey—up to Green River Overlook in Canyonlands, where twenty years before, on first moving to Moab, he'd drunk a beer, put a note to himself in the bottle, and buried it.

---

*As of October 1995.

Quaffing Cactus Ed's Kulmbacher, watching the sunset, Stiles has an epiphany: "MAKE EVERY MOMENT COUNT." Striking a tone somewhere between Thomas Wolfe and Ecclesiastes, Stiles shakes his "twenty-something friends" to get their attention, preaching: "[R]emember and absorb every sight and smell and store it away. . . . And remember what this town looked like when it *only* had eight franchise restaurants and the annual number of visitors to Arches [National Park] was actually less than a million." Having got this off his chest, Stiles writes a second note to himself, sticks it in Abbey's empty bottle, buries it, and vows to return in another twenty years.

Later I talked to Stiles, who sounded far less demagogic in person than on the page. "The basic problem isn't Moab," he said. "All over the country, people are out looking for a simpler lifestyle. They all descend on a quaint little town like Moab, but they bring their problems with them. In fact, they create the problems they were trying to escape.

"Am I pessimistic? Yeah—real pessimistic. I don't see it turning around. We're dealing with the nature of American culture."

In the view of purists such as Stiles, the ultimate sin a local can commit is to pen a guidebook. Just before my arrival, José Knighton, a witty iconoclast who moved to Moab from Salt Lake City five years ago, had not only published a guide to the La Sal Mountains east of town but also had defended the practice in a satiric letter to the *Zephyr*. This prompted the unmitigated ire of, among others, one Lucy K. Wallingford, who let *Zephyr* readers know that Knighton might as well "form a new COLORADO PLATEAU SELLOUT CHEERLEADER SQUAD. . . . JOSE IS ACTUALLY MARKETING ACCESS TO SACRED SPOTS THAT WE HAVE ALL GUARDED JEALOUSLY SINCE THE DAWNING OF THE AGE OF MOAB INUNDATION!!!!"

What, exactly, constitutes the Moab Inundation? A few facts are in order. The present population of the town is about 4,500. This is far from Moab's peak, which reached 10,000 during the uranium boom of the 1950s, but it is way up from the 1,200 who hung on in the nearly moribund town of the late 1970s. In the words of one local, "A house you bought ten years ago for $12,000 is worth $80,000 today." Moab realtors more accurately assess the property-value inflation during the last decade as three-fold to five-fold.

Moab has always huddled in a skinny sprawl across its own main drag. On Route 191 today, which becomes Main Street for some twenty blocks, about 700 trucks a day belch through town. To those in the Stiles–Wallingford camp, the look of Main Street is proof of Moab's imminent ruination. The town does have zoning laws, but they are feeble and honored in the breach: thus big signs trumpeting Arby's and Pizza Hut and the Apache Motel and Texaco drown out the indigenous architecture. Last year local outrage went off the voltmeter upon the erection of a McDonald's sign south of town urging travelers to "Visit Moab's Other Arches." The offending slogan was jeered off the billboard.

Speaking of indigenous architecture: unlike other western towns such as Deadwood, South Dakota, or Durango, Colorado, Moab's dilemma is not a case of handsome Victorian buildings avalanched under '90s kitsch. The prevailing architecture in Moab has the boxy, serviceable style of the 1950s. The town's early history was written not so much by Mormon settlers as by vagabonds and outlaws, and very few buildings from the nineteenth century still stand.

Moab indeed has a tacky surface today, but the flavor is a curious blend of fast-food joint and boutique. Cheek-by-jowl with Best Western motels are pricey gift shops with names like Moabilia. The T-shirt stores are dominated by three icons: Delicate Arch (the most celebrated span in Arches); the mountain bike; and Kokopelli, the hunchbacked flute player of Anasazi rock art. Some T-shirts show Kokopelli riding a bike down a vertiginous slickrock trail. Bumper stickers proclaim "Work sucks—I'm goin' bikin'!!" and "I brake for petroglyphs." As Steve Wilsker, who works at Back of Beyond Bookstore, puts it, "I'm just waiting for somebody to open 'Kokopelli's Authentic Anasazi Sushi Bar—Dine as the Ancients Did.'"

No matter which side of the virulent debate one takes, everybody agrees that the main reason for Moab's present boom is the mountain bike. And the credit for wedding bike and town goes to the Groff brothers. A Tweedledum and Tweedledee pair, grandly plump Bill Groff and leaner, stubbier Robin Groff still run Rim Cyclery, which they founded in 1983. Survivors of the uranium bust in the 1960s, the Groffs decided, as Robin puts it, "to capitalize on a renewable resource—scenic beauty." But when they opened a bike shop in the terminally depressed town, "people just laughed at us."

When mountain bikes became hot stuff around 1985, the Groffs started riding them, and stocked a few for novelty value. The breakthrough was the Slickrock Trail. As we sat on a bench in front of their shop, Robin recalled the sequence of events. "I had an old cowboy friend who camped out by Deadhorse Point. I'd help him with his cows, then we'd ride different trails. Rode everything we could. One day I said, 'Let's go try the Slickrock Trail.'"

The trail had, in effect, been invented back in 1969 by a brazen motorcyclist named Dick Wilson who, working in cahoots with Bureau of Land Management officials, worked out a cycle course on the sandstone plateau above town on the northeast. The trail had a brief vogue, but never saw more than 400 user-days a year. By 1985, almost no one rode it.

"We quickly realized," Robin Groff told me, "that the Slickrock Trail was much better for mountain bikes than for motorcycles." When *Mountain Bike* magazine touted the trail in its inaugural cover story in 1987, the fad was born. Today, the trail gets 90,000 user-days of play per year—of which only a tiny fraction are motorcyclists.

Like most of the Moab old-timers—people who lived through both the boom of the 1950s and the bust that succeeded it—the Groffs lean toward progress and development. When I observed that the most avid voices for keeping Moab small and pristine belonged to residents who had moved there relatively recently, Bill Groff nodded: "We call it the barn door policy. People come in here and want to slam the door behind them, not let anybody else in." Later another old-timer used a different metaphor: "Some folks have found our treehouse. Now they want to pull the rope up."

The Groffs scoff at the notion that the backcountry around Moab is being overrun. "I can go fifteen minutes from here on Easter weekend," insisted Bill, "and not see another soul."

Nor do the Groffs yearn nostalgically for the days when Moab was quiet. "I think it's a good thing," said Robin, "that you don't have to drive 110 miles [to Grand Junction] any more to buy a two-by-four or a washing machine."

For eleven years the Groffs have hosted the Fat Tire Festival, a mountain-bike Halloween weekend that draws some 3,000 riders and inclines toward the Bacchic. That and the Easter weekend Jeep Safari are Moab's best-known events; but it is spring break, when college kids descend on Moab, bike the hell out of the environs, and leave their beer cans everywhere, that has given mountain biking a bad image around Moab.

Says Jim Stiles, the pessimist: "A vast number of visitors will ruin a place no matter how environmentally sensitive they are. It's the sheer numbers of mountain bikers that causes the problem. If Moab were the macramé capital of the country, we'd all hate macramé makers."

To see what the fuss was all about, I rented a bike and pedaled up to the Slickrock Trail. I had mountain biked before on dirt roads and woodland paths, but never on raw bedrock. The sport turned out to be harder and scarier than I had expected. On steep uphills I couldn't keep the pedals rotating, and on downhills I was preoccupied with the fear of hurtling head over handlebars. On one bumpy ascent, I gently and clumsily fell off my bike sideways, banging and scraping various parts.

The Slickrock Trail, with its many loops, is painted on the sandstone in little white dashes like those announcing highway passing zones. For that matter, you could stay on track simply by following the dull black rubber swath smeared by a decade of user-days and the gouges grooved by pedals whacking rock. The trail is tough for beginners, and the trickier stretches, called "problems," are named and rated by both technical difficulty and physical demand. I rode, for instance, Faith in Friction, rated five/one—five out of ten in technique, but an easy one out of ten on the ergometer. I walked Prelude Primp and Thrust or Bust.

At one point I crossed paths with a blonde Amazon. "This is hard work," I blurted out in what I hoped she would hear as flirtatious accents. "Nah, it's *fun*," she corrected, speeding by without a backward glance.

After two hours I realized I wasn't having a very good time. I hid my bike behind a piñon, hiked off the trail up a slickrock dome, and sat down to ruminate. In the distance bikers swarmed. They had a tendency to yell and whoop. I analyzed my misgivings.

The white dotted line and the bike itself seemed buffers between me and the landscape. Cranking up a problem, trying to see where the trail went next, I felt out of touch with the nature around me; simply hiking up the dome had restored that touch. The fad of biking on slickrock struck me as one more example, like sport climbing and parasailing, of the modern vogue of reducing wilderness travel to a technical game. And bikers seemed far less capable than hikers of navigating on their own: at Echo Point, where a sudden precipice drops into Negro Bill Canyon, a yellow skull and crossbones had been painted on the rock. Mere hikers would probably have figured out all by themselves that a cliff was something you could fall off.

But who was I to gripe about bikers abusing the countryside? They could get their kicks as they pleased. I was glad that those 90,000 user-days got concentrated into an acre or two of slickrock near town, rather than seeping evenly across the wilderness.

As I HUNG OUT IN MOAB, I recognized that no two pundits had the same take on the controversy. Steve Wilsker, the bookstore clerk, lamented, "The north end of town is starting to look like the entrance to Gatlinburg, Tennessee. It used to take us thirty to forty years to destroy a lovely setting. Now we can do it in ten."

"So who are the bad guys?" I asked.

"Real estate developers," said Wilsker. "They don't care who buys property as long as the market churns."

But when I talked to Dan Holyoak, of Arches Realty, he didn't seem a bad guy. A lifelong resident of Moab and a former county commissioner, Holyoak recalled the sleepy days of the late '70s with no fondness: "This office had a hundred boarded-up, repossessed houses."

Moab's biggest problem, in Holyoak's view, was the lack of private real estate: ninety-five percent of Grand County is state or federal land. "So Moab really can't grow a great deal. The ultimate population of the county might be 15,000. It's 6,000 to 7,000 today."

Holyoak repeated a local joke about tourism: "What we'd really like is if the tourists just sent their money and didn't bother to come. But actually, most of us'd rather see the tourists, just to irritate the environmentalists."

He went on in a more serious vein: "Yes, I'd like to go back to the calm, quiet town of my boyhood. But I recognize that that was a dead community. I'd rather have a place where you can make a living."

If you want to stir a Moab environmentalist to fury, mention the Tram. "Stop the Tram" petitions circulating in town have the apocalyptic ring of predictions of nuclear winter or the icecaps melting. Word of mouth is equally scathing. "If you ask me," a waitress told me one night, "I think the Tram is disgusting."

The Tram is the brainchild of Emmett Mays, a forty-year resident who worked most of his life for the telephone company. Two decades ago he bought one of the prime properties around Moab: the northern point of the Rim, the plateau west of town that overlooks the Portal, where the Colorado River plunges south between thousand-foot cliffs. Mays has secured all the necessary permits to build a cable car that will carry visitors from Kane Creek Road up to a snack bar, a gift shop, and an amphitheater on the Rim.

I might have automatically signed the petition against the Tram before I met Mays, a gentle, old-fashioned westerner whom the controversy has turned a mite defensive. As we walked across his land, he pointed out how the tramway would be hidden from town inside a slanting couloir, how the expensive architect from Grand Junction was an expert at building structures that blend in with the landscape, how he's shelled out $6,200 to have a noise study done.

Mays led me to a boulder beneath which some Jeepers camped the previous Easter, building a fire that laid soot over a panel of ancient petroglyphs. For weeks, Mays has been cleaning the panel with a mild acid; he hopes to make a visitor exhibit of the rock art. Suddenly, the man's placid manner turned churlish: "For the last twenty years, I could have built a fence and kept people out. There's any number of ugly things I could have done. It's zoned commercial—I could have put in a pig farm!"

Mays observed that the European visitors who stay in a small motel he owns uniformly think the Tram's a good idea. Indeed, in the Alps, few hikers deplore the abundance of *téléphériques:* a good cable car, like a hut serving beer and beefsteak, is regarded as part of the civilizing furniture of a landscape that no one pretends is still wilderness.

But the wilderness dream lives on in Utah. It centers on the notion of "secret places" or, as Lucy Wallingford's diatribe in the *Zephyr* had referred to them, "SACRED SPOTS." Implicit in the passion about a secret place is the idea that it's great for me to go there, and even to tell my friends about it, but when outsiders discover the place, it's on the no-return road to ruination.

Jim Stiles, who used to work as a ranger at Arches, recalled the insidious paradox built into the question visitor after visitor asked him: "Where's some really beautiful place to go that nobody knows about?"

I asked José Knighton, the guidebook author, about the notion of secret places. He had a cogent response: "The legacy of secret-keeping is what gave us Glen Canyon Dam. The Place No One Knew." Then Knighton read me a favorite line from Terry Tempest Williams's *Desert Quartet:* "But I believe our desire to share is more potent and trustworthy than our desire to be alone."

Recently I received an equally cogent critique in a letter from Steve Lekson, one of the leading Anasazi archaeologists, who identified what he called the Four Corners mentality:

> This is my tag for people (local and imports) who want to keep the Four Corners wild/rural/ traditional/private/special. . . . I think we should be honest and admit that the Four Corners mentality is exclusive, reactionary, and elitist. It's interesting to watch populist, anti-government ex-hippies try to wriggle out of that conundrum.

Another point bears making. During the good old days of the 1950s, prospectors tore up the backcountry around Moab, using Jeeps and bulldozers to blaze tracks and landing strips to service their claims. Their impact was far more brutal than that of the most reckless Jeepers today. Yet many of the old roads that Lucy Wallingford and Jim Stiles now drive to their SACRED SPOTS were the work of these uranium cowboys.

To test my own perceptions about crowding in the Moab outback, I went on a pair of hikes calculated to produce opposite experiences. One was the mile-and-a-half stroll to Delicate Arch, the most popular walk in Arches National Park. In two hours, going and coming, I passed 136 other visitors. At the arch itself, the feeling was almost urban. People sat in clumps trying to commune with the graceful bridge, but when they walked over to get a closer look, they said to their friends, "Watch my pack, will you?"

The other hike was a thousand-foot ascent of a plateau only a few miles from Moab. Though the trail is listed in the guidebooks, in five hours I saw only ten other people, eight of them near the trailhead. On top of the plateau, I wandered in and out of a labyrinth of sharp fins so arcane it felt as though it had been decades since anyone else had come this way. Then I ate lunch beneath a panel of exquisite Anasazi petroglyphs: the *chef d'oeuvre*, carved by some prehistoric Picasso, was a deer-headed humanoid whose round torso enclosed a crescent-headed humanoid. Near the petroglyphs, several idiots had carved their initials. But one of the idiots had recorded his passing with a florid "C. A. R." and the date June 2, 1899. Until just a few years ago, the National Park Service and the Bureau of Lands Management (BLM) were still effacing nineteenth-century signatures. Now they have begun—rightly, in my book—to treat them as historic and therefore exciting to find.

ON FRIDAY NIGHT, I ATTENDED the high school homecoming football game. It was a revelation. The slick veneer of hip Moab is a town where you eat bagels over your morning *New York Times*, where location scouts for Holywood films hang out in the Slick Rock Cafe, where you can pick up the latest copy of *le Nouvel Observateur* and *Vogue Hommes*. But at homecoming I saw the bedrock Middle American town beneath the veneer. I felt as though I had been transported back to the 1950s, to one of those eastern Colorado cow towns like Fort Morgan or Sterling where my Boulder High Panthers did autumnal battle.

The Moab Red Devils, ranked for the first time ever number one in state (Double A level), were taking on the Monticello Buckaroos. Nestled among parents and grandparents in my four-dollar bleacher seat, I asked how come the Red Devils were so good this year. A graybeard clapped me on the shoulder and bellowed, "I've got two grandsons on the team, that's why they're so good!" Another fellow amplified the analysis: "A lot of 'em been lifting weights."

The cheerleaders, who looked about fourteen years old, pumped out, "Devils, Devils, what's your cry?" The crowd answered: "V-I-C-T-O-R-Y!" Moab scored the first touchdown, whereupon a fire truck in the end zone turned on its siren and lights. Everyone around me sang the alma mater:

Old Grand High,
You're dearer than the rest,
Old Grand High,
The school we love the best.

I left in the third quarter, with Moab on top twenty-five to zip, as the cheerleaders started tossing Frisbees into the happy throng.

The next day I headed up the Portal Overlook trail to Poison Spider Mesa. This clever path, which sidles through sheer cliffs up a thousand-foot climb, is used as a short-cut descent by mountain bikers closing a long loop on the backside of Poison Spider. Comments in the trail register captured the trail's ambiance: "Poison Spider kicked my butt." "Virtually unrideable: ranges from gonzo to absurd. Swallow your pride and preserve your life! Still, kinda cool. . . . "

The crux comes near the top, where the trail narrows to a steep grassy ledge above the void. It was still an easy hike, but I would have been petrified to try to bike down it. And with good reason: a few years ago a biker went off here, falling 400 feet to his death, while another lost it, unintentionally jettisoned his bike, which slid over the precipice, and self-arrested with his fingernails just before taking the big ride himself.

My intimations of danger on the Slickrock Trail were apparently well-founded. The previous August, two twenty-year-olds from Iowa took a wrong turn on the Porcupine Rim trail east of Moab, got rimrocked, abandoned their bikes, scrambled down something they couldn't climb back up, and died of dehydration before anyone could find them. (After a massive search, their bodies were spotted from a helicopter.)

It was something of a wonder that no one died on the 1995 Eco-Challenge, which caused a furor around Moab rivaling that over the Tram. An imitation of the Raid Gauloises, the Eco-Challenge put 500 contestants and monitors on a ten-day wilderness race ranging from the San Rafael Swell to Horseshoe Canyon, involving 370 miles of rappelling, biking, running, horseback riding, and rafting. Despite stringent opposition from such luminaries as David Brower, Yvon Chouinard, and Richard Bangs, the Eco-Challenge talked the BLM into sanctioning the race—in part, by promising to pack out human waste and to promote low-impact hiking in the MTV show covering the event.

Some observers fear that "adventure racing" (Chouinard: "There's no real adventure involved—it's a race for weenies") may become the next outdoor fad, the triathlon of the late 1990s. Says José Knighton: "'Eco-Challenge!' Doublespeak straight out of *1984*. It's just such an arrogant idea."

Adds Richard Bangs: "The title is correct. They did challenge the ecology."

But a pilot who'd flown support for the race demurred: "Environmental impact? Five hundred people for ten days?" he muttered. "Compared to one single weekend of hikers and bikers and Jeepers? Give me a break."

In an odd way, even José Knighton seemed to agree. "Frankly, I don't give a damn what goes on in town. It's the backcountry that I'm worried about. And livestock—which is permitted by the BLM, the Forest Service, the state—is the threat. Even Jeepers don't do the damage that cows do."

THE DEBATE OVER MOAB quickly devolves into an angst-ridden pandemonium about proper and improper ways of being in nature. Each spokesperson who takes a stand cherishes the illusion that by adopting the right set of rules, he or she can find a guiltless high in the outdoors.

The absurdity of this quest came home obliquely to me one morning as I drove into Arches National Park. The sign at the gate read, "Der Kampingplatz ist voll. Camping complet." It was only 8:00 A.M. Vacancies had gone on the market half an hour before, but crowding is so intense the sign—in German and French, no less—never goes into storage. By some measure, Arches has become too popular for its own good.

Yet a few minutes later in the visitor center, I beheld a cutesy exhibit titled "Don't Bust the Crust!" Extolling the wonders of cryptobiotic crust, the tabletop display implied that if the hiker managed never to crush any cryptogam underfoot, he would wend a virtuous path through the wilderness. (Tell *that* to the cows, I wanted to say.)

In the Southwest, "Don't bust the crust" has become the environmental piety of the moment. I was reminded of the "fragile arctic tundra" of the 1960s pipeline wars in Alaska, and recalled the outburst of a Republican congressman, "I'm sick and tired of hearing about the goddamned fragile tundra."

For a piety, especially in the form of a slogan (like the Sierra Club's hoary "Take nothing but pictures, leave nothing but footprints") substitutes a simplistic codex for the ambiguous and hesitant internal dialogue that ought to attend all our deeds in the wilderness. Who are the rangers at Arches, who have sold their stone bridges wholesale to European travel companies, whose trail to Delicate Arch was dynamited out of the bedrock to provide a dramatic arrival, to tell me how to walk in the desert?

At its most extreme, in the strictures of eco-fanatics who would teach us never to step on a meadow or camp within sight of a stream, to drink our own dishwater, to shit into plastic bags and pack them out, a germ of nihilistic misanthropy is at work. Rather than an arena for play, these watchdogs imply, the backcountry is such a deadly serious place that it can only be approached in a spirit of self-expunging asceticism. Only a short logical step leads from those strictures to their *reductio ad absurdum*: the best way to treat the wilderness is never to go there at all.

KARLA VANDERZANDEN IS DIRECTOR of the Canyonlands Field Institute, a local outfit pushing the oxymoron of "ecotourism"—filling the backcountry with paying clients in groups of twelve under the pretext of teaching them how to treat the country right.

VanderZanden first came to Moab in 1980, and she hankers after the dead old days as passionately as does Jim Stiles. But she has an interesting take on her own nostalgia.

"It's hard to separate Moab's growth from your own personal change," she told me. "We all feel, 'Gee, I remember quieter streets, when life was simpler, we were closer to our new friends, and the place felt really open, not closed and discovered.' But so much of what we're sad about is that *we've* grown up and changed. It's our old lives we're nostalgic for, not the old Moab."

In 1973, in *The Country and the City*, the Marxist literary critic Raymond Williams brilliantly analyzed the English equivalent of the Moab syndrome. The stimulus for the book was his own nostalgia for the "lost" village of his youth beneath the Black Hills on the Welsh border, combined with reading a new book about country life, whose first sentence struck Williams as improbable: "A way of life that has come down to us from the days of Virgil has suddenly ended."

Williams traced this *où sont les neiges d'antan* melancholy back from the present through F. R. Leavis, Thomas Hardy, and George Eliot, to George Crabbe, John Clare, and Oliver Goldsmith, eventually landing on Sir Thomas More, who in 1516 had deplored how "good holy men turne all dwellinge places and all glebeland into desolation and wildernes." Every generation of English bucolic writers had mourned, in Williams's pithy phrase, "those successive and endlessly recessive 'happy Englands of my boyhood.'"

The brilliance of the book lies in Williams's analysis—too complex to summarize here—of how that lost Edenic longing is an inevitable by-product of capitalism, with its "real social processes of alienation, separation, externality, abstraction." Whether or not one agrees with this critique, Williams's caveat against such childish sentimentalities as the Moab syndrome thunders home.

During my two days alone Jeeping, hiking, and camping in a pair of canyons outside Canyonlands National Park, I thought long and hard about all this. I walked through a wilderness the equal of anything in Arches or Canyonlands, and in two days crossed paths with but a single other party. The trail register in the first canyon recorded only twenty-seven visitors during the whole month of September; in the second, only fourteen.

As long as I could have days like this in southeastern Utah, it would be unlikely that I would regard the growth of Moab as a tragedy or believe the backcountry was being overrun. All it took was what it had taken in my own boyhood, among the high peaks of Colorado: if you did your home-work and were willing to hike, you could always find Edens in the outback that few others knew about.

The last night, camping on a shelf above the dry streambed, I engaged in a brief and half-hearted debate with myself, then gathered dead juniper and piñon sticks. According to the official regulations governing the par-cel of federal land I had laid my sleeping bag on, campfires were not al-lowed. Tough shit, I said to the bureaucrats in my head, desk-bound ghosts in Moab and Monticello.

Of the small fire I sat beside for three peaceful hours, as Cygnus and Lyra wheeled overhead, not a trace would remain when I left in the morn-ing. My collecting foray had made an infinitesimal dent in the stock of dead branches decomposing on the shelf behind me. The reason for my fire was neither warmth—it was a mild night—nor cooking.

I built a fire because that was what my ancestors had done in the Neolithic. The fire was to stare into, to muse upon, to pry open the senses with. The wilderness was there to be touched.

ED VIESTURS
CONFESSIONS OF AN ALTITUDE JUNKIE

"No, Scott, not there," Ed Viesturs shouted over the storm. "We've got to go more to the right!"

It was a small moment, coming near the end of an expedition that had already lasted fifty-two days. It was also the difference between life and death.

That day in 1992, three of the strongest Himalayan mountaineers—Americans Charlie Mace, Scott Fischer, and Ed Viesturs—were fighting their way down from the summit of K2, the second-highest mountain in the world and one of the most treacherous. For weeks, bad weather had stalled the climbers at base camp. Then a strong assault by Fischer and Viesturs had turned into a dicey rescue of a weaker climber in trouble on the mountain. By mid-August, these setbacks had all but consumed the trio's chances for the summit.

But on August 16, there was a slight break in the weather. Setting out from their highest camp at 1:30 A.M., going extraordinarily light for speed (they carried no food, no bivouac sack, not even their packs), the three men reached the summit well before their agreed-on turnaround hour of 2:00 P.M.

As they had climbed, a sea of clouds had risen slowly beneath them. Of the three men, only Viesturs seemed fully to comprehend the threat of those clouds. "It was eating me up inside," he reflects today. "I'd stop and say, 'Hey, guys, what do you think?' Scott and Charlie just said, 'Let's keep going.'"

Now, as they descended, the once-clear features of the mountain blurred to a gray smudge. The storm thickened into whiteout; billows of spindrift engulfed the men, and small slab avalanches cut loose on either side. The trio pushed on, each man wrapped in a solipsistic fog of hypoxia and fatigue.

To lose the thread of the route now would be fatal. As Fischer started to head down the wrong gully—an ill-defined runnel of snow that looked like a dozen others near the summit, but that led to a blank precipice rather than to camp—it was Viesturs who corrected the error. On the way up, he had acutely memorized every wrinkle on the mountain. Now Viesturs's attention to detail made the difference.

"Ed was really focused," Fischer said later. "He was the star getting down." Yet at the time, Viesturs was seized with a dark thought: *This is it. We're really going to die.*

Viesturs's fussy vigilance kept the trio on-route. At 5:00 P.M., they reached Camp IV, where at last they collapsed in the luxury of food and drink and shelter.

It was a brilliant triumph, the first American ascent of the Abruzzi ridge, a nervy dash in marginal conditions, without bottled oxygen, to the top of a mountain that had killed scores of expert mountaineers. Most of the legendary Himalayan climbers who have pushed their limits to such a thin edge and got away with it have tended to congratulate their own daring.

Not Viesturs. "When I got back to camp," he remembers, "I was really pissed at myself. I said to myself, 'God, you stupid idiot, don't ever do that again.' It was the one mistake I've made in mountaineering."

Four years later, Scott Fischer and Ed Viesturs met up again, on Mount Everest, though they were on separate expeditions. Fischer was guiding clients, while Viesturs was part of a team making an IMAX film. On May 10, 1996, once again a perfect summit day deteriorated into storm. Once again, Fischer pushed his limits. This time he didn't get away with it. Along with ten others, in the worst disaster in Everest's history, Fischer perished, of hypothermia and possible cerebral edema.

Two weeks later, Viesturs reached the summit of Everest—without oxygen and without incident.

THIRTY-SEVEN YEARS OLD, a veterinarian and Seattle resident, Ed Viesturs is only beginning to be known beyond the close-knit fraternity of climbing. Yet it is hard to quarrel with the notion that he ranks at the moment as this country's most accomplished high-altitude mountaineer. Viesturs's quest is to become the first American to reach the summit of the fourteen 8,000-meter peaks, a feat first performed by Reinhold Messner and matched by only four others since. Viesturs has snagged nine of the fourteen. No other American has more than five.

In the eyes of the lay public, the deed of ascending the world's fourteen highest mountains is overshadowed by the far less impressive Seven Summits—the climb to the highest point on each of the continents. The Seven Summits were first bagged by Dick Bass, a Texas millionaire and novice mountaineer who was guided up Everest, Aconcagua, Denali, and the Vinson Massif. Since Bass, many others, some equally inexperienced, have claimed the septet.

The fourteen 8,000ers, in contrast, define the elite of Himalayan mountaineering, as well as a campaign of the highest peril. Messner narrowly beat his rival, the splendid Polish climber Jerzy Kukuczka, in the race for first; Kukuczka subsequently died near the summit of the south face of Lhotse. In a later race to become the third to accomplish the feat, the Frenchman Benoit Chamoux lost out to the powerful Swiss, Erhard Loretan. Driven by his ambition, Chamoux also lost his life, near the summit of Kangchenjunga.

Unlike Messner, Kukuczka, or Loretan, Viesturs has never been in the forefront of technical alpinism. He has put up no big walls in Yosemite, no fiendish new routes in Patagonia. He freely admits that as a rock climber, he's not comfortable leading anything much harder than 5.9. As he became a mountaineer, he realized that technical difficulty held little allure for him.

"I'm an altitude junkie," he says. "I'm not a thrill-seeker. Danger doesn't appeal to me at all. My goal is to get up a mountain and get back home. In the Himalaya, my passion is to go to a beautiful place—a place lots of people don't visit—and challenge myself."

In his purism, Viesturs insists that each of his ascents of the 8,000ers be accomplished without supplemental oxygen. Yet despite the good style of this pilgrimage, Viesturs's quest has inspired curious rumblings of criticism. *Outside* magazine ran a brief profile of Viesturs peppered with invidious putdowns by several other Himalayan veterans. The unstated premise seemed to be that Viesturs was a mere peak-bagger, not a cutting-edge alpinist.

This vituperation puzzles and hurts Viesturs, who by all odds is one of the nicest guys ever to excel at mountaineering. Pressed to come up with evidence of conflict between himself and his colleagues, he says sheepishly, "I don't really know anyone who doesn't like me."

153

FROM HIS FIRST HIGH-ALTITUDE expedition, to Everest in 1987, onward, Viesturs learned that he adapted remarkably well to altitude. Nine years later, after seventeen Himalayan expeditions, Viesturs can claim that he's never really felt "out of it" on a mountain, never stumbled along in a stupor, as so many top-notch mountaineers have. Making the IMAX film last May, David Breashears, who himself has climbed Everest three times, caught up with Viesturs at the South Summit, 300 feet below the highest point. Breashears was using supplemental oxygen, Viesturs was not.

"I'm used to seeing the faces of climbers up high without oxygen," Breashears says. "They usually look like survivors of some terrible event. But Ed looked as fresh as anyone using oxygen. He's the closest thing to Superman I've ever met."

What allows one strong mountaineer to adjust well to rarefied air while another collapses, along with what causes a climber to perform well on one expedition but succumb to pulmonary or cerebral edema on the next, remains a considerable biological mystery. There are some startling bottom lines, however. As high-altitude expert Dr. Charles Houston (himself a veteran of the 1938 and 1953 K2 expeditions) first pointed out, if you took even a climber as strong as Viesturs and transported him from sea level to the top of Everest, he would die within two minutes.

There is also an absolute barrier, somewhere around 18,000 feet, above which human beings inevitably deteriorate. A striking confirmation of this frontier came years ago in Peru, where native workers had toiled for years at a mine at about 18,500 feet, descending nearly a thousand feet each night to sleep in their village. When the company offered to build the miners a new town adjacent to the mine, they refused. Generations of adapting to altitude had taught these hill people that though they could work above 18,000 feet, they would die if forced to live so high.

Thus climbing an 8,000-meter (26,256-foot) peak without oxygen requires a tricky balancing act: one must spend time up high to acclimate, yet minimize the deterioration that insidiously attacks the body above 18,000 feet. Each high-altitude ace works out his own formula, carrying loads high but retreating to base to recuperate; there is as yet no common wisdom how best to pull off this bargain with the devil of thin air.

Viesturs himself is somewhat at a loss to explain his knack for acclimating. Above 8,500 meters, Reinhold Messner has reported being seized with the conviction that an invisible companion marched along beside him. Descending Everest, Erhard Loretan saw vivid hallucinations of climbers cavorting through an icefall, dressed in carnival attire. Peter Habeler, who with Messner made the first oxygenless ascent of Everest in 1978, came back from the mountain convinced his concentration and memory had been permanently damaged.

Viesturs insists, after seventeen expeditions to 8,000-meter peaks, that none of these debilitations or hallucinations has come his way. He can, on the other hand, give a vivid demonstration of what it means to climb Everest without gas. Seated in a conference room in Seattle, he says, "At 8,500 meters, breaking trail through deep snow, it would take me ten minutes to reach that wall over there." He waves at a partition a mere ten yards away, then gets up to give an agonizing demonstration of the Everest shuffle. "Five breaths, one step," he says, panting dramatically. "Five breaths, one step. If your mind wanders, you lose the rhythm."

Viesturs is the first to assert that the mental aspects of performing well at altitude are paramount. "You have to be this patient, determined machine," he explains. "If you set the summit as your goal, you'll get too frustrated and overwhelmed. So you break it down into steps. You fix your eyes on that rock forty yards away. You say, 'I'm not going to stop till I reach that rock.' Then you choose your next goal.

"One thing, though. The summit day is always five to ten times harder than any load-carrying day before it."

In person, Ed Viesturs comes across as clean-cut, hearty, ingenuous. Of modest build—a shade under six feet, 165 pounds—he's obviously in great shape, but he's the farthest cry from the macho stud who kicks sand in weaklings' faces on the beach. His favorite exclamation is "Geez." With his big brown eyes, his bushy hair, his ear-to-ear grin, he bears a certain resemblance to Alfred E. Newman, the "What, Me Worry?" kid of early *Mad* magazine. A woman his age, meeting Viesturs recently at a Seattle office, blurted out, "Look at that face! No frown lines."

Viesturs's home in West Seattle is a museum of clutter: papers and photos strewn on every available surface inside, climbing gear overwhelming the patio, paint cans and rose bushes holding the house hostage. The clutter is surprising, for Viesturs is one of the best organized, most methodical of mountaineers.

The nice guy is more than skin deep. Says John Cumming, founder of Mountain Hard Wear, Viesturs's principal equipment sponsor, "Ed's the strongest climber I've ever seen or heard of. But he's also just a genuine person. There's no pretense whatsoever. In the world of climbing, that's a rarity."

John Roskelley, the leading American in the Himalaya a decade ago, testifies, "Ed always seems to be healthy. In the high mountains, I'm sick as a dog half the time. Ed has this low-key demeanor, no bravado. He's the kind of guy, you say, 'I'd like to be like him.'"

David Breashears sums up Viesturs in a pithy epithet: "He's the Chevy truck of Himalayan mountaineering. Nothing flashy. He just goes day in and day out and never breaks down."

Viesturs grew up in the flatlands of Rockford, Illinois. He's the son of a design engineer from Latvia and a beautician from Germany, both of whom were refugees from the Russian army in World War II. On reflection, the climber credits his parents for instilling a sense of modesty and a work ethic: "I was always aware of what they'd been through in a refugee camp in Germany. They gave me the sense that you could never take life for granted, that you don't complain about the minor things."

A varsity swimmer in junior high and high school, Viesturs caught the exploration bug when he discovered, in his hometown library, the heroic chronicles of Scott, Shackleton, and Mawson in the Antarctic. On the next shelf was Maurice Herzog's *Annapurna*—the book that has inspired more youngsters to climb than any other ever written. "On the surface of it, you'd think, 'Why would I want to go off on a climb like that and lose my fingers and toes?'" muses Viesturs. "But the book had the opposite effect on me. It was a last-ditch effort, with the team running out of time. They gutted it out and made it."

Viesturs and a high-school pal made their way to Devils Lake, Wisconsin, where they taught themselves to rock climb. Unlike most autodidacts attacking local crags, Viesturs never had a close call. He went on to the University of Washington to be near the mountains, studied hard, and hitchhiked to Rainier and the Cascades on weekends, pairing up with strangers met through climbing-store bulletin boards. After college, Viesturs earned his doctorate in veterinary medicine at Washington State University in Pullman. "I always loved animals and bugs," he reflects. But climbing had him hooked. "I thought, 'Geez, what if I could work as a guide on Rainier?'" In 1982, he landed the coveted summer job.

"With another guide named Andy Politz, I invented what we called the Load Wars," recalls Viesturs. "We had to carry all the food up to Camp Muir for the senior guides. We'd just load up our packs as heavy as we could cram in, eighty-five or ninety pounds, then go for Muir, bent over double. It wasn't a race, because we had to go at the clients' pace. We let the other guides judge who'd carried more. Sometimes you'd sneak a rock into another guy's pack. We just thought it was good for us."

Unlike other guides who aspire to mountaineering stardom, Viesturs never regarded Rainier as the drudgery that paid his bills. Even today, he professes to get a kick out of taking friends up the tourist slog on Rainier.

In 1983 and 1985, Viesturs guided clients to the top of Denali, where the mysteries of altitude first whispered their seductions in his ear. On his first Himalayan expedition in 1987, he turned back on Everest only 300 feet below the top. Though the setback was disappointing, "it was logical to turn around," says Viesturs. From the start, he was learning the kind of judgment that would be reflected in John Roskelley's high praise a decade later: "Ed's one of those rare people who knows himself well enough to back off." Today, Viesturs's favorite apothegm is, "Reaching the summit is optional. Getting down is mandatory."

Soon the triumphs began to tick off: Kangchenjunga with Roskelley in 1989. Everest in 1990, then again the next year, and in 1994 and 1996. K2 with Scott Fischer in 1992; Lhotse two years later. Though some of these expeditions, like K2, were marathons stretching over two months, Viesturs also pulled off some stylishly fast ascents of 8,000-meter peaks, including a four-day dash up Makalu and a thirty-hour climb of Gasherbrum I, both in 1995.

Through these whirlwind years, Viesturs attracted a series of girlfriends, but the climbing always took its toll. "When they first met me," he generalizes, "climbing was cool. Then a trip would come up, and another, and they'd say, 'Oh, you're leaving again?' I could feel the tension in the room. I'd realize I couldn't be with that person."

Two years ago, however, Viesturs met Paula Barton, a pretty, feisty children's therapist. Though Paula knew nothing about climbing, Viesturs was instantly smitten. The two were married in February 1996. The last two years, Paula has served as base camp manager on Ed's Everest expeditions. So far, the tension in the room has been kept at bay, but it remains to be seen whether marriage will blunt Viesturs's all-out ambition.

K2 WAS VIESTURS'S "EPIC." The trip seemed jinxed from the start. Unable to mount their own expedition, Fischer and Viesturs bought their way onto a Russian assault, hoping they could ignore the crowd and climb as an autonomous duo.

Early on, as they descended through an icefall, a block of ice shifted under Fischer's weight, plunging him into a crevasse. Sticking out an arm to cushion his fall, he badly dislocated his shoulder. The pair had to appeal to the Russians for rescue and medical help. For weeks after the accident, Fischer was *hors de combat;* the Russian doctor, resetting the shoulder, had told him, "The climb is over. Go home."

The dogged Fischer languished for two weeks at base camp, however, then set out with Viesturs for a try at the top, even though his arm still throbbed with pain. By August 4, the two men were installed at Camp III, around 24,000 feet, prepared to wait for a break in the weather.

Here, once again, the illusion that Fischer and Viesturs could operate as an autonomous pair vanished. A call for help came over the radio. Above them, at Camp IV, the American Thor Kieser and the Frenchwoman Chantal Mauduit were in trouble. The day before, as a storm gathered, Mauduit had pushed hard to make the summit, becoming only the fourth woman to climb K2. Kieser had turned back only a few hundred feet below the top. Now Mauduit was snowblind and exhausted. Kieser wasn't sure he could get her down without help.

In weather they would otherwise have waited out, Viesturs and Fischer headed up—not to go for the summit, but to aid other climbers on the mountain. Conditions were hideous: wind, whiteout, heavy snowfall building up hair-trigger avalanches. On one steep section, Viesturs, with his acute sensitivity to danger, realized the whole slope was ready to slide. But he and Fischer had just heard the shouts of Mauduit and Kieser, perhaps 500 feet above.

In a frenzy, Viesturs started to dig a hole with his ice axe. This was no tried-and-true mountaineering tactic, but a desperate instinctive reaction to an untenable plight. If the slope went, the climbers might just duck beneath it in their hole.

Before Viesturs could complete his excavation, the avalanche hit. Fischer, higher on the slope, was swept off. Viesturs jumped into the unfinished hole, planted his axe, and hung on. He had just begun to think, *Hey, it worked,* when the rope came tight to Fischer, now hurtling with the avalanche far below his partner. The sudden pull jerked Viesturs out of his hole like a toothpick.

With both men tumbling out of control toward ineluctable death, Viesturs thought calmly: *Rule number one—don't drop the axe.* Somehow in midflight he managed to get the axe beneath him, laid the weight of his body on it, and tried to drive the pick into the slope. At first nothing happened. Then the pick bit, stopping first Viesturs, next the helpless Fischer, as the avalanche thundered on.

Viesturs's self-arrest was one of the exceptional deeds in mountaineering history. It deserves to enter the realms of legend, like those two previous team-saving acts on K2: Fritz Wiessner's self-arrest in 1939, Pete Schoening's ice-axe belay in 1953. But other climbers scarcely know about Viesturs's heroic feat. Much of the blame is Viesturs's own: with his characteristic modesty, when he wrote about K2 for the *American Alpine Journal*, he devoted one dry sentence to the act: "After a 200-foot slide, I managed a self-arrest and held Fischer."

It is a testimony to Viesturs's and Fischer's courage that, having coming as close to death as you can in the mountains, they persisted in climbing up to Mauduit and Kieser. The American had spent himself belaying Mauduit down from Camp IV; now Fischer and Viesturs took up the burden. During the next two days, they safeguarded every step of their colleagues' descent to base camp. Mauduit was so exhausted she several times fell asleep standing up.

After so many setbacks, after such a brush with death, most mountaineers would have packed up and gone home. Yet Viesturs and Fischer lingered on. Finally, eleven days after their rescue of Mauduit, the two, with Charlie Mace, summitted on K2, then made their way in storm back to Camp IV.

Like Viesturs's heroes on the 1950 Annapurna expedition, he and Fischer had gutted it out and made it. *Annapurna* is Maurice Herzog's elegy to the skill and bravery of the French team, the first ever to climb an 8,000-meter peak. But Viesturs sees pushing to the top of K2 only as a mistake. "It was too thin an edge," he says. "I feel I pushed it too hard."

UNLIKE VIESTURS, WHOSE NAME draws a blank for the average American, Chantal Mauduit is a celebrity in France. Her star is hitched to success on the world's highest peaks, and it is not in her best interest to dwell on the aid she may have had getting safely down. Last spring, Mauduit came back from a solo attempt on Lhotse, nonchalantly claiming the summit. Other climbers on nearby Everest, having seen a tiny figure moving far too slowly up the Lhotse face, found it inconceivable she could have summitted. No one has come out to call Lhotse a fraud, but the grumblings are rampant.

In 1994, Mauduit attempted the summit of Everest, but collapsed near the South Summit. As luck would have it, Viesturs, guiding clients for Rob Hall, was in position once more to save Mauduit by getting her down the mountain. Another climber involved in the rescue put it bluntly, "We hauled her down like a sack of spuds."

Mauduit remembers K2 and Everest somewhat differently. Of Fischer and Viesturs's role in getting her down the former mountain, she says, "They helped a little. I was going down. It was nice to see them." Asked about her rescue from Everest, Mauduit laughs charmingly, then says, "No, I didn't collapse. I arrived later than the others. I waited for help to go down."

On Mauduit's last day at K2 base camp, she crept into Viesturs's tent and seduced him. Understandably dazzled by the Frenchwoman's glamour, Viesturs went to Chamonix to climb with her for two weeks. Somewhat ruefully, he says today, "It didn't matter who she was seeing, she was always seeing someone else." The relationship fizzled out, though Viesturs insists the two are still friends. But he adds tellingly, "I don't want to climb with her. She's not safe."

Mauduit met Paula Barton at Everest base camp in 1995. Now she says, "I'm very happy for Ed. He deserves to be happy with a woman. For me, I'm too much flying. . . . "

A CHARACTERISTIC OF MOST OF THE WORLD'S best mountaineers is that at some deep level, when it comes to contemplating their own mortality, they are deeply superstitious. Viesturs is no exception. With his hyper-rational approach to risk, he would like to think that he has cut the odds of disaster to the barest minimum.

A careful study of the fatality rate on 8,000-meter peaks concluded that on any given expedition, the odds of dying are one in thirty-four. If this is true, a simple exercise in probability reveals that by going on seventeen expeditions so far to 8,000-meter peaks, Viesturs has run a forty percent chance of getting killed. As he goes back again, after Nanga Parbat, Annapurna, Dhaulagiri, Manaslu, and Broad Peak—the five summits he needs to complete his fourteen—the odds will have risen to above fifty percent.

Whether or not the one-in-thirty-four rate is accurate, the statistics correspond to one's gut-level sense of just how dangerous Himalayan mountaineering is. Another measure of the risk is a pair of cold figures: on Everest, since the first attempt in 1921, there have been some 630 successful ascents and 143 deaths. Even more intuitively, Viesturs's double close call on K2 testifies to the inevitable peril of high-altitude mountaineering.

But Viesturs greets all such talk with incredulity. Without naming names, he argues that the numerous bozos on high mountains—ill-trained climbers who shouldn't be there—inflate the death rate. To no avail, it is pointed out to him that the rate also includes climbers in support roles who do little more than shuttle loads to lower camps along routes fixed with rope—far safer toil than going for the summit.

Asked what he subjectively considers the risk he's run so far in the Himalaya, he says, "I don't go there with the thought of a chance of dying. Maybe one in a hundred."

At this well-buried level, most climbers on the cutting edge recite private mantras that explain their survival. Says Erhard Loretan, "Fear and dread are my life insurance."

Viesturs takes a different tack. "I believe in the Karma National Bank," he says. "You put in deposits by doing good things for people. Sometimes maybe you need to make a big withdrawal."

AT DINNER IN A SEATTLE RESTAURANT, less than two months after the Everest tragedy, Ed and Paula go at the question of risk in a more visceral, emotional way. It begins with talk about kids.

"Paula would like to have them yesterday," Viesturs jokes. "Her idea is four. My idea is two."

Paula, who's twenty-nine, adds, "Ed wants to wait till he's finished the fourteen summits. But I don't want to wait five years."

"I could put it off," Ed urges.

"I could wait, too, but I might get pissed off."

Erhard Loretan has said, "If you have a family, you can't commit yourself in the same way." Viesturs hopes that's not true. "Now," he claims, "after an expedition, I can't wait to get home to Paula." He glances uneasily at his wife. "But on the climb, I guess I compartmentalize my emotions. I have to conserve my emotional energy."

Completely unfamiliar with mountaineering when she met Ed, Paula embraced his passion head-on by going to Everest twice as base camp manager. Last May, what it really meant came home with a vengeance. Over the radio, Paula had stayed abreast of every excruciating detail of the loss of Scott Fischer, Rob Hall, and nine others. At the time, Viesturs and Breashears were at an intermediate camp, biding their time for a summit thrust.

As the deaths piled up, Paula assumed that all further attempts on the mountain would be called off. Deeply shaken by the debacle, she anticipated only reunion with her husband and the hike out.

Then Paula heard David Breashears's matter-of-fact voice over the radio, talking to another climber, "We're going to come down and regroup before we go up again."

"That's when I lost it," Paula says now. "I just flew down to my tent and started crying really hard. I had to hike down to Thyangboche and back by myself, five days, to work it out."

But the solo trek wrought a change. By the time she got back to base camp, Paula stood firmly behind Ed's decision to go for the summit.

Late in the evening before his attempt, Ed radioed his wife from the South Col. "Paula, I'm going to bed. We'll get up to go at 11:00 P.M."

"OK," Paula answered. "I won't talk to you again till you're on the summit."

"Roger that."

"Climb this mountain like you've never climbed it before."

Paula's challenge decompartmentalized Ed's emotions. "I was so choked up," he says today, "I couldn't answer her. Because of this inspiration she was giving me. I literally couldn't speak."

Now, in the restaurant, contemplating the string of expeditions in Ed's future, Paula puts a brave face on it. "I'm going to live like you're coming home," she says. They're holding hands.

"I *am* coming home," says Viesturs.

ROB HALL AND SCOTT FISCHER were coming home, too—or so they told their wives. Hall was one of Viesturs's two or three closest climbing buddies: together they had climbed on Everest, Gasherbrum I, Gasherbrum II, Makalu, and Lhotse. And a tight bond between Fischer and Viesturs had been fused by their harrowing escape on K2.

In May 1996, Fischer and Hall were each leading expeditions with paying clients on the South Col or "standard" route. A cooperative competitiveness stamped their interplay; the two veterans had markedly different styles of guiding, but each agreed to help the other out on the mountain.

Style meant nothing, however, on May 10, when a storm not unlike the one that had engulfed Fischer and Viesturs on K2 turned a ringing success on Everest into a full-scale catastrophe. Rob Hall died of hypothermia high on the mountain, between the South Summit and the top, in large part because he would not abandon his doomed client, Doug Hansen. Fischer, who had felt out of sorts and lethargic for days, dragged himself along behind his own party, reached the summit last, and ran out of steam on the descent below the South Summit. Nearly incoherent remarks to the last climbers who saw him alive suggested that cerebral edema might have befuddled Fischer's thinking.

With their audacious project to make an IMAX film all the way to the top, Breashears and Viesturs had cooled their heels, giving other parties the first shots at Everest. Finally, late on May 22, twelve days after the disaster, Viesturs set out by headlamp, without oxygen, at 11:00 P.M.; Breashears and two Sherpas, with oxygen, set out an hour later. The plan was for Viesturs to break trail in the knee- and sometimes thigh-deep snow until the film crew caught up. After sunrise, Breashears would film Viesturs, the star of the movie, on the home stretch.

Breashears describes what happened. "As soon as I set out, I said to myself, 'My God, that headlamp's a lot higher than I thought it would be.'" All morning, Breashears and the Sherpas struggled to catch Viesturs. Breaking trail in deep snow at altitude without oxygen is a nearly superhuman task. Viesturs somehow performed it faster than the savvy Sherpas, sucking oxygen and stepping in his footsteps, could follow.

Several times Viesturs waited for his partners to catch up. But without oxygen, to stop still is to invite instant hypothermia. Breashears managed to join Viesturs on the South Summit, but the Sherpas, some of whom were vomiting from the effort, never caught up. In the end, Viesturs made what amounted to a solitary ascent of Everest (his fourth), and Breashears had to build the summit footage around the Sherpas.

Of Viesturs's astounding feat, Breashears testifies: "I got off-line and had to break trail for a hundred feet, and I was exhausted."

As Viesturs had headed out from the South Col in the middle of the night, he knew that the bodies of Fischer and Hall still lay in place on the mountain. In all his climbing, Viesturs had never seen a partner die. In fact, he had never suffered the loss of any friend in a fatal accident.

During Hall's ordeal on May 10 and 11, he had been in intermittent radio contact with others low on Everest. Early on May 11, at Camp II, Viesturs had been radioed by Paula, at base camp, who had just heard a fading Hall say, "Hey, is anybody coming to get me?" Now Paula urged her husband, "Get mad at Rob, get pissed, get him moving."

On and off for six hours Viesturs exhorted his close friend over the radio. "Rob, you gotta get moving. Put that pack on, get the oxygen going, get down the hill." He cajoled Hall with friendly badgering: "We're going to get down, and we'll go to Thailand, and I'll get to see you in your swimsuit with your skinny legs." Hall's wife, Jan Arnold, herself an Everest summiteer, was pregnant with their first child. "You're lucky, Rob," Viesturs needled desperately, "your kid's going to be better-looking than you."

Viesturs recalls Hall's response: "He laughed. He said, 'Geez, thanks for that.' He sounded totally positive. We told him, 'Don't talk, just listen.' We thought he had started moving down. Then, three hours later, we heard him say, 'I haven't even started moving. My hands are fucked, and my feet are gone.'" Weeping with grief and frustration, Viesturs cut off his own broadcast to spare his friend. Then, along with many others on the mountain, Viesturs had to listen to Hall's poignant last words to his wife, who had been patched through to the radio from New Zealand.

Both Fischer and Hall were among Ed's favorite climbing partners. "Scott was the photographer for Paula's and my wedding," he reflects. "All of Paula's sisters fell in love with him, he was so charismatic. In the mountains, he was always positive: 'We'll pull it off, Ed.'"

Viesturs was even closer to Hall. "Rob was articulate, intellectual, conservative, and safe. He always had his t's crossed, his i's dotted. We had enormous respect for each other."

It was thus with no little anxiety that Viesturs set off for the summit early on May 23. "Around 1:00 or 2:00 A.M.," he remembers, "I came over a rise, and my headlamp shined on Scott's legs. I knew it was him. I said to myself, 'Well, I want to see him, but I'll see him on the way down.'" Viesturs climbed past Fischer's body, then, after sunrise, past Hall's. He waited with

Breashears on the summit for the lagging Sherpas, but cold drove him down before they could top out.

Both Hall's and Fischer's wives, knowing Viesturs was going for the summit, had asked him to retrieve some keepsake—a ring or a watch—from their bodies. "I came to Rob just above the South Summit. He was lying on his side, in a wind-formed crevasse. His face was covered with snow. I couldn't bring myself to roll him over."

Viesturs pushed on down the mountain. The weather was nearly perfect. He came to Fischer's body. The last teammate who had tried to bring Fischer down ten days before, finding him dead, had covered his face with a pack. Now Fischer's body, like Hall's, was partially frozen into the slope.

Fischer, Viesturs knew, bore a treasured ring on a necklace dangling on his chest. "I just couldn't do it," he says. "I couldn't make myself get it off," he says. "I couldn't roll him over. If it was somebody I didn't know, maybe I could have done it."

Instead, Viesturs sat down beside his friend. "Hey, Scott," he said softly, "how you doing?" Only the wind answered him. "What happened, man?"

RECOLLECTED IN
TRANQUILLITY

THE HEARSE TRAVERSE

Basically, I hated Harvard. Majoring in math, I degenerated in four years from a natural sprinter to a has-been crawling on his knees toward the finish line. My professors deserved much of the credit: uninterested in teaching, they slapped equations on the blackboard in a scribble of chalk, and it was our duty to copy down these runes, go back to our rooms, and stay up all night trying to figure out what they meant. I have forgotten the classes I nodded through in psychology, expository writing, and history of science, but I recall with keen regret the training in snobbery that was Harvard's relentless subtext. We wore coats and ties to breakfast, lounged like barons in our common rooms, and had our bathrooms cleaned for us weekly.

In high school in Colorado I had led a normal social life, asking girls out to the movies, then on lucky evenings making out with them at the Twinburger Drive-In. Back east I froze, witless and sweaty, at Wellesley mixers and Radcliffe jolly-ups. Every November there was the terrible threat of not having a date for the Harvard-Yale game, a failure that demonstrated to your hypercompetitive peers that you were indeed the drooling cretin they had taken you for. What parties I did accomplish passed in a stupe-faction of rum-and-coke, the Kingston Trio on full blast, the anonymous girl at my side as incapable as I was of striking up conversation, let alone romance.

The obligatory Harvard style of those years, 1961 to 1965, was glib, cruel, and invulnerable. Admitting you needed help, confessing pleasure in another's friendship, uttering an unironic sentiment—all such behav-ior was decidedly uncool. I consulted my academic advisor for fifteen min-utes each year, and at that length only because the initial meeting was mandatory. Flattened in my freshman year by a setback of the heart, I sneaked off to a college shrink. He told me to read C. S. Lewis and every-thing would be all right.

Slogging across that desert of privilege and affectation, I managed to land on an oasis called the Harvard Mountaineering Club (HMC). I had climbed before college, but it was thanks to the HMC that I became a se-rious mountaineer. The club at the time was in fact the most ambitious collection of undergraduate alpinists in the country. But within Harvard, we were a small band of misfits, apostles of an arcane cult whose rites might lead to that most pitiful of heresies—taking a year off. The HMC was barely acknowledged to exist by the university, which let us use a moldy closet in the basement of Lowell House for a clubroom. When we trudged back to our rooms on Sunday night after a weekend at the Shawangunks, grubby and hung with carabiners and rope, our bridge-playing roommates looked as if some animal had barged in and peed on the floor.

Twenty-five years after my graduation, the only Harvard friends I stay in touch with are my climbing buddies. The HMC was the most spirited gang of cronies I have ever been part of; it forms for me a lasting model of how friendship ought to be organized. And its curriculum amounted, I feel now, to the best possible way to learn climbing.

The club didn't recruit; you had to find it among the fine print of the extracurricular. In my last year of high school, I had climbed the east face of Longs Peak while it was legally closed on account of bad snow condi-tions—a bold stunt, I thought, but hopelessly minor-league compared to the exploits I had read about since I was twelve, in library books by Euro-peans who went to places called Annapurna and Nanga Parbat. Boys from Boulder could never climb in the great ranges: only gods with names like Herzog and Buhl were admitted.

Yet in the fall of 1961, I wandered into my first HMC meeting pre-pared to patronize. This was Massachusetts, after all: Were there moun-tains at all in New England? I thought HMC activities would resemble the dowdy outings of the Colorado Mountain Club back home, with their campfire singalongs and blister clinics—an anathema of chummy backpacking to the avid loner I was at seventeen.

At that first meeting, I had my socks knocked off. Two fellows—a senior and a junior—had just come back from an ascent of the east ridge of Mount Logan, the second-highest peak in North America. Five or six others were reuniting after a raucous month in the Coast Range of British Columbia, where they had bagged Waddington, Tiedemann, Stiletto Needle, and dozens of other difficult mountains. The slide show confirmed it: guys only two years older than I were putting up new routes on mountains whose names were to me only hazy rumors from the geography of the impossible.

On my first HMC trips to Quincy Quarries, Joe English, and the Gunks, I learned how much better rock climbers these blithe veterans were than I. And on Cannon Mountain, I discovered that there were cliffs in New England equal to the east face of Longs. I went to every HMC meeting, where I mustered the nerve to say hello to the mountain men who ran things. I envied their camaraderie, their shared allusions to shaky rappels and unplanned bivouacs, with a longing as sharp as hunger.

The four juniors who dominated the club that year and the next bore the brunt of my hero-worship. They were Ted Carman, tall, boyish, sandy-haired, the eldest of four brothers who would climb and attend Harvard; Hank Abrons, a melancholic from Scarsdale who looked more like a librarian than a climber; Charlie Bickel, a grizzled gnome with the soul of an anarchist; and the hirsute, soft-spoken Rick Millikan. Rick had a tough act to follow, genetically: he was the grandson of George Leigh Mallory, who had said "Because it is there" and vanished near the top of Everest in 1924; his other grandfather, Robert Millikan, had snagged the 1923 Nobel Prize for his oil-drop experiment.

The turning point for me came at term break in my freshman year, when the HMC conducted its annual ordeal by masochism, an attempt to traverse the Presidential Range in New Hampshire at the end of January. This was a serious undertaking, but the club let anybody come who could walk in snowshoes, regardless of experience. On Friday night we drove north in Ted Carman's hearse, in the back of which—unheated, as hearses are—we rookies hunkered. I had never winter-camped before, and it was a bona fide thirty degrees below zero. Despite having been issued two army mummy bags, I was fairly sure, with the glum fatalism of youth, that we were all going to die, or at least lose many digits to frostbite. At midnight near the train depot in Randolph, New Hampshire, we piled out of the hearse and, under Rick and Ted's inspired hectoring, got our tents pitched quickly on the hard snow and our bodies inside. After three sleepless hours I had just gotten warm and drifted off, only to awaken to a distant train whistle. An engine chuffed in berserk rage, the ground shook, the Doppler wail bent the whistle, and the nightmare passed. In the morning, we saw that we had pitched our tents six feet from the drifted-over railroad tracks.

After that it got easier. We lost our trail on the Howker Ridge, bush-whacked in circles, and got stormed off Mount Adams on the third day. But Ted and Rick praised my trail-breaking and one night let me cook glop, and by the spring term I was almost one of the gang.

The HMC had been founded by Henry Hall in 1924, the year before he took part in the storied first ascent of Mount Logan. Four decades later, Henry attended every meeting, as he would continue to do until his death in 1987 at the age of ninety-one. By the early 1960s, he was starting to be a little fuzzy about sorting out each crop of undergraduates, but then somebody giving a slide show about a recent jaunt in the Canadian Rockies would mislabel an obscure peak, and Henry would burst in, "I think you'll find that's Mount Unwin. Mary Vaux is out of sight from there."

Thanks to Henry, we had a direct link to the great mountaineers who had peopled the club in the 1930s, for at regular intervals they would come to meetings to relive—always with cavalier modesty—the deeds of their own youth. Terris Moore projected glass slides from his extraordinary conquest of Minya Konka in 1932; Adams Carter took us up Nanda Devi with Tilman and Odell in 1936; and Bob Bates recounted the daring 1938 attempt on K2. In the imposing sanctum of his presidential office atop Boston's Museum of Science, Brad Washburn invited us to paw through his collection of aerial photos, as we searched for challenges worthy of the tradition of this preeminent mountaineer in Alaskan history.

Another pair of faithful guests was the English critic and philosopher I. A. Richards and his wife, Dorothy, who as Dorothy Pilley had written the classic *Climbing Days*. We got the feeling that, in his eighth decade, Richards had perhaps grown less interested in the Meaning of Meaning than in seeing dusty slides of the Bugaboos and Vowells, where the two of them had made first ascents in lightning times in the 1930s.

Before our thrice-yearly "banquets"—ordinary dining-hall meals dignified by a separate room—the club's advisory council met with the HMC president. The protocol was ancient and precise. It would have been a grievous faux pas, for instance, not to serve Duff Gordon amontillado sherry, the aperitif of Henry Hall's choice. Henry, of course, never told anyone this: rather, it was part of the lore handed down by the outgoing president to his successor. Yet these were genial affairs, where old lions like Ken Henderson and Ben Ferris and Henry himself, men who turned down invitations to be on boards of directors of corporations, solemnly deliberated whether we ought to get a new stove for the HMC cabin.

The roster of HMC activities was rich. In addition to the banquets, there were meetings with slide shows every few weeks; rock-climbing trips every fall and spring weekend to the Gunks, Cannon, Cathedral, and Whitehorse; impromptu dashes to Quincy Quarries on sunny afternoons; ice-climbing trips to Mount Washington's Huntington Ravine every weekend in February and March; the infamous Winter Traverse at term break; cabin-building frenzies; first aid courses; and a Climbing Camp every other summer in a remote part of Canada. Often members seized Christmas vacation to mountaineer out west, and in the summer as many as three or four expeditions sought out unclimbed summits in Alaska, Canada, or the Andes. The club also published a ninety-page journal every two years. This required dunning the graduate membership for funds, a campaign whose inevitable deficit Henry Hall always covered out of pocket.

At any given time, the HMC had only 25 or 30 undergraduate members, out of a student body of nearly 5,000. Perhaps eight or ten grad students, teachers, and affiliates also came to the Gunks with us. Yet these ranks comprised a remarkable collection of characters and eccentrics. There was Pete Carman, the best natural climber I ever saw, stocky yet limber, as aggressive as a pulling guard; his standard greeting, in lieu of a verbal salutation, was to bop you on the head with an empty Clorox bottle. There was tall, squint-eyed John Graham, who smoked cigars, tended to get lost in the woods, and fancied a career as a double agent in Africa. There was the absent-minded biologist George Millikan, Rick's older brother, who once accidentally locked his professor inside a bird cage. Our number boasted the mad inventor Art Shurcliff, who believed that adding rubber blobs to ski-jumpers' ski tips would prevent eye injuries; glowering Mike McGrath, who devised his own rating system for top-rope climbs (it began with "Glad to Get Up," went on to "Ecstatic to Get Up," and so forth); Paul Rich, a leftist Unitarian minister who got us bombed out of our minds every Christmas at his eggnog party; the professional salvage expert and doomsayer Ritner Walling; and Bill Putnam, who had successfully proposed his dog for membership in the American Alpine Club on the basis of his (the dog's) actual climbing record.

In those days, when Radcliffe was still largely separate from Harvard, when the Draconian parietal hours made cohabitation as rare as marijuana (and it was not until after Harvard that I saw my first joint), we had a single 'Cliffie, named Mary Ann Hooper, who came to our meetings and went on our trips. Mary Ann was not a member, however, because Henry Hall was old-fashioned about those things, and after all, it was sort of *his* club, and the question had never before come up. The Harvard Dean of

Students ruled that if Mary Ann were to attend a cabin weekend, she had to have a chaperone—a regulation we happily ignored. Three or four of us took turns dating her, but (speaking for my benighted self) there seemed something faintly incestuous about smooching with someone you might have to belay the next morning.

Like the Class of '63, with Rick, Ted, Hank, and Charlie as the club's dominant clique, my own Class of '65 was a strong one. Among five or six promising acolytes, two of us emerged as particularly dedicated. The other was Don Jensen, from California, a heavy-set fellow who had spent weeks alone in the High Sierra, a math major like myself. Don was warm-hearted but given to deep funks, and his long-pondered speech was the antithesis of glibness, for which traits he would pay dearly at Harvard. He quickly became my best friend.

The Class of '66 was a weak one, with only one outstanding rookie. We noticed Matt Hale from the start, because he got up every climb we tried to stump him with, but he was as mute as a Carmelite, whether out of shyness, deference, or plain stupidity, it was hard to tell. Then one day in the spring of his freshman year, at a party in Rick Millikan's room, Matt swallowed a couple of beers and suddenly started blurting witticisms. This revelation of character, along with his skill on rock, admitted him to the gang.

By the late 1960s, the vagabond passion of the HMC might have earned us a certain cachet within the college. But this was an altogether different Harvard from the one the police raided in '69. In our day the annual May riot was not about Vietnam but about whether the diploma should be in Latin or English. Timothy Leary was still a tenure-grubbing teacher in the psychology department. Erich Segal was a marathon-running classics tutor—widely regarded as a nerd, or, to use the Harvard phrase, wonk—who was sure he was going to become a famous writer, but whose only claim to fame was the doggerel in the Dunster House Christmas skit.

Had we rowed crew, or played ice hockey, we might have been Harvard stalwarts. But climbing was as weird then as caving is today. We were no doubt wonks ourselves. One cold January night in my senior year, as practice for Alaska, I bivouacked on my fifth-floor window ledge, tied in to the radiator inside my room. My roommates threatened to unclip my anchor, and other friends threw snowballs, but on the whole I thought they respected my vigil. A week later, in a chat with a stranger at dinner in Lowell House, the HMC came up. "You're a climber?" he asked. "Did you hear about that asshole over in Dunster House who slept out on his windowsill?" "No," I muttered. "Really?"

During freshman year, every Harvard student had to earn three "PT credits" each week to certify that he was of sound body. You could rack up a credit for an hour of softball, golf, or swimming, but it took a vigorous petitioning of a dubious dean to let us slide by with two full days of climbing ice gullies on Mount Washington.

On top of official incomprehension, we suffered from the conviction that by going climbing every weekend we were ruining our academic careers and thus our futures. This was not an illusion. Some of us dropped out, and none of us graduated with distinction. Ten years after Harvard, we would find ourselves teaching Outward Bound, manufacturing gaiters, farming on the ranch back home. Yet within the HMC we took gleeful pride in our feckless scholarship. When Ted Carman, a history major, let his climbing slough off in his senior year while he labored over a thesis on Walter Bagehot, we taunted him as a deserter.

As oddballs on the fringe, we indulged in all manner of antisocial antics. It would be nice to see in these juvenile outbursts the germs of the protest marches and sit-ins we would soon take part in, but our deeds were mere hijinks. An annual event was the Halloween ascent of the neo-Gothic Memorial Hall, which regularly roused the cops. One year Charlie Bickel got nabbed because his tennis shoes protruded conspicuously from the ledge where he was hiding. He spent a night in the clink after suggesting to the apprehending officers that their time might be better spent looking for the Boston Strangler.

There was the Hearse Traverse, a clamber out one window of Ted Carman's car, across the roof, and in the opposite window, all at sixty miles per hour. The Winter Traverse could be counted on to produce follies, such as the time Matt Hale and Rick Millikan had to prod a neophyte with their ice axes after he sat down exhausted in a blizzard and said, "It's all right. Just leave me here. I'll catch up later." Pete Carman and Rick Millikan went off to the Tetons one summer and came back with a whole new vocabulary. When it was "grue" out, they waved their fists at an Australian god and yelled, "Send 'er down, Huey!" There was never a question of "crumping." From one ridge Rick would yell, "Yo ho ho!" Pete would respond from afar, "Yo fucking ho!" One grim, drizzly day in November Pete and Rick, whom the Tetons had turned into first-rate rock climbers, failed to find the start of a route called the ConnCourse on Cannon Mountain. They ended up forging a desperate line up horrible rock, lassoing spikes as they went. By the time "November" was repeated, more than a decade later, it had become so apocryphal experts doubted the first ascent.

The best building climb ever done in Cambridge was Pete and Matt's ascent of the tower of Saint Paul's Catholic Church, 150 feet of direct aid in the dark on a loosely stapled lightning rod, passing two overhangs near the top. The victors left an undershirt flying from the cross. A few days later I saw Pete in the Dunster dining hall conferring with a pair of solemn priests. I thought they had his number, but it turned out the clerics were seeking advice and had been steered to the best climber at Harvard. "Would it be possible," they asked, "for mountaineers to climb our tower?" "Possible," said Pete judiciously, "but they'd have to be damned good." He offered, for a fee, to attempt removal of the impious undershirt. The church hired scaffolding instead.

For each of us who got hooked, the HMC started out as fun; then it became more than that. The most meaningful rite of passage of my life came in February 1963, when Hank and Rick invited me, a mere sophomore, to join their Mount McKinley expedition that summer. Though the prospect of attacking the mountain's unclimbed Wickersham Wall terrified me, there was no way I could say no. Boys from Boulder could after all be admitted to the great ranges.

With our expedition to McKinley, climbing became an obsession for me, by far the most important thing in life. The weekend trips, the slide shows, even Paul Rich's eggnog parties, had laid the groundwork. We didn't know it at the time, but we stood on the threshold of a golden age in American climbing. At the Gunks, where nowadays the hordes elbow their way toward favorite routes, we sat around a single campfire with the best climbers in the east, men such as Jim McCarthy, Art Gran, and Dick Williams. There was no guidebook yet: only tattered, mimeographed copies of a master list of routes. Everybody knew each other, and unless you were an Appie (a card-carrying member of the Appalachian Mountain Club, notorious for rulebound overcaution), you were welcome to the inner circle. At the Gunks that circle was the Vulgarians, whose wild cavortings gave us glimpses of the mysteries of drugs, sex, and 5.10.

Out at Camp Four in Yosemite, a band of kindred souls, penniless and idealistic, was pushing the steepest walls in the continental United States. Their names came to us already freighted with legend—Chouinard, Robbins, Frost, and Pratt—but within a few years we would meet these bold warriors and share our common enthusiasm. In Alaska and Canada, the hardest peaks were still unclimbed, and whole ranges lay unexplored.

Within the HMC, in large part because of the legacy of Henry Hall and Brad Washburn and their peers, we still regarded rock and ice climbing not as an end in itself, but as training for expeditions. Of our gang, only Pete Carman and Matt Hale ever went on to set new standards at local crags. But in the big ranges, we made a mark not unworthy of comparison with that of Washburn's generation.

On McKinley in 1963, my partnership with Don Jensen was lastingly forged. Harvard took it out of Don. He had already dropped out once, in the spring of his sophomore year. Don rationalized his defection with a scheme to do "independent study" somewhere near the High Sierra, but, like a drunk kicked out of a bar, he couldn't quite get it together to leave Cambridge. He moved surreptitiously into the HMC basement clubroom. I would drop by with dining-hall leftovers, to find Don shivering in his down jacket, staring at Alaskan photos in old journals or sketching designs for revolutionary ice pitons.

Don never returned to Harvard for his senior year. The HMC meant as much to him, however, as it did to me, and on three successive expeditions—to Mounts Deborah and Huntington, after McKinley—we carried its figurative banner onto the untrodden glaciers of the Alaska Range. The obsession had only begun. I was to climb in Alaska for thirteen years in a row, and when it came time to make a living, I found that, paradoxically, the métier I devised owed more to the HMC than to all my other schooling put together.

I live in Cambridge today, not far from Harvard Square. When I walk across Harvard Yard, sometimes I pass the building in which I nearly flunked a course called Theory of the Functions of a Complex Variable, and a Dickensian chill never fails to settle in my spine. But the other day I biked down the alley where Ted Carman's hearse had pulled away from Lowell House in January 1962 on the way to my first Winter Traverse. I saw the addled eighteen-year-old hunkering in thirty-below cold in the back, staring at the precious fingers he was about to lose to frostbite, and I felt good all over, because I knew how the story went from there.

BIKING THROUGH
TIANANMEN SQUARE

"This is becoming a cliché," said our guide, Mr. Sung, waving an impatient hand at the tents in Tiananmen Square as we bicycled past. "You can have a full report in *Time* or *Newsweek* magazine."

It was May 30, 1989, our first full day in China. For more than a month, the demonstrators in Beijing had camped out between the portrait of Chairman Mao and the Monument to the People's Heroes. The State Department warning against travel to China was still in effect, but things had quieted down just before our departure, and our group had unanimously decided to go ahead with our expedition.

We had signed up for a twenty-four-day tour of China, much of it by bicycle. Within our group of six, the pedaling experience ranged widely. Bob, a towering, crew-cut twenty-five-year-old given to sudden yelps of good feeling, had actually propelled himself across the country in an ordeal called the Trans-America Bike Trek. At the other end of the spectrum, I was content to putter around the back streets of Cambridge on a Raleigh Golden Arrow that my father had bought half a century ago.

Never before had I seriously focused my attention on China. The world's most populous country had always loomed like some dizzying, high-powered subject in school—the nuclear physics of world affairs. As the trip neared, however, I started reading Paul Theroux and Fox Butterfield and an assortment of guidebooks, and their intimations merged with the daily news from Tiananmen Square to make China vivid for the first time. Among the members of our group, as I was soon to learn, curiosity about China varied more or less inversely with enthusiasm for biking.

During our four days in Beijing, we admired a marble boat at the Summer Palace, poked through the tomb of a Ming emperor named Ding Ling, stomped on a stone to hear the triple echo at the Imperial Vault of Heaven, and strolled along the Great Wall. Mr. Sung hustled us through a flurry of temples, a blur of dynasties, so that we wouldn't be ten minutes late for lunch or dinner. We made rear-numbing forays of up to thirty kilometers at a stretch on our spiffy Japanese fifteen-speed mountain bikes. The best fun was biking in Beijing traffic, weaving with abandon through tight phalanxes of trishaws and Flying Pigeons (the Chinese bike of choice).

I beguiled myself with bicycle data. The Chinese word for the contraption is Zixingche—literally, "car that runs by itself." There are 7 million bikes in Beijing; in the whole country, 100 million machines, roughly one for every ten people. To buy a bike you have to get a permit, for which the wait can be long. The cost of a new bike is a month's salary for an average worker. To park downtown, you pay an attendant who assigns you a space.

Mr. Sung had not wanted to take us by Tiananmen Square that first day, but I had insisted. He was grouchy as he spirited us past; no doubt his superiors had told him to keep the Americans clear of political unrest. But I kept prodding, and later our group returned on foot to spend several hours wandering through the square.

Tents drooped and billowed; scrawny intellectuals lined up for food handouts; the pedestals of maudlin revolutionary statues were plastered with bulletins; and banners blazed with slogans, a few in English: "Victory belongs to us forever!" "Bank up our brave brothers and sisters." When we took pictures, some of the students flashed two-finger V's. Competing loudspeakers flung government propaganda and people's rhetoric across the concrete. The plaster Goddess of Democracy had just been erected. I joined a knot of spectators gawking at the two-handed torchbearer, murmuring their approval.

Like much of the world, I was completely fooled. The long demonstration seemed to be winding down. The hunger strike was over, and the remaining students looked tired, ready to go home. The government, which everybody said had showed admirable restraint, was offering them free train passage to their home towns. That night I wrote my parents, "The square looks like Woodstock. You have to keep reminding yourself that the students are there at some risk to their lives."

On June 2 we flew to Xian. In each city, we were assigned a new Chinese guide. The thin young man who greeted us at the airport was agitated; when he found that I was interested in the turmoil, he whispered to me that on April 22 twelve protesters in Xian had been beaten to death by police. Later I mentioned this shocking news to some hotel staff; they laughed and said no, nobody had been killed in Xian.

How could I verify any rumor in this alien land? So far my Chinese vocabulary amounted to three words: "hello," "thank you," and "beer."

We climbed the Wild Goose Pagoda, traced steles with our fingertips in the Shaanxi Museum, and drove out to Qin Shi Huangdi's astonishing army of terra cotta soldiers. On the morning of June 4, on the way to the airport, our guide told us that the students in Beijing had kidnapped some troops, but by now we were skeptical of such alarmist gossip. We flew to Nanjing, where we settled into our swanky rooms in the high-rise Jinling Hotel. Among the days ahead lay the heart of our bicycle pilgrimage: a series of pastoral trundles from Nanjing down the Yangtze River—to Yangzhou, Changzhou, Yixing, Wuxi, Suzhou, and at last Shanghai.

LATE THAT AFTERNOON I STOPPED at one of the hotel shops, where I found an odd scene. Four or five clerks were huddled behind the counter, near the floor, one of them holding a small radio. They were listening, it turned out, to the illegal BBC broadcast in Chinese. To our western eyes, the Chinese countenance is indeed hard to read—whence all the old canards about the inscrutable Orient. But I knew shock when I saw it. One woman was weeping soundlessly.

She stood up, embarrassed, to wait on me. I asked what had happened. The man with the radio said softly, "The troops have attacked Tiananmen. The tanks have rolled over people. Thousands have died."

A British tourist who had wandered in said, "No, no, no. Only about forty dead. I wonder if I might see—" He pointed to an item in the case. The salesperson served him.

I pumped the man with the radio for all he knew, then ran to tell the rest of our group. We spent the evening chasing further information. *China Daily*, the heavily censored English-language newspaper, had not arrived that morning (nor would it for more than a week). The comparably sanitized

TV news never came on. Some of us got through by phone to relatives in the States, who gave us scraps of fact. The brunt was inescapable: there had been a massacre in Beijing.

Norm, our American tour leader, faced a particularly cruel dilemma. An expert martial artist who had made eight or nine trips to China and who speaks the language well, he had fallen in love with a Chinese woman. The previous year he had asked her to marry him. While we were in Beijing, she had found him and given her assent.

The marriage, however—which would entail her emigration to the United States—went against her parents' and teachers' wishes, and would be frowned on by the state. During their brief hours together in Beijing, Norm and his fiancée had had to observe a Victorian decorum. There was no chance of their spending the night together. Our group had gone to an acrobatics show one evening; I was touched to see Norm and his beloved sneak handclasps under cover of the crowd's absorption in the show.

Now Norm judged it too risky to his fiancée for him to try to contact her, even indirectly. For all he knew, she had been at Tiananmen Square on the night of June 3. It would be weeks before he could learn anything about her welfare, and then, depending on the course the crisis took, it might be impossible for her to leave China.

Like any tour group with a prepackaged itinerary, we found it hard, so to speak, to shift gears. The next morning we sat in the lobby of the Jinling waiting for our bicycles to arrive. I had spent the night in a half-waking delirium of hallucinatory news dispatches, and now our bike vigil seemed absurd. But Mr. Ling, our Nanjing guide, was eager to proceed as planned.

The question was moot. Nanjing was paralyzed by a horde of protesters; it was hard to cross the city on foot, let alone deliver bicycles by van. Now Mr. Ling urged us to stay put in the sanctum of our hotel. It was not an order, though, so around 11:00 A.M. I walked toward Drum Tower Square, at the city's center.

The short hike was a powerful experience. Buses and trucks sat useless, halted at barricades made by men and women holding up lengths of string. A ritual funeral procession marched up the center of the street, its mourners chanting a dirge. I saw only one or two other Caucasians among thousands of pedestrians. When I paused at a corner, fifty Chinese surrounded me. A girl boldly asked, "What do you think of the Chinese people?" I expressed my support for the demonstration, and a man begged, "Please tell the world what is going on in China." In Drum Tower Square, the flag was flying at half-mast above a huge white drape with a single character painted on it—"sorrow" or "tragedy," a stranger translated.

Another banner, I was told, read "Hang Li Peng." The square was packed solid with people listening to speeches; unable to fathom a single word, I could feel the emotion like a wind. I started taking pictures, and a cold-eyed fellow in the crowd shook his hand to threaten my camera.

Separately, the others in the group had made their own way toward Drum Tower Square. Back at the hotel we agreed that, for all our confusion about what was going on, the scenes we had witnessed were galvanizing. Norm, who had fought in Viet Nam, was more leery of street crowds than the rest of us; his caution gave me pause. In Tiananmen Square on May 30, he had seen not Woodstock but the full peril of the situation, and the students' courage had deeply moved him.

Yet now there was nothing to do but sit around and wait. I had never before been in a country where you couldn't buy a newspaper to find out what was happening, and I felt the deprivation like a physical craving. Rumors were our only knowledge. The numbers of dead ranged from the British tourist's 40 to 5,000, the sum proclaimed by a solemn German engineer I met on the elevator. The tanks had crushed people in their tents, we heard; students had thrown Molotov cocktails; journalists were missing; the troops had cremated the dead on the spot with flame throwers. Already many of the tourists in our hotel were packing up to leave China.

At lunch I met a psychiatrist named Phil, part of a large group of American doctors having a get-together with their Chinese counterparts. He had been in Tiananmen Square on the evening of June 3: the first charge of soldiers had gone right by him, and he had seen the demonstrators stop the troops and beat them up. Too surprised to be scared, he had pulled out a camera and started snapping pictures.

Now he related with disgust how his group, aware of the massacre, had gone ahead on the morning of June 4 to visit the Summer Palace before heading to the Beijing airport. They had waited ten hours for their plane to Nanjing. By now, Phil had all but abandoned his colleagues. "It seems obscene to go ahead with our tour of Sun Yatsen's Mausoleum," he said, "and I had to get away from the ladies, who just want to go shopping." At that moment an American woman rushed up to our table. "Did I hear you mention 'tour'? Because for some reason our tour has been canceled, and I wonder if I could go on yours."

Our own group, which had never showed much promise of being cohesive, was fraying at the edges. In the dining room, where we took all our meals, a single tape played over and over—an obsessive meditation on two chords by a Japanese Keith Jarrett with a synthesizer. Sitting down to lunch, I had said, "Ah, my favorite music." For such cracks I had won the reputation of being "negative." Ravenous for news, unable to reach the United

States embassy in either Beijing or Shanghai, I kept pumping the others for the contents of their calls home. One woman who had reached her mother confessed, "I didn't actually ask anything. I just told her not to worry about me." Another woman had bragged of a friend in Hong Kong who was a TV journalist. "She'll know what's going on," the woman kept saying. Each time I asked if she had called her friend yet, however, she made an excuse. Finally she said petulantly, "I decided not to call. Why should I? I can't change anything." Norm himself seemed to be slipping into a narcoleptic torpor.

I went back alone to Drum Tower Square that night. There were still thousands of people in the streets, but I saw no other westerners. Hand-lettered broadsides, many on bright red or yellow paper, had been posted on every wall and billboard. Residents were reading these by cigarette lighter. The first photos from the massacre had appeared—faxed from Hong Kong and the States, I later learned.

Yet in the Jinling Hotel, you could have imagined that nothing was amiss. On the mezzanine, the Jinling Quartet robotically played Boccherini and Tchaikovsky. In the dining room, the waitresses smiled and brought more quarts of Nanjing beer. The communist party members in the hotel administration had called a meeting and urged all staff to be "sensitive" to the guests—i.e., to talk about Beijing on pain of dismissal or worse. Yet the tourist exodus was on: the Jinling grew more deserted by the hour.

It is the nature of group tours in foreign countries to render their participants passive; the clientele may even self-select for timidity. Every time I joined such a trip, I had to fight my own passivity. Why, in a whole week, had I learned only a handful of Chinese words? It always irked me how travelers in a group will stand around plaintively asking each other: "When did they say the bus was coming?" "What time are we having dinner?" "Where did June and Melvin go?" For some reason, I tend to be the focus of these anxious bleats, and now, living up to my negative reputation, I snapped back, "Why are you asking me? Ask Mr. Ling."

For two days I had felt frustrated and on edge. Some of the protesters I had photographed a few days before were no doubt dead by now. There was no way to gauge what was going to happen next in China. A train, we heard, had run over six demonstrators in Shanghai, killing them: that city might be the next to blow. Mixed with my outrage was a weird exhilaration: it was breathtaking to be caught in the midst of such a cataclysm. Among the masses of mourners in Drum Tower Square, I had fought back tears. None of the sit-ins, strikes, or marches I had joined in the late sixties had felt this powerful.

There seemed a self-evident mandate to *do* something. But I was not

Chinese; the most I could do was to bear witness. And how did one ac-complish that? By hanging out on the streets, taking pictures, vowing to tell friends in America what I had seen? My urge to act was heavy with a sense of impotence.

My fellow travelers seemed to have no more idea than I did what to do, and so, on June 6, we went biking. Disobeying his superior, Mr. Ling outfitted us with a fleet of decrepit Flying Pigeons. (His boss wanted us to sit tight another day in Jinling; what he really hoped was to pass us on to the Yangzhou guide and wash his hands of us, but the highways were blocked.) We managed to pedal east, away from the center of Nanjing, and reached Sun Yatsen's Mausoleum. The snack and souvenir stalls were shut down; only a few busloads of Taiwanese loitered about the grandiose monu-ment. I tried to concentrate on sightseeing, but I was hopelessly distracted.

The latest rumors held that Deng Xiaoping was dead, or that Deng and Li Peng and the other top leaders had fled to the provinces. Suddenly Tom, the quietest member of our group, blurted out, "If all the bosses are in Inner Mongolia, who's minding the store?" Mr. Ling grinned in nervous incom-prehension. "WHO'S MINDING THE STORE?" Tom shouted in his face.

On the morning of June 7, our group held a meeting to decide what to do. All the other tourists in the Jinling had left or were preparing to leave the country. Norm said we had two options: to get out ourselves, or to go on to Yangzhou and continue our bike trip. The Yangzhou guide was sup-posedly trying to drive to Nanjing that morning to greet us.

The decision had the potential to be one of the most important any of us had ever made. If civil war erupted, our freedom, even our lives, could be at stake. I had no further interest in biking, but I didn't want to pull out of China. I raised the possibility of staying in Nanjing. Norm showed a rare flash of anger as he burst out, "That's bullshit. If we stay in Nanjing, it's only to get out of China."

Bob, the marathon biker, chirped, "Let's ride." A kind of machismo seized the group. One woman, who the night before had been desperate to leave the country, now said, "Norm, I'm ready to ride." The others mur-mured their pledges. You would have thought we were GI's, volunteering to storm an enemy fortress. I pleaded for further discussion, but the woman cut me off: "Norm, just make a decision for us." Exasperated, I said, "But we have to come to a consensus." The woman said, "I've come to my con-sensus," and walked out of the room. Another woman left with her.

Norm went downstairs to see if the Yangzhou guide had arrived. He was back a few minutes later. The president of the bike touring company, who had been monitoring the situation from Virginia and trying to reach us, had got through with a telegram. "The whole thing is academic," Norm announced. "Li Peng has been shot. The troops are firing on each other. We're getting the hell out."

WE FOUND OUT LATER THAT NEITHER rumor was true, but both had been reported in the American news. As it turned out, we were so far down the waiting list for airplane seats that it took us three more days to get out of Nanjing, and then we could fly only to Guangzhou (Canton), where we took a train to Hong Kong.

Having the decision to end our trip made for us seemed to lift the others' spirits. They started laying plans for ways to spend their "extra" days back in the States. There was talk about whether we'd get back in time for the Pistons-Lakers playoff games.

With the decision, my colleagues' interest in China came to an end. To Norm and me, the situation had never been more fraught, but the others no longer even feigned curiosity. For them the hotel became an airport waiting lounge. Only shopping continued to hold their attention. My relations with the group had reached a new low, epitomized in an absurd moment. Doris, a hefty redhead with an eye for the shops, appeared in the lobby one morning burdened with packages. Thinking to make a pleasantry, I said, "You're going to be overweight." She stared at me, aghast. At last the ambiguity of my remark dawned on me.

We still had our Flying Pigeons; I rode all over Nanjing on mine, but the others never touched theirs. Mr. Ling arranged a sightseeing outing by bus. The Cliff of the Thousand Buddhas seemed an eerie harbinger of what might be in store for China. In the Cultural Revolution twenty years before, every one of the ancient rock-carved Buddhas had been beheaded by the Red Guards with their sledgehammers. The women in our group didn't want to hike up the short path to see the statues. On the way back, we stopped to look at some Bixie, huge, bizarre stone chimeras carved in the sixth century. Most of the group didn't leave the bus.

On June 9, our last day in Nanjing, the city was transformed. Overnight every wall bulletin had disappeared, along with the banners, the "sorrow" drape, the mourning wreaths in Drum Tower Square. We heard that martial law was in effect; if so, it was now illegal even to stand around talking politics. During our last hour in Nanjing, Norm and I took a final tour by bike. In Drum Tower Square, traffic cops hustled cars and people through; yet a group surrounded the two of us, and a young man Norm talked to in Chinese suddenly squeezed his hand with fervor.

We had almost reached the Jinling when we came upon an extraordinary scene. A crowd of forty had gathered around a tree in a vacant lot, where a new yellow protest poster had been hung. The top character, said

Norm, was "blood." Leaning with his back against the tree was a skinny young man with glasses. He held up a tape player with a small megaphone in front of it. We drew within listening range. On the tape we heard gun-fire and screams: somehow the man had got hold of a recording made in Tiananmen Square during the massacre. The man's arms were shaking, and his eyes frantically scanned the neighborhood, checking for police. He was ready to bolt: his act, after all, was treason. But as I took his picture, he stood there, proud and distraught.

In Hong Kong, I went on an orgy of newspaper and magazine reading. After China, a free press tasted like water in the desert. Our farewell din-ner was a dismal affair. Seated next to Doris, I commented that the tour operator had done all anyone could in an impossible situation. She didn't agree; the company owed her compensation, she thought. "So what are you going to do about it?" I baited her. "I'll wait a few days," she said, "then if I don't hear from them, I'll put it in the hands of my lawyer. I'm too busy to deal with this piddly stuff."

I had decided to stay on in Hong Kong for four or five days. The others shopped till their last moment. I went out to photograph the savage politi-cal cartoons that were sprouting on building walls. When I got back, to my relief, the others were gone. They hadn't left me a farewell note.

On a cruise boat in the harbor I ran into Phil, the psychiatrist I had met in Nanjing. He seemed at loose ends, too. "You know," he said, "I feel guilty for leaving China. For being able to." That hit a nail on the head for me. His group of doctors had tried to go on a bus outing, but had been stopped by the protesters who had taken over the Yangtze River Bridge, one of the main links between northern and southern China. Their tour guide was crying; even the bus driver seemed overcome. Suddenly one doctor asked a question about dynasties and architecture; another blurted out, "Are there any snakes in China?" Phil lost his cool and upbraided the latter in front of the group. At their farewell dinner, he said, his group had given him the "Haight-Ashbury Award."

"What happens to tourists to make them act like that?" I wondered.

Phil shrugged. "It's a defense, I guess."

"Against what?"

"Involvement. Empathy."

During my days alone, I puzzled over my colleagues' behavior. From the first days in Beijing on, none of them seemed to ask any questions. Nor had they brought any books on China, except for the guidebook that the tour operator issued with the company T-shirt. Geographical ignorance goes hand in hand with lack of curiosity. In 1985, when tourists were terrified to fly to Europe, it had surely been the least-informed, the ones who could hardly tell Hungary from Portugal, who had been most certain that an Arab with a bomb was on board every TWA flight.

It made sense that shopping was the last refuge of the bewildered tourist. Susan Sontag had written that a camera becomes a shield against anxiety; to take snapshots in a foreign land is to tame its strangeness. In a similar way, shopping reduced a country to a boutique, and to drive hard bargains with vendors, as Doris and the others delighted in doing, passed for connoisseurship.

But in the midst of my analyzing, I realized that I was enjoying my scorn. The group was right—I was a negative sort of fellow. I was wallowing in *Schadenfreude*, and I could discern its function. It was more satisfying to gnaw on my disdain for the others than to surrender to the anguish and impotence and confusion that had beset my spirits since June 4. When one of the great spasms of history performs its convulsions before your eyes, and you cannot figure out how to respond to it, then to deride someone else's response serves as a sop to conscience.

My guilt peaked as I settled into my plane seat at the Hong Kong airport. China was slipping away, and I, too, was glad to go back to the States. From my briefcase I took a piece of paper that a demonstrator in Nanjing had thrust into my hand. To hold it now was to hang on to my stake in the Chinese tragedy, if only for a few minutes longer. The paper was a copy of a handwritten message. The scrawl of delicate characters was meaningless to me, but a few days before I had handed the paper to Mr. Ling and asked him to translate the opening. In a toneless voice he had recited, "I was one of the last to leave Tiananmen Square. My friends are gone forever . . . "

QUIET DAYS IN THE
BROOKS RANGE

On my second night in the Brooks Range I couldn't sleep. The problem was the perpetual daylight of midsummer. At one in the morning the sun lay low in the north, its rays washing the un-named peaks to the south with a muted clarity. Inside my tent, I turned over once more. The tundra under my sleeping bag was so soft it seemed to chide my insomnia.

I heard a deep, gravelly cough. One of the other guys, I thought with satisfaction, must be having trouble sleeping, too. I hoped, however, that he wasn't coming down with something contagious.

In the morning I discovered, a couple of yards from my tent, a sizable mound of fresh excrement, unmistakably that of *Ursus horribilis*. A grizzly bear had walked through our camp in the balmy night. The "cough" had been an altogether different sort of eructation.

We were camped at Angiaak Pass, near the headwaters of the Noatak, one of the major rivers in the western Brooks Range. Stretching 600 miles across the northern half of Alaska, the Brooks is the greatest unbroken wilderness left in the United States. Only the infamous pipeline, with its dirt service road, penetrates this fastness of intricate valleys, low but jagged peaks, purling streams, glassy lakes, and vast plains of tundra. Most of the range is north of the limit of wooded land. For nine months each winter, the countryside lies frozen under the arctic snows. But from June to August the land is seized by a riot of life and motion. The dwarf fireweed, bright magenta, blooms down its stalk; the heliotropic arctic poppy bends with the arc of the Zodiac; pods of Alaska cotton stream in the wind; and the ground-close web of willows, mosses, and grasses that makes up the tundra itself turns slowly from dull brown to full green, before expiring in an autumn blaze of russet and orange. The rivers flood loose in May in the ice cataclysm called breakup; trout and grayling begin to leap in the lakes; great clouds of mosquitoes hang over the land; the arctic tern and the long-tailed jaeger soar over the valleys. And all summer long, there is no night.

From Angiaak Pass we hiked down the Reed River, named for a United States Navy ensign who was guided by the Inuit to a sacred hot springs in 1886. Our intention, during a lengthy expedition, was to make the first ascent of Mount Igikpak, the highest peak in the western Brooks Range.

Angiaak is Inuit for "stone scraper," and Igikpak refers to the two fierce rock towers that form the top of the impressive mountain. There are Inuit names all over the Brooks Range, for the place was that people's ancestral home. But with the exception of the fifty-odd denizens of the anomalous village of Anaktuvuk Pass, the Inuit themselves have not inhabited the range since the 1890s, when a mysterious decline in the great caribou herds forced these inland nomads down to the coast to new trading settlements like Barrow and Nome, where they were to live in much greater unhappiness than they had aboriginally known. The Inuit live in those squalid towns today, and the Brooks Range remains a haunted wilderness.

That day in 1968, this fact came home to me with sudden force. A few miles below the pass, we crossed a talus slope spilling from a peak on one side of the valley. On five prominent boulders, someone had propped angular rocks, two or three atop each boulder, like Matisse cut-out heads. Lichens had grown across the cracks, indicating age, and the strange constructions were utterly unlike the cairns that white men build. It was clear that they were the work of Inuit. In the eighty-two years since Reed himself, very few people had been through Angiaak Pass; we might well have been the first whites ever to see these small towers. I puzzled for the rest of the expedition over their significance, and later combed the anthropological literature. My best guess today—by no means a certainty—is that the cairns were built as human effigies, shapes which the caribou, as they were chased up the valley, would mistake for hunters, shy away from, and so plunge into an ambush on the other side of the valley.

That summer I fell utterly and completely in love with the Brooks Range. Over the years since I have gone on three month-long climbing expeditions there and five other two-week fishing trips with my father. Before 1968 I had climbed quite a bit in the glacial treacheries of the Alaska Range, farther south. The Brooks, I found to my astonished delight, was warm (up to eighty degrees Fahrenheit), dry, and had generally good weather. But it was the light, more than anything, that lured me back year after year: that slanting effulgence, as clear as cold water, that wheeled diurnally through the points of the compass and never dimmed into night. Only north of the Arctic Circle does the sun actually stay above the horizon at midnight. And the Brooks Range is the only part of Alaska north of the Circle.

The trips with my father were wonderful. A workaholic scientist, he had scarcely taken a vacation all during the years I grew up, and it had not been part of our family pattern for him and me to go hiking or fishing together, even though he had been an angler of no small repute on the trout streams of Colorado. But my reports of the Brooks Range got under his skin. Dad had taken up flying as a hobby and had bought a small two-engine plane. In 1970, when he was fifty-five and I twenty-seven, we made the first of our arctic explorations together.

With assorted cronies, we would fly his plane up the Alaska Highway, overnighting at Fort Nelson or Whitehorse or Tok. In Fairbanks we would load up on expedition groceries, then fly north to the tiny arctic crossroads called Bettles. There a real bush pilot took over. Paul Shanahan would throw the FAA regulations out the window, pull up his fishing waders, load us and our groceries to the ceiling in his Cessna 185 on floats, and take off from his dock on the Koyukuk River. An hour and a half later we would be landing on "our" lake. We spent our blissful weeks, in successive years, on Omelaktavik, Selby, Alatna, Kurupa, and Shainin Lakes; not once did we have to share the camping with another party.

Each year, I would put together my Klepper foldboat and paddle Dad out to the middle of the lake, where he trolled deep for trout and northern pike, or cast in the inlet for grayling. We made scrubby fires out of willow twigs and the fuel boxes left by government parties from the 1950s; the same boxes became camp stools. We played baseball with a spheroid made of tundra wound in duct tape, the bat a tent pole. Sometimes there was a forest fire out of control, eighty miles to the south; the wind would blow a sweet-smelling smog our way, and the sky was hazy for days with wood smoke. On the shore of Shainin Lake we discovered an undercut bank in which, three feet deep in the black soil, an astonishing collection of animal bones lay buried. Clearly this had been for generations a summer campsite for the Inuit, where they had trapped and eaten caribou and bear. I would hike off and "bag" the easy peaks in the distance, none of which had ever been climbed before. On one such walk I stumbled upon the interlocked antlers of two buck caribou, the skulls attached; thus had these proud beasts died in rutting combat. The antlers had moss growing all over them, and they looked fragile; but I couldn't pull the two sets apart.

The midsummer light seduced us into staying up late. Some nights we never slept at all. We sat on our Blazo stools in our big canvas tent, brewing up cup after cup of coffee and hot Tang, and, as Callimachus put it, "tired the sun with talking as we sent him down the sky." Except that he never quite went all the way down—sometimes he would dip beneath a mountain ridge for an hour or two. My father, an astronomer, had spent thirty years studying the sun, and one memorable night on the Alatna Lakes we saw the exquisite, rare green flash as a distant peak eclipsed the sun: saw it not once, as mortals count themselves lucky to do, but many times, at will, by walking up the hillside behind us to cause the sun to set again and again.

In August there were blueberries in limitless profusion, and whole afternoons went to piling our plastic eating bowls full of them. We ate fish until we were so sick of them, even Spam tasted great. For hours we lay on the luxurious tundra and watched the sky, which always seemed to be changing. Although it was a standard, rueful joke, we half hoped Shanahan would forget about us and we would have to winter over, there on Kurupa or Omelaktavik. By flying off to the Brooks Range, and flying in and sending our pilot away, we had given ourselves permission for two glorious weeks to be boys again.

Two of my climbing expeditions were in the Arrigetch (Inuit for "fingers of the hand outstretched"), the finest mountaineering challenges in all of the Brooks Range. At the end of both trips, rather than fly out with Shanahan, we chose to boat down the Alatna River. In the Alaska Range, where everything was "serious," my expeditions had been made up only of experienced climbers. But in the Brooks Range it was perfectly reasonable for my wife, Sharon, who climbed only a little, to come along. She spent some lonely days at base camp while the rest of us were off on the peaks. But on the Alatna, as the two of us paddled our Klepper, she was in her element.

After a month of activity centered on the cluster of tents we called base camp, there seemed a blissful freedom in floating down a river, always on the move. One day Sharon and I glided quietly along a sweeping bend in the Alatna, while a wolf, invisible in the alder bushes on shore, moaned plaintively. Another time we floated up to within a few yards of two wolf cubs playing on the beach: they are still the only wolves I have seen in the wild. We camped on grassy shelves above the river, and gave ourselves, now that we were back in timbered country, the privilege of great bonfires of spruce and alder each night.

Before my first trip down the Alatna, I made my way alone upstream to the mouth of Kutuk Creek, where I found the ruins of Bud and Connie Helmericks' cabin, which the young couple had built in 1944. Connie had written a long, chatty book called *We Live in the Arctic* about their lonely year as homesteaders, and I had read it just before our trip. Yet no accumulation of domestic vignettes in her prose had the force of the hour I spent poking through their cabin. The windows were gone, and there was a big hole in the roof, but the handmade chairs still sat waiting to be used, and on a knick-knacky shelf there was a jar with old tea bags in it. On the back of the door I found a penciled note which Bud and Connie had left on their departure. "You are welcome," the note said in part, "to use this cabin as long as you like and anything in or about it. . . . Visitors may sign below." I signed, only the fourth visitor to do so in the twenty-five years the note had hung there, brittle and yellowing, in the dry arctic air.

Near the end of our second trip down the Alatna River, Sharon and I were camped off in the bushes one drizzly night. The other tents were out on the gravel bar, near our boats. I woke from a light sleep around two A.M., because the ground beneath me was undulating ever so gently. As I came to my groggy senses, I realized that what was shaking the packed sand was the regular tread of an animal. I also realized that the only animal capable of vibrating terra firma like that was a grizzly. It was apparently passing only a few feet from our tent. I held my breath and let Sharon sleep on.

We had lugged a 30.06 rifle with us for more than a month. Now it lay, unloaded, on one of the rafts out by the river. We hadn't seen a bear the whole trip. After a few minutes, to my inexpressible relief, the thudding tread grew more distant. I woke Sharon and cautioned her to be quiet. Then we dared open the door of the tent.

In the gray light the first thing I saw was *Ursus horribilis* himself, his rear end toward me at a distance of about thirty feet. He was a good-sized one, and he was headed straight for the high-peaked, gaily colored four-man tent. I considered yelling to warn the quartet inside, but the rifle was as useless to them as it had been to me. As I watched, the bear walked up to the tent and paused. He lifted a paw, lowered it, then thrust his great muzzle against the fabric.

Recoiling abruptly, the bear jerked his head away from the tent. Again he paused, then turned and started toward a raft—the one with our gun on it, as well as all our food. But at the last minute he veered off, waded into the river, effortlessly swam across, and disappeared into the bushes on the other side.

Nobody else had seen the bear, and in the morning the others were reluctant to credit my story, until I pointed out the tracks in the sand. One person in the four-man tent, however, remembered that he had been having a nightmare. Every day of the expedition, each of us had been allotted two candy bars. In the man's nightmare, someone else on the expedition had discovered his secret stash of Butterfingers. The other fellow was trying to cut his way into the tent to pilfer the precious chocolate. To save his stash, the dreamer lashed out with his fist and connected with a solid blow. The intruder had vanished. In the nightmare, the blow had seemed quite vivid. And no wonder: our friend may have been the only person in Alaska history to punch a grizzly on the snout and not even know he had done so.

During my three climbing expeditions, I made thirteen first ascents in the Arrigetch and the Igikpak area. The best of them was an 1,100-foot-high needle of granite called Shot Tower. On a warm morning in 1971, Ed Ward, who had become my regular climbing partner, and I started up the soaring western arête of this beautiful peak, which had been named by a previous party but never attempted. Twelve hours of continuous rock climbing later, we neared the top; but we had run into the hardest single pitch on the whole thing, a dead vertical wall split only by a meandering thread of a crack.

I belayed Ed as, quite tired and low on pitons, he took this crux lead. When he was thirty feet above me, a piton pulled out and he fell a short distance. I too felt almost too exhausted to go on, and even if we got up, we had the whole tricky descent ahead of us. We were nearly out of drinking water. I was worried. If one of us got hurt, it would be real trouble. We were fifteen rope-lengths of hard climbing off the ground; three days from the nearest place a plane could land; and 300 miles from the nearest hospital. We had no radio, and our pilot wasn't due for weeks. Ed plugged onward. There was nothing I could do but stand there, pay out the rope, offer the odd word of encouragement. Yet suddenly, in the midst of my worrying, I felt swamped by contentment. At the moment, Ed and I were doing the thing that we cared most about in life, and doing it as skillfully as we ever had.

He hooked a bent wrinkle of steel over a tiny flake of granite, stood on a nylon sling attached to it, and gained two more precious feet. I let the rope inch out. "I think it's going to go," Ed said quietly. It was a little be-fore midnight. I looked at the sky in the north. It was June 22, the summer solstice, the longest day of the year. The sun stood several degrees from the horizon, a yellow fire above the black silhouettes of other mountains.

On sleeting, late November nights in Boston, where I live today, it comforts me to think of the Brooks Range, to know it still abounds with nooks and ledges where no one has ever been, and that all it takes to get me there is another summer and the flimsiest excuse.

THE GUNKS REVISITED

As I topped the rise on Route 299 at Jenkins and Lueken Orchard, where we used to buy gallons of a Hesperidian cider, an old shiver—three parts exhilaration to one part dread—seized me. There, suddenly, the cliffs of the Shawangunks stretch high above you, like some wall at the end of the world, insisting that you come to grips with its stern demand.

For the last forty-five years the Gunks, as they are known worldwide, have been the most popular rock climbing crag in the East. A series of bands of shiny white conglomerate rock ranging as high as 300 feet, the Shawangunks amount to a long east–west ridge that serves as a foothill to the Catskill Mountains of central New York State. For a beginner on the first visit, the Gunks are intimidating: so steep is the precipice that every route looks desperate. But a quirk of geology—a consistent twenty-two degree dip in the sedimentary strata—seams the cliffs with horizontal ledges abounding in perfect, jug-like handholds. Nowhere in the world can you find easy climbs with such breathtaking exposure.

It was at the Gunks, as much as anywhere, that I learned to climb in the early 1960s. In those days, the crag was at the cutting edge of the arcane sport of rock climbing. The scene was dominated by a rowdy, brilliant gang of anarchists called the Vulgarians. Thirty years later, their hijinks remain the stuff of legend. On prime fall and spring weekends stolen from my college education, I gravitated to the periphery of the Vulgarian campfire. Climbing for me, and for all my best friends, was by far the most important thing in life. I took what I learned at the Gunks and applied it, for thirteen straight years, to the assault of unclimbed mountains in Alaska.

The old shiver at Jenkins and Lueken, then, was joy at the prospect of testing my youthful nerve against the void, tempered with the knowledge of just how scared I could get up there on the third pitch, twenty feet above the last piton, with my arms turning to jelly and no holds in sight. Now, in 1995, the shiver had blurred to a mild tremor, for in my fifties I was teaching myself to climb for fun, not out of wild ambition. It was not "desperates" but "classics" that drew me back to the Gunks.

On my first weekend last October, I was leading Gargoyle, the second route ever put in at the Gunks, yet, oddly, one I had never done before. A genuinely moderate route at 5.5, Gargoyle nonetheless packs a stunning assortment of weird maneuvers—body-stretching stems, awkward chimney scuttles, overhangs with hidden handholds—into a single dead-vertical pitch. As the guidebook says, "Who but Fritz Wiessner would pick out such a bold line?"

It was Wiessner, one of the greatest mountaineers in history, who discovered the Gunks for climbers. One afternoon in 1935, as he toiled at an inferior crag near the Hudson River, Wiessner watched a thunderstorm cleanse the sky and saw a precipice gleaming in the northwest. Two weekends later, he put up Gargoyle.

During the three decades since I had served my Gunks apprenticeship, rock climbing had been revolutionized. In our day, pitons formed the only protection we could place. Soon nuts, then later friends, transformed the sport into a gentler, more ingenious pastime; but standards soared so quickly that, all over the United States, the hardest routes began to demand strings of expansion bolts to safeguard their crackless itineraries.

When bolts first reared their ugly hangers at the Gunks, a great outcry went up, not least from the Vulgarians, the avant-garde of the decade before. By common consensus as well as by law, bolts cannot today be drilled at the Gunks. So the crag that had always been at the leading edge became a backwater, while such heretofore obscure cliffs as the New River Gorge in West Virginia and a canyon outside Rifle, Colorado—where nearly anything goes, boltwise—have become state of the art.

But for the huge majority of climbers incapable of getting up a 5.14, the Gunks remain one of the happiest playgrounds in the country. On that sunny weekend last October, as I belayed my partner from the top of Gargoyle, some 800 other devotees were swarming about the cliffs. (In the 1960s, we seldom saw 80 on the most perfect autumn Sunday.) Yet the Gunks are so extensive, with some 1,000 routes listed in the guidebook, that by walking a little ways from the car, you can always find a route where you don't have to wait in line.

I was pleased, on this 1995 outing, to discover that despite its burgeoning popularity, climbing remains little understood by the public. On that beautiful weekend, the area was also aswarm with walkers headed for Skytop, a grandiose stone tower built in 1921 to promulgate the most lordly panorama in the Gunks. Upon finding me seated at the top of the cliff managing the rope, pilgrims asked, "What are you doing?" and "Are you going down?" The top of Gargoyle lies close to the exit from the Crevice, a huge natural fissure splitting the precipice, festooned with wooden ladders that tempt hikers with a good old Victorian scramble. As I sat belaying, a pretty young woman, having been egged up the ladders by her boyfriend, surfaced out of the Crevice, crying, "Now that's sick!" Then she caught sight of me, and of my partner just hauling himself over Gargoyle's lip. "But not as sick as *those* guys," she declared.

Late in his life, but early in mine, I got to know Fritz Wiessner fairly well, a happenstance I consider among the luckiest in my career. Well into his eighties, though hobbled with arthritis, Fritz still climbed at a high standard. Back in 1918, on the cliffs near his native Dresden, Fritz had put up the hardest pure rock climbs then accomplished anywhere in the world. After emigrating to the United States in 1929, Wiessner sought out crags all over North America where, characteristically, he not only forged the first routes but also blazed the lines that would become the classics.

The great deed of his life—which turned into his sorest tribulation—had come in 1939 on K2, the world's second-highest mountain. Spearheading an American team, most of whose members had faltered low on the mountain, Wiessner singlehandedly solved all the technical difficulties of the route without artificial oxygen and stood, late on the afternoon of July 19, with only 700 feet of easy snow slope between himself and the summit. But his partner, a Sherpa, terrified of rousing angry spirits by climbing into the night, held the rope tight, telling Wiessner, "No, sahib, tomorrow."

Fritz never got a second chance. Later, with the weather deteriorating, three Sherpas died in a heroic effort to save a weak American trapped in a high camp. Wiessner came home to find, in the gathering clouds of World War II, that he was blamed for a "Teutonic" attitude that supposedly led to the tragedy. Fritz kept his proud silence. Only in the late 1960s did a younger generation salute Wiessner's own heroism on K2 and hail the man as a mountaineering genius decades ahead of his time. None of the world's fourteen highest summits would be reached until 1950; K2 not until 1954, and then by a massive Italian team using supplemental oxygen.

Throughout the late 1930s, then again after the war, a small band of climbers put up routes at the Gunks. Their leaders were Wiessner and Hans Kraus, five years Fritz's junior, an Austrian doctor who had fled the Nazis and come to the United States in 1938. Though both in their forties, Hans and Fritz, with their rigorous training in the Alps, were probably the best rock climbers in America.

Until his death at age ninety in the spring of 1996, Kraus still visited the Gunks regularly, though arthritis had ended his climbing a decade before. As remarkable a man as Wiessner, Kraus served as President Kennedy's back specialist (not to mention Katharine Hepburn's and Rita Hayworth's), and in the 1950s was hired by President Eisenhower to revolutionize America's school fitness programs. Way back before the First World War, in his native Trieste, Kraus had been tutored in English by James Joyce, who was writing *Ulysses* in his spare time.

Over the years, Kraus put in some forty-seven new routes at the Gunks, a figure topped only by Vulgarians Dick Williams and Jim McCarthy. One of Kraus's absolute classics is High Exposure, a line teased with Wiessner out of one of the steepest cliffs in 1941. Led by Kraus, its top pitch, which vectors straight up an overhanging prow above 200 feet of empty space, may be the most photogenic in the Gunks.

By the late 1950s, the Shawangunks scene had come under the thrall of the Appalachian Mountain Club. In response to the first fatality at the crag in 1958, the Appies hoped to appease the Smiley family, who owned the land and might well have closed the cliffs to climbing, by developing a rigid and ultimately ridiculous certification system through which only "qualifying leaders" were allowed to go first on the rope. At their most grandiose, Appie potentates strolled along the carriage road below the cliffs ordering unqualified leaders off the routes.

It was in opposition to the Appies that the Vulgarians coalesced. Urban counter-culturalists, sprung at first from the City College of New York Outing Club, the Vulgarians snubbed their noses at the Appie-ratus and simply went out and climbed whatever they felt like. Stalwarts such as Williams and McCarthy and Art Gran put in the hardest routes in the Gunks, far beyond the dreams of the bravest Appie, but they also cavorted with a will in their hours off the cliffs.

In effect, the Vulgarians for the first time wed extreme climbing to dropout politics, hallucinogenic substances (including limitless pitchers of beer), and sex. Their antics turned the Ivy League men's club that had long ruled American mountaineering on its head. For us neophytes in the early '60s, it was impossible not to gaze on with awe and envy.

For one thing, in those days when women in the sport were few and far between, at the Gunks the best female climbers (as well as the most desirable) became Vulgarians. Unabashedly calling themselves the Vulgatits, they made the first all-women's ascents of many a route.

The Vulgarians delighted in shocking tourists and Appies alike. Directly beneath a highly visible overhang on a route called Shockley's Ceiling (put up in 1953 by later Nobel laureate Bill Shockley), the last hairpin on Route 299 formed a theater for motorists who stopped to gawk. To entertain the crowd, Dick Williams led a trio one sunny Saturday on the first nude ascent of Shockley's.

The Vulgarians hung out at two nearby taverns, known as Charlie's (aka the Bavarian Inn) and Emil's (the Mountain Brauhaus). But, as long-time Gunks ranger Tom Scheuer recalls, "When climbers walked into Charlie's, the owner would pull off the tablecloths." No one remembers whether it was this slight or another aggravation (some say a punch-out with local firemen) that one evening provoked Dave Craft, in many respects the shyest of the Vulgarians. Craft ended up on the roof of Charlie's, urinating on customers as they left the pub.

A sophomoric crudeness was the trademark of the Vulgarians, who published their own short-lived yet memorable journal, called *Vulgarian Digest* (*V. D.* for short), full of scatalogical in-jokes and bad photos of high times in the Tetons and Bugaboos. Even when they blundered, the Vulgarians blundered with style. One memorable "epic" ensued when a veteran who had a talent for epics got benighted in fog high on a long route. Rappelling off in the dark, he lost track of his whereabouts. Thinking himself on the Grand Traverse Ledge, with a 200-foot abyss below, he belayed his party on a hypervigilant crawl across the carriage road, where on normal afternoons graybeards strolled with their dogs.

The great thing about the Vulgarians, as we acolytes learned, was that they demonstrated that climbing was not some stern school of character, but a hedonistic romp in the *grand guignol* of the good life. They had not a trace of snobbery about them. As the gang's historian and panegyrist, Joe Kelsey, reminisced a few years ago in *Rock and Ice,*

> A naive climber once approached me in [Yosemite's] Camp 4, said he'd heard I belonged to the Vulgarian Mountain Club and, since he was moving East, wanted to apply for membership. I tried to explain that if you thought yourself a Vulgarian, you were.

OBSESSED WITH CLIMBING, year after year on my visits to the Gunks, I headed straight for the cliffs. Only on my 1995 return did I venture farther afield, and discover what a splendid outback the Shawangunks form in their totality.

Glimmerings came to me during a half-day hike out of Minnewaska, a gem of a lake dropped into a conglomerate basin on the summit of a high hill. I headed west on one of the many carriage roads that branch in an intricate network through the woods. These roads were built around the turn of the century by laborers each earning a dollar a day, with the help, as local historian Bradley Snyder reports, of "picks, shovels, wheelbarrows, crowbars, sledge hammers, stone boats, horses, a hand-cranked derrick, and a portable boiler called Black Maria." The roads have begun to attract mountain bikers, who some traditionalists fear are about to overrun the place. Yet on my ten-mile ramble through a perfect afternoon, I crossed paths with only half a dozen hikers and a dozen bikers.

The leaves were just turning yellow and red. Crickets sang in the hemlocks. I paused to rest on a shelf of bedrock poised like a beach above a sea of space, and with my fingertips traced the striations and chatter marks left by the last glaciation, 14,000 years ago. At Castle Point I lolled for an hour, staring into the gloom around Lake Awosting, as the sun wheeled low in the west. I had known the Gunks always as a social scene, a gathering of climbers: here was a solitude that would have gladdened Thoreau.

The Shawangunks, all told, form a patchwork of some 20,000 acres of forest, vale, and cliff. Parts of it, such as Minnewaska, lie in state park preserves; the heart of the ridge, formerly private land, has been incorporated as the Mohonk Preserve; and 2,100 acres, centered by the old hotel called the Mohonk Mountain House, are still owned by the Smiley family.

Glenn Hoagland, executive director of the Mohonk Preserve, estimates that 100,000 visitors a year come to the Shawangunks. I was beguiled to hear Hoagland pronounce the name "Shongums," and to learn that all locals in the know stick to that pronunciation. The original meaning of the Delaware Indian name—rendered also over the years as Chawangong and Schunemunk—is obscure: some say it comes from the word *schawaneu*, or "south."

This part of New York State was settled first in the seventeenth century by French Huguenots. Later the Dutch and Germans came in. Over the centuries, a series of esoteric minor industries brought in hundreds of laborers, who with back-breaking toil tried to squeeze a living from the countryside: tanners who wrung an elixir out of hemlock bark, charcoal makers who burnt down whole forests, barrel hoop makers and millstone quarriers, and legions of huckleberry pickers who thrived into the 1950s.

197

As you stand on some Shawangunk aerie and gaze across the landscape, your eye will come to rest on scores of abandoned farms slowly being swallowed by the forest. For all its scenic glory, the Shongums are more thinly populated today than they were during the Civil War.

I stayed for five days at the Mohonk Mountain House, one of the grandest and quirkiest hotels in America. First opened in 1870 by twin brothers Alfred and Albert Smiley, it has been added onto over the decades in such eclectic fashion that today it looks like the sort of sprawling jeu d'esprit mad King Ludwig might have concocted had he transplanted his fantasy castles from Bavaria to New York State. (From one well-used fourth-floor chimney, a mysterious and hardy black birch protrudes, having somehow reached ground with its tap root and survived fifty years of fireplace blazes.)

The hotel hugs the northern lip of Lake Mohonk. The cliffs that enfold the waters are strewn with clever paths that give onto wooden gazebos ("summer houses," in Smiley parlance) perched on stilts on panoramic ledges. I know of no more exhilarating short hike in the country than the stroll from the hotel along Eagle Cliff Road. From its high point, called Huntington Lookout, you behold the finest view in all the Gunks—an eagle's eye prospect west along the spine of the range, each cliff distinct within the lapping woods.

The Smileys were Quakers who for decades forbade card playing and dancing and drinking. Even today, there is no TV in the rooms and no bar in the hotel, though since 1971, guests have been able to order wine with dinner or discreetly sip from their bottles in their rooms. The joy of the Mountain House comes from its invitation to repose—on the many balconies that brood over the postcard lake, or in the sitting nooks that festoon each floor. As you walk the undulant, creaking wooden hallways, you pass bookshelves laden with bound sets of Carlyle and Dickens and mounted, signed photographs of such august guests as William Howard Taft, Rutherford Hayes, and John Burroughs.

Elms Cottage, a house down the hill behind the hotel where Dan Smiley lived until his death in 1989, has been turned into a research center and museum. For seven decades, this self-taught naturalist obsessively collected not only specimens and artifacts but also his own observations in the woods. The 16,000-odd note cards on which Smiley patiently recorded each day's data turned out to be a treasure trove of lore, documenting many a phenomenon—the onset of acid rain in Shawangunk lakes as early as 1931, for instance, or the near extinction of the wild turkey around 1910—that virtually no one else at the time thought to record.

Curator Paul Huth, who continues Smiley's work, pulled out drawers to show me his mentor's stuffed birds and rodents. A handsome Allegheny wood rat bore a laconic tag: "Killed 5 Dec. 1958. Mohonk House, in the linen room. Trapped. Ivory soap had been disappearing."

And Huth took me on a short drive along an out-of-the-way carriage road to an Archaic Indian site, in a gloomy rock shelter near a rhododendron swamp. The site was first explored by Boy Scouts led by Dan Smiley in 1931, then dug by an archaeologist from nearby SUNY New Paltz from 1982 to 1983. Here the scholar found fifty-five Neville points—chert projectile blades dating from at least 8,500 years ago—and demonstrated that the shelter had most likely been a hunting camp for millennia before Columbus. As I stood in the dank hollow and contemplated the prehistoric pursuit of bear and deer, I was suffused in a far richer appreciation of the Shongums that I had been able to glean from mere ropework on its shining cliffs.

NONETHELESS, ON THE SECOND weekend of my return visit, I headed back to the precipice, joined by a quartet of cronies I had recruited for the task. We met at Rock and Snow, the climbing shop in New Paltz run by charter Vulgarian Dick Williams (who in his late fifties leads 5.12 routes). The store is far more than a gear emporium: it serves as one of a pair of social centers for the climbing community. The bulletin board distills the arcane syntax of the sport, covered with hand-written notes only climbers can decipher: "Motivated individual wanted for fall projects. Need to know basics. Equal time on sharp end."

The other social center is the Uberfall, a stretch of carriage road beneath the cliff at the west end of the Trapps (from a Dutch word for "staircase"), the most popular cliff at the Gunks. The Uberfall first became a scene because it stands at the bottom of the normal descent route from Trapps climbs. Nowadays, however, virtually all the younger climbers rappel off each route after bothering only with its first pitch. The trail through the woods along the clifftop, where in our day handy tree trunks had turned glossy with wear, is growing over with weeds.

At the Uberfall, the Mohonk Preserve ranger hangs out in his pickup, trading gossip and collecting a daily use fee. (We used to sneak past this official, even though the charge was only fifty cents a day!) A kiosk carries notices, and a brass plaque mounted on a boulder pays homage to Fritz Wiessner and Hans Kraus.

In the hungry days of youth, we used to cram six or seven hard climbs into a manic day. Now I was content to polish off two or three classics. Wending my way up a route I had first climbed three decades before, I felt the nostalgia of the half-remembered in my fingertips. One evening, as I leafed through the guidebook, I counted 95 Gunks routes I had climbed over the years: nearly every one was still attended with a special memory. (Only 900 to go, I mused. . . .)

The peculiar beauty of the Gunks struck me all over again. Many routes wander across "open books," where a pair of walls face each other aslant, allowing you to watch your partner's progress as though you had the best seat in the house. Time and again, just when a sequence of moves gets thin enough to scare you, the ample hold arrives that guarantees security once more. Nuts and friends slot snugly into the blessedly frequent cracks. The rock of the Gunks even has its own unique smell, the pulverized essence, perhaps, of the black *umbilicaria* lichens that sprouts everywhere; the scent clings to your fingers for hours after the day's climbing is done.

Just as I was starting to get into good shape, awakened to the stirring of an old ambition, Saturday dawned cold with torrents of rain. With my colleagues, I drove to Poughkeepsie to visit an old friend I hadn't seen in more than ten years.

Way back in 1968, Al de Maria and I had made the first ascent of Igikpak, the highest mountain in the western Brooks Range of arctic Alaska. A founding Vulgarian, Al had settled down as a math teacher. I had heard through the grapevine that he'd moved back to New Paltz.

Despite his participation in some of the more raucous of Vulgarian antics, Al had always been one of the safest climbers I knew. Short, grizzled, gnomelike, he had a fussy, methodical streak that sorted out danger and cast it aside. But to renew our friendship, I headed now to Saint Francis Hospital. A mere week before I had arrived at the Gunks, Al had suffered the only serious accident of his thirty-five-year climbing career, when he had fallen twenty feet and hit a ledge, breaking both ankles.

Suddenly, there in bed was Al, grayer and more grizzled than ever, but unmistakably himself. His left ankle was bound with conventional plaster, but his right calf sprouted a gruesome metal contraption called an external fixator. As we, his visitors, cringed and winced, Al calmly narrated his mishap.

He had been leading the second pitch of a route called, ominously enough, Twisted Sister. As he had done thousands of times before, he reached up to the top of a hefty-sized block sitting on a ledge and started to pull himself up. In the mountains, Al would have tested the block, slapping a palm to judge by the sound how well fixed in place it was. But at the Gunks, the rock is so solid, everyone shortcuts the old precautions.

The block—the size of a filing cabinet—came loose in Al's hands. With an unconscious instinct, as he fell he shoved the potentially fatal stone away from himself. He landed on both heels twenty feet below, and knew at once he was badly hurt; then, as he crumpled on the ledge, he watched the block smash a few feet to his left.

Miraculously, the block missed both the rope and his belayer. It was a Friday afternoon, and the Gunks were still not crowded: on Saturday or Sunday, the stone, hurtling 100 feet to the base of the cliff, would probably have killed someone starting up a nearby route.

Al talked on in his matter-of-fact way, blaming himself for the accident. I couldn't take my eyes off the medieval torture implement attached to his right leg, pins drilled through flesh to stabilize bones that it had taken hours of surgery to sort out. He would be three months in a wheelchair. Though none of us said as much, it seemed unlikely that Al would ever climb again. He would have to relearn to walk.

And yet, such is the strength of climbing camaraderie, within minutes we were all joking about old exploits and buffooneries.

None of the Vulgarians was ever killed at the Gunks in a climbing accident. Yet along with their storied parties and brave ascents, the Vulgarians knew tragedy. Perhaps the saddest episode had to do with a talented youth named Howie.

Howie fell in love with an older woman, the wife of one of the leading Gunks climbers, herself one of the best women climbers at the crag. Their brief affair flamed, then flickered out. She called an end to it.

One drizzly day when no one else was climbing, Howie walked to the base of a line called Jackie. The route had been "their climb." Howie soloed up the two pitches of Jackie, stood on the ledge at the top, then, with no one to witness, jumped off the cliff. There were those who wanted to believe that Howie had slipped in the rain, but the friends who knew him best said that, rain or no rain, he was too good a climber to have "come off" Jackie by accident.

Saturday evening, at dinner, chastened by the sight of Al in the hospital, I asked Rich Goldstone, one of my quartet of cronies, about Howie, whom Rich had known well. Rich retold the old tale—as climbers meeting in pubs have done again and again over the decades, until the remembered deeds gain the shape of myth. But then he added a detail I had not heard before.

"Shortly after Howie died," said Rich, "I climbed Jackie just to look at the ledge from which he'd jumped. I wanted to see if I could even imagine doing it." Rich paused. "He must have taken a running start. It really shook me up."

Yet on Sunday, the clouds slowly burned away, and the afternoon grew bright. It was the kind of day on which, sixty years earlier, Fritz Wiessner had made his discovery of the Gunks. And with the clouds, the edgy misgivings that visiting Al in the hospital had provoked, burned off, too.

There was time for one more climb. With Rich Goldstone and Matt Hale, I set out for the Near Trapps to climb Yellow Ridge, a 5.7 climb that was one of Wiessner's blithest creations. Matt and I had climbed for thirty years together, including three Alaskan expeditions. And years ago, Matt and Rich, feeling their oats, had traveled together to the Needles of South Dakota and the Bugaboos of British Columbia and done the hardest climbs in those two cutting-edge ranges.

Now Matt led the first pitch, up a steep protruding corner to a shelf out of sight from the ground. Rich and I followed, then he took the second lead. As Matt belayed, I snapped pictures, for the route traverses for fifty photogenic feet above an abyss of empty air before angling wildly toward the sky.

Rich, who climbs only once or twice a year, had complained about being out-of-shape. Now, however, I marveled at the balance and economy of movement for which he had once been famous. He placed each toe precisely on each minuscule conglomerate rugosity, using his hands, it seemed, only to caress the holds, not to hang from them. He climbed as though solving a chess puzzle.

Yellow Ridge finishes with the most improbable acrobatics, as you crane out over space to breach a ceiling that looks from below like a stern dead end. Half an hour after Rich had showed the way, I stretched my limbs into the requisite contortion, found the holds above, and poked my head above the last overhang. Rich sat there, tied to a tree, tending the rope.

"Good old Fritz," I gasped, out of breath from my effort.

Rich grinned, awash in his own memories of his friend Wiessner. "Good old Fritz!" he echoed.

INTO THE
LOST PAST

BANDIAGARA
THE DOGON AND THE TELLEM

With 100 feet of empty space beneath my feet, secured by a climbing rope, I pulled myself past a final overhang of sandstone and stood on the threshold of a small cave. Before my eyes, filling the grotto to half-height, stretched a pile of bleached human bones. There was no sense of order about this grisly mausoleum: scores of skulls tilted randomly upon a talus of ribs and femurs. There were animal bones mixed with the human. Dusty bits of cloth, bearing faded indigo checkwork, lay snagged among the debris. Knotted pieces of rope woven from tree bark trailed in and out of the bones. In a space that would accommodate no more than ten living persons, some 3,000 skeletons had been packed like so much landfill. A musty, acrid odor filled the air. I took a first step inside the cave, and winced as I felt bones grind and snap underfoot. The skulls grinned in the ocher dimness.

Who were these dead? How had they reached this graveyard in the sky? Why had this inaccessible cliff been chosen as a burial site? For even with modern techniques and gear, it had required a difficult climb to reach the cave. Why were the bones heaped in such chaotic disarray?

Below me wound a dry, narrow valley called the Toloy Couloir, shaded by the occasional acacia tree; in its center, a small field of millet lay fallow. As I peered out of the cave, I saw two women carrying jars atop their heads as they stepped barefoot up a rocky path, silhouetted against the morning sun. The hazy air was so still that I could hear them chatting from a mile away. Beyond the women, a brown plain, parched and flat, stretched to the horizon.

The cave full of skeletons lies near the center of a long escarpment called the Bandiagara. This convoluted cliff, ranging up to 500 feet high, stretches across Mali 150 miles south of Tombouctou, in the heart of one of the last wildernesses in West Africa to be explored by Europeans. The women I saw, like the men who had planted the millet field, were Dogon, who remain one of the least assimilated peoples in Africa. For the last four centuries, the Bandiagara has been their home. According to their own legends, the Dogon came to the escarpment in the fifteenth century from a once-paradisaical land called Mandé, somewhere to the south or west. When they reached the Bandiagara, they found a strange race of beings living in caves high in the sandstone cliff. They named these people *Tellem*—Dogon for "we found them."

Four of us—photographer Jose Azel, Joe Lentini, Matt Hale, and I—had come to Mali in the relatively cool, dry season of December. We wanted to hike and camp among the Dogon villages, to visit their markets, watch their dances, admire the extraordinary architecture of their mud houses and granaries, and see *in situ* their granary doors and carved pillars, which art collectors in North America and Europe so covet that the finest examples have begun to disappear from the country. And, as rock climbers, we hoped to gain a firsthand appreciation of the vanished Tellem, who, despite the brilliant archaeological probe of a Dutch team during the last two decades, remain a prehistoric mystery.

According to some Dogon tales, the Tellem were dwarfs. There is no doubt that they possessed a powerful magic. The contact between races, some say, was amicable; other accounts have war breaking out. In any event, the Tellem abandoned the cliffs soon after the Dogon came. No one knows for sure where they went, or whether they died out as a people. Perhaps the finest ancient climbers in the world, the Tellem seem to have left little more than their enigmatic caves, some filled with the jumbled bones of their dead, to testify to their achievement.

WE RENTED LAND CRUISERS in Bamako, Mali's capital, bought food and supplies, and drove 450 miles east to Sanga, the best-known Dogon village. Behind the wheel were our canny Bambara drivers, Namory and Moussa. In Sanga we hired Oumar, one of the top

Dogon guides, a well-educated thirty-year-old with a wry manner and an unflappable disposition.

Almost no one in Mali understands English. The only European language spoken widely is French; in colonial times, the country was French Sudan. To converse with our drivers and guide, we thus had to use French. Namory and Moussa spoke to each other in Bambara, which Oumar also understood. In the villages, Oumar spoke his native Dogon.

In recent years, European tourists have begun to come to the Bandiagara. Both Muslim and Christian missionaries have been hard at work among these animists for a century, but converts have come slowly. The researches of a whole school of anthropologists inspired by the great Marcel Griaule, who came to Sanga in 1931 and died there in 1956, have won for Dogon culture an admiring audience far beyond the borders of Mali, particularly in France. Griaule's discovery of a complex Dogon cosmology, in which every gesture and object was rich with symbolic meaning, served as a pioneer thrust in overturning the patronizing assumptions of nineteenth-century ethnography in Africa.

Yet few tourists venture much beyond Sanga, and few stay for more than a day or two. As we ranged along the 150-mile escarpment in our Land Cruisers, the farther we got from Sanga, the scarcer were the signs of western acculturation. And we came to realize that in some ways, despite Griaule and tourism, the Dogon remain almost as much a mystery as the Tellem who preceded them.

On one of our first days, we walked to Ireli, a town of about 2,000 Dogon people that lies at the foot of the Bandiagara precipice. From a distance, Ireli was nearly invisible: all we could see at first was a sandy brown scattering of talus, grass, and baobab trees. Gradually we realized that what looked like boulders strewn across the slope were the buildings of a vibrant community.

A man hiking out of town crossed our path. Without breaking stride, he and Oumar exchanged the ritual greeting that is de rigueur every time two Dogon meet:

"Po," said the man—"Hi" in Dogon.

"OK," answered Oumar; then, after a pause, "How are you?"

"Fine."

"How's your family?"

"Fine."

"OK."

"Then how are you?"

"Fine."

"How's your family?"

"Fine."

"OK."

As we reached the outskirts of Ireli, naked boys and girls came running, screaming their favorite French phrase, "Ça va?" The bolder children insisted on taking our hands to escort us through the narrow lanes; others hid behind houses and peeked out at us. Chickens flew underfoot, and runty dogs yapped in outrage. When we stopped to look at something, boys knelt and began pulling the irksome stickers called *krem-krem* out of our socks.

We were stunned by the strangeness and beauty of the granaries, square towers crafted out of mud and straw, set on low stilts above the ground. The thatch roofs protecting them from rain looked somehow comic, like jaunty caps atop the vaguely anthropomorphic buildings (a trio of granary windows could easily approximate a face). Some of the wooden granary doors were mesmerizing. The lock is made of wood with a toothed wooden key, and the panel, Oumar explained, is a rigorously prescribed résumé of the Dogon myth of creation.

There were more granaries in Ireli than houses. Soil is so precious along the Bandiagara that the natives had built some of their houses on top of boulders, in order to save a few square yards that could be planted with grain. The *ginna*, or family house, is laid out in a shape that imitates the human body, as we later saw when we gazed down upon a village from clifftop: a circular enclave resembles the head, oblong side rooms look like burly arms dangling at the side, and the central plaza approximates the human trunk. We passed the house of the *hogon*, the spiritual chief of the village. Its facade was scored with eerie undulant columns and hung with fetishes (monkey skulls, jewelry, braided cords). In the heart of the village we came across a *togu na*, the men's shelter, where no women were allowed. The elders loafing on the stone floor inside gazed at us with sleepy disdain. On this hot, dusty afternoon, the *togu na* was the coolest place in town. The roof, about eight feet thick, was made of dried millet stalks laid in sheaves. The pillars supporting the roof, made of a kind of adobe, were engraved with figures representing the eight mythical Dogon ancestors.

Even on an ordinary day, Ireli was swarming with activity. The previous afternoon we had visited the market at the small town of Banani. The Dogon keep to their traditional five-day calendar. Organized by the women, the trading fair in each village occurs every fifth day, and the Dogon take care that neighboring villages have different market days. Amused by our presence, the women sitting behind their piles of goods raucously pressed us to buy roasted goat meat, millet porridge, onion balls, and—yes—plastic flip-flops. We squeamishly declined, assailed as we were by the mixed aroma of charred meat, goat dung, sweat, and dust that wafted among the makeshift stalls. I did try millet beer, which tasted like a kind of insipid, mealy lemonade.

No market is considered a success unless it slides in the afternoon toward a drunken fête. That night, as we camped near the Banani well, we were kept awake after midnight by drums and singing, wild laughter, and drunken taunts shouted back and forth in the gloom.

At dawn, we woke to the bantering of women as they drew their bags of water from the well, hauling them up on long ropes that slid through the polished grooves of log sills laid long ago to preserve the sandy edges of the deep hole. When they saw us poking our heads out of our tents, eager with our cameras, they shrieked and shook fingers, fleeing as soon as their vessels were full.

As we hiked toward Ireli, we passed many pairs of women pounding millet. Bare-breasted, they faced each other over the wooden *mortier*, alternately raising their long *pilons* to bring them smashing down on the grains of millet. To while away the tedious hours, some of them sang in the cadence of their teamwork. Even ten-year-old girls took part in the grueling work. The endless seesaw of this ancient labor became our most familiar image of Dogon life.

The daily routine of a village masks the deeply spiritual life that the Dogon lead, which they have woven into the very fabric of the landscape. Often Oumar would warn us not to walk off the trail—waving at some nondescript hollow in the weeds, he would say simply, "It's forbidden." One day I spotted beside the trail a carved wooden object that looked like one of those monopod stools spectators use at golf tournaments. I reached out to grasp it, and Oumar hissed, "No! Don't touch it!" The wayside relic, it seems, was indeed a seat, but one used only on that holiest of occasions, the *Sigi*, a ceremony that takes place once every sixty years, when the Dogon save and rejuvenate the world. The rest of the time the relic guarded a locality against evil spirits. From a distance, we often saw strange mounds of clay that the Dogon consecrate as altars; usually they were stained with streaks of white or rust, the residue of sacrifices of millet porridge and animal blood. We were forbidden even to approach these altars.

The Dogon name prominent rocks in and about their villages, and even name the baobab trees: in the vicinity of Sanga, according to Griaule, some were called Ancestor, High Bosom, Gravel, Little Bulk, and Small Seeds.

No place in the Dogon world is more sacred than one of their own graves. Above every village at the foot of the Bandiagara escarpment, the rock wall is honeycombed with caves, in many of which stand the remains of Tellem buildings. The Dogon themselves do not build or live in the caves, but they do bury their dead there. Traditionally, most Tellem caves were of little interest to the Dogon, but each village has appropriated a certain number of them for its tombs. In a precisely stylized funeral rite, they purge their grief in the luxurious choreography of masked dances. At the end, the dead person, tied to a wooden bier, is run head-high through the village while the women wail and shriek; then the corpse is raised to a cave in the cliff. In many villages, this final ascent is accomplished by hauling with ropes made from baobab bark.

To visit a Tellem cave—even one the Dogon do not use for burial—we had to apply for permission to the chief of the nearest village. This was always a drawn-out exercise in diplomacy. On learning our request, little boys scampered through the alleys to inform the chief, then guided us to his house. In a courtyard under a roof of thatch, this grave dignitary offered us the best stones to sit on. Younger men, girls, and dogs clustered around to gawk. The chief took out his pipe and smoked it. Then he offered us millet beer. Through Oumar we made small talk: Had it been a good year for the rains? Were the crops abundant? At last the question came up. The chief looked dubious; his fellow elders frowned. No, it was out of the question. Oumar made more small talk. Perhaps, if a trusted villager went with us, and if we could make a small contribution to the community. . . . We negotiated the price down to the equivalent of about eight dollars. The chief nodded and stood up. We shook hands all around.

After our climb to the cave of the 3,000 skeletons, we set our sights on another section of cliff in the same Toloy Couloir, which looked even more inaccessible. As climbers, we had been astounded from first glance at the wild eyries high in his 350-foot overhanging wall where the Tellem had somehow built small structures of mud bricks and mortar. The Dogon insist that these buildings high in the cliff caves were Tellem houses, but the Dutch archaeologists proved they were granaries. (Where the Tellem built their houses remains a great mystery: not a single Tellem house has been found.)

The one weakness in the precipice was a long, wide ledge 150 feet off the ground. We saw no way to climb to the big ledge from below. Our plan instead was to descend to it from the top of the cliff.

Joe Lentini rigged up an elaborate lowering system. The gear this required—custom-made metal chocks and cams, a battery-powered bolt gun, six perlon ropes, and a walkie-talkie—gave us pause when we thought of our Tellem predecessors.

Tied in to a chest and waist harness, I backed slowly down the steepening slab. It is a scary thing to be lowered off a cliff, and as I moved past the lip of the ceiling and suddenly hung free in space, my heart was pounding. We had assumed that it would be an easy matter to land on the 150-foot ledge, but now we discovered that the wall was so steep the lowered person would sail past the outermost rim of the ledge. I had brought along a long stick to the end of which I had taped a small metal device called a skyhook. When I was 140 feet down, level with the ledge, I told the others over the walkie-talkie to hold me in place. Leaning to the utmost, I could just scrape the rock with the skyhook. By catching a nubbin, I could start myself swinging. After about twenty pendulums, I managed to seize the lip of the ledge and scramble to safe ground.

I tied off my rope, then spent an enthralling hour exploring this horizontal island in the midst of a vertical wilderness. There was no sign that the Tellem sites had ever been disturbed. By traversing right and left, up and down, I was able to visit some dozen caves. The most intriguing was a small necropolis open to the sky, in which I counted fifteen skulls. Some of the skeletons lay just as they must have been deposited, still wrapped snugly in their indigo-patterned cotton shrouds.

There were potsherds all over the ledge, including several handsome fragments from the lips of larger vessels. I found an ornamented piece of wood, perhaps part of a wooden bowl or a headrest. Beneath a small bulge lay a ten-foot Tellem ladder. I lifted the black, hollow log with its notched steps, and was surprised by its heaviness. Most of the buildings were empty, and the delicate interior brickwork shone semitranslucent in the morning sun. I saw potsherds built into walls to strengthen them, like pebbles in concrete.

Despite some brave scrambling, I had to give up trying to reach at least twice as many cave sites as the dozen I poked through. With a major effort, we might have landed two climbers on the ledge together; with rope and technical gear, we could then have climbed to several sites that I was unwilling to attempt unroped. But there were others still that I had no idea how to get to. The highest Tellem sites, tucked beneath the ceiling sixty feet above my head, looked all but impossible. Most tantalizing was a pristine burial-ritual cave, below the ledge and forty feet to the left. I could see a pair of ritual pots with ring bases in perfect condition, and a walled-off sepulcher that I knew must house untold secrets.

At last I tied in again and gave the signal to lower me the rest of the way to the ground. As I glided slowly down 150 feet of thin air, I watched my shadow flit across the face of one abandoned sanctuary after another. My mind reeled with a single thought: *How had the Tellem done it?*

EVERY DOGON VILLAGE ON the escarpment has one or two men who are specialists at climbing. The expert from the village of

Pégué showed up as we were completing our rope-lower. Amadomion was a rugged thirty-eight-year-old wearing a blue tunic and a tan three-cornered cap. He claimed to have climbed to some of the caves beneath the ledge I had been lowered to. We asked him to tell us how.

Amadomion led us to a spot at the foot of the cliff and gestured upward. Forty feet above the ground, a black stick protruded horizontally from a small cave. At that level, a ledge led 60 feet to the right, where we saw that the bottom end of a thin doubled rope had been tied. This rope dangled sixty feet farther upwards in a loose arc, free of the constantly overhanging cliff, to a second black stick 100 feet off the ground. Looped over the stick, the rope dangled in place.

This upper stick protruded from a dark ledge, beneath an enormous ceiling that jutted over the void. Craning our necks, we could glimpse several mud buildings tucked away in that gloomy recess 100 feet above us.

The black sticks, Oumar said, were "boulins"—a French word I did not know. They had been placed by the Tellem, many hundreds of years ago. Yet the rope, woven in braids of baobab bark, was recent, of Dogon manufacture.

With a grin of pride, Amadomion pointed at the upper boulin and the mud granaries and told us that he had been up there three times. He would bring his own baobab rope, which was perhaps 120 feet long and an inch in diameter, to the cliff. After tying one end to a piece of wood, he would throw the rope in the air until it caught over the lower boulin, 40 feet up. The piece of wood was heavy enough so that he could then feed the rope out until it hung doubled, both ends on the ground. Amadomion then simply climbed the rope, his legs wrapped for grip as he hauled himself up like a kid in gym class.

Reaching the first ledge, Amadomion would pull his rope up after him, then edge his way along the ledge sixty feet to the right, to the bottom end of the rope left dangling in place. This cord, being only about a quarter-inch in diameter, was too frail to climb. Instead, he tied the end of his heavy rope to the end of the light one, then pulled on the latter to hoist his own rope until it hung doubled over the upper boulin. He climbed this rope and reached the upper recess, trusting his life to a stick wedged in a crack perhaps seven centuries ago.

The reason for this daring ascent? Pigeon dung. Amadomion would fill a large sack with handfuls of the fragrant droppings, prized by the Dogon as a first-class fertilizer. Later in the week he would take his bag to the market in Sanga and make a killing.

I asked Amadomion how the Tellem had placed the boulins so high in the cliffs—let alone built granaries in such an impossible spot.

Amadomion laughed and said, "They were very strong."

"Stronger than the Dogon?" I asked.

"Yes." Amadomion had a brief exchange with some friends from Pégué who had stopped to gossip. All the men had views on the Tellem. Oumar translated the gist. "The Tellem could climb a single thread. And they had a way of making the thread go up there and attach itself. They had a very strong magic."

I had heard other local explanations of the Tellem ascents. During droughts, the Dogon said, their predecessors could fly into the sky, poke holes, and produce rain. To get to their caves, they could make ropes stand on end, or they could change themselves to giants, take a single step up to the highest caves, and change themselves back into dwarfs to live there. Some even said the Tellem were such powerful orators they could simply talk their way up to the caves.

I remained baffled. Amadomion's explanation of Dogon climbing was hair-raising but plausible. But everything depended on those boulins being already fixed in place. How the Tellem had first ascended the blank cliffs was still beyond our grasp. Often at night around the campfire, the four of us wrangled over theories of Tellem climbing.

It was not until the 1960s that any explanation of the Tellem achievement other than that offered by the Dogon existed. Returning year after year, a team of archaeologists from the University of Utrecht carried out intensive research in the Bandiagara. Using a bizarre aluminum cage which they hoisted up and down with cables hundreds of feet long, the team, led by professors Johan Huizinga and Rogier Bedaux, managed to enter several dozen caves, including the grotto of the 3,000 skeletons.

Over two decades of extraordinary work, the Dutch discovered many things about the Tellem, often in contradiction to Dogon belief. These prehistoric climbers were not dwarfs, but men and women of normal height. They never lived in the cliff buildings, as the Dogon claimed, but only built granaries and buried their dead there, and possibly retreated to them in times of crisis. Extensive carbon-fourteen datings placed the Tellem unambiguously in the eleventh to fifteenth centuries. Rather than being the ancestors of any other known African tribe, the Tellem, Huizinga and Bedaux think, had died out by the sixteenth century.

The Dutch found a dazzling array of grave relics, including beautiful carved wooden headrests (the oldest manmade wooden objects yet found in sub-Saharan Africa); ceramic pots patterned by rolling cord or cloth across the wet clay; finger bells, twisted volute pins, and bracelets of iron; quartz lip plugs and hexagonal carnelian necklace beads; bows, quivers, and hoes broken when they were laid with the dead; the pieces of a wooden harp; and a single flute, blown end-on like a recorder. Tellem men wore a tight cotton skull cap, and beautifully dyed red-and-black tunics. Women wore knee-length fiber aprons hung from a waistband, looking vaguely like hula skirts.

In one cave the Dutch found three tattered leather boots, much like those the Dogon use for riding horses. On the basis of this find alone, Huizinga and Bedaux believe that the Tellem domesticated horses, even though no equine bones have been found and horses remain rare today along the Bandiagara. In the cave of the skeletons, the archaeologists found bones of sheep, cow, antelope, buffalo, bushbuck, gazelle, and ostrich, suggesting that hunters may have been buried with specimens of their prey, herders with tokens of their flocks. Puzzled by this chaos of skulls and skeletons, the Dutch concluded that because of a shortage of space, one generation of Tellem must have simply flung aside its ancestors' bones to bury the newly dead.

Despite their definitive work, the Dutch raised as many questions as they answered. Where did the Tellem live? Do all their houses lie under current-day Dogon villages? To what extent were the Dogon influenced or even taught by the Tellem, with their "strong magic"? Cultural similarities—of pottery style, in the hauling by ropes of the dead to cave tombs—seem too strong to be coincidences of adaptation to the same landscape. Yet despite Dogon tales of war or friendship with the Tellem, Huizinga and Bedaux insist that we cannot even be sure that the two cultures overlapped in history. It is possible that the Tellem had disappeared by the time the first Dogon band wandered in from Mandé.

All the things we most want to know still lie beyond our comprehension. What did the Tellem believe? How was their society organized? Who were their enemies? What were the tales they told over the campfire in the prehistoric night? Who were their heroes, what were their tragedies? And why, after all, did they go to such enormous effort and risk to erect what must be from a technical point of view the ultimate cliff buildings in the world?

THE GRIAULE SCHOOL IMPUTES to Dogon culture an all-embracing belief system, a sophisticated astronomy, and a rich lore of abstract thought. The Dogon is sage, bucolic, genial, and reserved—a noble savage whose every stroke of the hoe or turn of the weaver's shuttle springs from a deep consciousness of the workings of the universe. Others, however—missionaries, members of other tribes, and dissenting anthropologists—have insisted on a darker side to the Dogon world. Dogon sorcery is a real force in village life, yet Griaule discovered almost nothing about it. Old tales of human sacrifice, poisoning, and even cannibalism have never been completely debunked. Here and there, as we traveled through Dogon country, we had our own glimpses of a darkness Griaule scarcely acknowledged.

At the edges of several villages, we found gloomy hovels covered with symbols representing the mythical serpent Lebé and with monstrous images of female sexuality; here, menstruating women are required to hide themselves. Some Dogon sites have become virtual ghost towns: the dwellings tucked under the cliff high on the talus have been abandoned in favor of more prosaic settlements on the flats below. In one such place, called Teli, near the southwest end of the Bandiagara, guided by a swarm of boys, we stumbled upon an old woman lying sick on the stones of a smelly alley; she screamed at us, and the boys scattered as before a witch. Elsewhere we puzzled over empty granaries covered with ancestral chimeras in bas-relief; mystic swaths of red, black, and white triangles painted on the overarching wall; and baleful rows of primate skulls plastered to the wall, fetishes to appease the spirits. Twice we happened upon caches of tiny blue *canari* cups, which we should not have seen, for the *hogons* use them in secret funeral rites.

In recent years, as African art has become fashionable, European collectors have come to the Bandiagara offering huge prices for Tellem grave goods. The most highly prized artifacts may fetch as much as $4,000 apiece. The doleful result is that the Dogon have become hard-core grave robbers. No one knows what percentage of the Tellem caves the Dogon have ransacked, but the damage is significant. Only twenty years ago, the Dogon retained a healthy fear of the Tellem mortuaries as strange, sacred places; they felt no inclination to enter any caves except those they had appropriated for their own burials, or in quest of rarities like pigeon dung.

Over the centuries, the Dogon had probed some of the Tellem caves and discovered many ancient objects. None seemed of much interest to them except the small wooden statuettes, usually from one to two feet in height, which the Dogon believed to possess a great power. They removed these sculptures and incorporated them in their own sacred rites. Inevitably, these strange figures—highly abstract humans with their hands raised above their heads, often encrusted with a patina of sacrificial droppings—caught the fancy of Malian dealers in antiquities.

One night in camp Oumar told us a sinister story. The events had taken place in Ireli shortly after the last *Sigi*, which ended in 1973. The Tellem sites at Ireli, ranging 200 feet above the village in a smooth, constantly overhanging wall, were among the most dramatic we had seen anywhere. The people of the town, said Oumar, knew that a pair of Tellem statuettes reposed in one of the highest caves. The old men said that the Tellem had had an altar there; when they had left the Bandiagara for good, they had made sacrifices at the altar and told the Dogon about the statuettes. In consequence, the Dogon had always forbade their removal.

Some Malian antiquaries, however, talked two Ireli boys into going after the statuettes. At sunset, the boys furtively fixed a rope on the cliff; then in the night they climbed it to the cave. As the lead boy reached into the granary to seize one of the statuettes, he fell, knocking the second boy off the rope. Both boys plunged to their deaths. The antiquaries fled in the darkness.

We asked Oumar what would have happened if the Ireli men had caught the antiquaries. "They would have been murdered," he said mat-ter-of-factly. The statuettes are still in the cave.

ONE NIGHT, AS WE CAMPED just outside the town of Tireli, the village chief sent one of his wives to bring us a special feast. The prize dish was pieces of scrawny chicken cooked in a rich peanut sauce and served over rice. We had already grown to like millet pancakes and the plain white bread the Dogon bake from imported flour. But no amount of good will could compel us to swallow much of the gooey, green sauce of baobab leaves served over millet porridge that is the Dogon staple (it tastes like a mixture of baby-food vegetables, cream of wheat, and library paste).

Besides millet, the men grow rice, sorghum, and the minuscule grain called *digitaria*, which has a charged mythic significance. They also grow cotton for cloth, which they weave into handsome blankets dyed with in-digo. In Ibi, we had bought blankets from a lean, implacable graybeard who then let us watch him work at his loom. The nimble dance of his bent, arthritic fingers, which were stained a permanent indigo, was dazzling to see. We hiked on through Ibi, then, guided by a fifteen-year-old boy named Akouni, climbed up a hidden side valley. A group of women was bathing at a fern-enshrouded spring: warned by Akouni of our approach, they hastily pulled on their cloth skirts, then stared as we self-consciously hiked past.

We suddenly came to a fertile garden in the midst of a more umbra-geous forest than we had seen anywhere else along the Bandiagara. Oumar named each plant for us in Dogon, then in French: eggplant, tomato, red pepper, watermelon. We saw several vegetables that looked quite unfamil-iar, and indeed, Oumar searched in vain for their French names.

Later, on a dawn hike above the town of Dioundiouru, we came upon a large field of onions, the prize Dogon crop, which was introduced to them by Griaule. As we watched, silent, muscular farmers plodded from stream to onion field, shouldering calabashes full of water which they patiently poured upon the terraced plots of soil. When the onions are ripe, the men crush and roll them into firm green balls, which they trade as far as the Ivory Coast.

The Dogon live also by gathering: from a land so dry and stony, they harvest a surprising abundance of wild fruits, berries, and edible plants. Out on the plains beyond the millet fields, their livestock graze, often tended by a boy with a switch. They raise cattle for milk and beef, donkeys as beasts of burden, goats, sheep, and chickens for food and ritual sacrifice. And the Dogon still hunt, although the game have dwindled drastically. Within our century, carrying flintlock rifles crafted by their own blacksmiths, using potash refined in stone kilns as powder, hunters brought down monkeys, baboons, birds, and even panthers. The fox, however, is a sacred ancestor, whose tracks in the sand diviners read to forecast the future. The Dogon hate to be away from their villages after dark, and so the hunter, who sleeps in trees and prowls through the night, remains for them the exemplar of courage.

Because the people are vitally dependent on the rain, which falls only from July to October, Dogon life can be precarious. Terrible droughts in 1973 and 1985 stunted crops and forests and took their toll in human lives. In 1973, white residents told us, as you drove through Dogon country you would find people lying dead along the road. Dogon fathers, blaming themselves for the famine, committed suicide by hanging. In the 1913–1914 drought, according to an early missionary, the Dogon had thrown their children off the cliff rather than watch them starve.

We saw shadows of this marginal existence everywhere. All the children sported the bulging stomachs of malnutrition. We met an inordinate number of deaf-mutes among the Dogon population. At night in our campsite, we had to get used to a throng of children who stood, utterly rapt, around us as we drank tea or wrote in our notebooks. Once I casually tossed an empty tuna can to the ground. Six or eight boys dived to seize it, and a free-for-all broke out in the dust. Kids would lick every corner of one of our discarded food wrappers for a trace of the exotic taste.

One afternoon we climbed in parching heat to the high, lonely site of Koundou Goumon. A town where perhaps fifty or sixty Dogon had once lived—perhaps within the last generation—under a gigantic roof of sandstone, with a spring dripping deep in a cave, was now all but abandoned. Here a single reclusive family hung on. A pair of scrawny dogs yipped and snarled at our approach. We found the mother and her four children at work in the gloomy shade. The father was away at market. Naked to the waist, mother and daughter alternated blows of the *pilon* as they pounded the eternal millet; the little boys boiled down potash on a clay kiln. The youngest, too small for work, played with his own toy wooden *mortier* and *pilon*. Oumar talked the mother into lending us her ten-year-old, a big-bellied boy named Amadou, as guide to the Tellem sites in the cliff above.

The age-old route lay up a deep and frightening rock fissure to the left. We climbed unsteady Dogon log ladders, used handholds carved in the sandstone, and inched our way around a spooky traverse above a fifty-foot drop. Perhaps a Dogon had fallen here in the past, for ten feet below the traverse, a half-dozen branches had been wedged in a loose grid across the gap as a sort of safety net. I guessed that if you fell off, there was a fifty-fifty chance the branches would catch you. Although some of the moves for the barefoot ten-year-old were at the very limit of his reach, Amadou cruised up the vertical path with utter nonchalance.

Some eighty feet above the hidden village, we found heavy ropes hanging from the Dogon tombs. Amadou let us handle the ropes, but we could approach no nearer. We moved back into the fissure and climbed another sixty feet, then headed out across a sloping ledge. At once we found ourselves surrounded by Tellem artifacts. In open granaries, we found overturned pots and calabashes, many with holes poked in the bottom. Was this defilement part of a burial ceremony? We could only guess.

We saw skeletons wrapped in white-and-indigo blankets, women's fiber skirts, heavy baobab ropes, and a thing like a feather duster. (Even Oumar, who usually had a ready explanation, was at a loss to define the function of this last item.) In a tiny niche Oumar found a covered leather bag, a leather knife-sheath, a locket of leather on a cord, and many small hexagonal wooden beads. (Here, as at every Tellem site we visited, we disturbed nothing and kept not a single potsherd.)

Our ledge blanked out in an overhang, but twelve feet below, another ledge stretched into the distance. We had neglected to bring a rope, and now we stared in frustration at a pair of granaries surrounded by a wall-to-wall carpet of inverted ceramic pots. We could easily have jumped down to the lower ledge, but we would have marooned ourselves by doing so, for it would have been impossible to climb back up.

As we descended, I found myself wondering about Amadou's family. Why did they choose to live alone, among abandoned houses, in the dark shade of the high overhang? Had they committed some offense that left them ostracized by the others? What would the fate of the children be when they grew up?

ALL TOLD, THERE ARE ABOUT 300,000 Dogon today, scattered among 700 villages that lie not only along the Bandiagara, but on the Gondo Plain south of it and atop the plateau to the north. Despite their marginal life, their numbers seem to be increasing. Griaule tended to treat the Dogon as if they were a single people, adhering to a marvelously intricate but uniform belief system. Recent research, however, has argued that this unitary view will not hold up. One French ethnographer has found that in the plateau village of Sibi-Sibi, only twenty miles from Sanga, even the basic creation myths are different from those recorded by Griaule. There are at least thirty-five distinct Dogon dialects, many of them mutually unintelligible. We noticed that once we got more than twenty-five miles from Sanga, Oumar had great trouble conversing with other Dogon.

Many aspects of Dogon life are still veiled in primal secrecy. It is clear that sorcery, for example, plays a vital role among the Dogon, but anthropologists have been able to learn almost nothing about it. And because graves and burial ceremonies are off-limits to outsiders, we know very little about the Dogon view of death or treatment of the dead.

The ethnographers have tended to cluster around Sanga. Far from that village, on the outskirts of Dogon land, dwell people whose lives are all but unknown. At the easternmost swing of our jaunt by Land Cruiser, we passed ten miles south of a remote plateau called Oualo. We saw it floating in the haze like a vast blue cloud. There are Dogon living there, we learned, who have never come down from the plateau, people who thus have yet to encounter a white person. Even Oumar knew nothing about them.

WITH OUMAR ONE AFTERNOON, Matt Hale and I started traversing below the cliff toward a Tellem site we had seen in binoculars. No Dogon village stood on the talus anywhere near this site, and though we knew that a town called Yawa was situated somewhere above on the plateau, Oumar thought it unlikely that the low caves were under its jurisdiction. Perhaps we could visit a Tellem site without having to go through the rigmarole of obtaining a village's permission. We were picking our way through tall weeds, perhaps a hundred yards short of the caves, when we heard shouting. Squinting up into the sun, we could just make out a trio of heads peering over the edge of the cliff 250 feet above us. Oumar answered the shouts, then told us, "They say we must go back."

We turned on our heels and started to walk away from the caves. Suddenly something crashed in the weeds nearby. Another, closer explosion followed, then another. From far above, rocks as big as volleyballs were being thrown, evidently with full intent to hit and kill us. Matt and I started to run. But Oumar was of another mind: perhaps he had lost face. He insisted that we hike the long way up to Yawa and deal with our attackers. Jittery and perplexed, Matt and I reluctantly agreed. Half an hour later, as we entered Yawa, girls greeted us with smiles. We poked along the edge of town, coming at last to three men reclining on the rock. Oumar traded elaborate salutations with the men, and we shook hands all around.

"What was that all about?" I asked Oumar as we left.

"They said, yes, it was we who yelled at you, but it was the boys who threw the rocks."

"Why?"

"They said they have to guard their tombs. They have spies looking for them."

"But who are the spies?" I wondered.

"Us," said Oumar.

On the outskirts of town, I noticed a teenage girl who seemed to be yelling at someone in the distance. She was bare-breasted, had a vacant look on her face, and walked in a strange shuffle. All at once I saw that her ankles were encased in heavy iron leg cuffs, like the ones Arabs had used to shackle slaves. I felt a chill back of my shoulders. "What is the matter?" I asked Oumar, indicating the cuffs.

"She's not normal," he said without breaking stride. "She's crazy." The girl's treatment, I reflected, was analogous to the Dogons' hobbling their donkeys to keep them from straying. In a way the leg cuffs may have been humanitarian—to keep the deranged teenager from wandering into the wilderness or falling off the cliff. All the same, I was glad to put Yawa behind us.

In a town called Tireli Sud, Matt and I had our most interesting exchange with the Dogon. It was our luck to find four of Tireli's oldest men lounging in the open courtyard beside the *togu na*. The senior was a thin blind man whose left hand shook uncontrollably. Another bearded elder had wrapped himself tight in a blanket against the December chill. A third sat in the Dogon "thinker's pose," elbows on knees, hands atop head. The fourth had a look of perpetual outrage on his fierce face. Through a translator, I gently prodded the men to learn what they might tell us about the Tellem.

The interview got off to a bad start. "Look at where he's sitting," one of the elders said to another, indicating Matt. Knowing no better, Matt had plopped himself down on top of what turned out to be a special stone in the middle of the courtyard. Now he scuttled to a safer seat.

When he was asked about the Tellem, the blind man snapped, "How do I know? I wasn't here." Gradually, however, the elders warmed to our curiosity. One teased another: "Tell them what you really know. Don't go making up stories." They spoke in turns after long silences, pausing to spit in the dirt or shoo away noisy children.

The people of Tireli, we learned, came originally from Aru, where today the great *hogon* of all the Dogon lives alone in his hilltop sanctuary. When the Dogon came, the men agreed, the Tellem had already departed from the cliff. There was no doubt that the Tellem lived in the cliff: they were hunter-gatherers, not growers, and they knew how to find water in some of the caves.

The Tellem, the old men went on, were definitely smaller than Dogon. I asked how the Tellem had managed to build on such outlandish perches. The elders could not say, but they knew it was done by magic. I played the devil's advocate: Hadn't the Dogon actually driven the Tellem away? A scornful sneer came over the blind man's ravaged face. "How," he said sternly, "could we have driven out people who had such powerful magic?"

They had heard, the elders went on, that the Tellem could ride horses straight up and down the cliff. They could ride on the wind itself. (Later, as we explored the cliff face above town, the chief of Tireli, a relatively young man, pointed out two boulins wedged in a crack above forty feet of dead-vertical sandstone. Those, he said, were hitching posts the Tellem had used to tie off their horses.)

The old men were reluctant to talk about the Dogon in general. As one put it, "You can only talk about your own village. You can't talk about another village." In Tireli, unlike the Sanga area, the people did not use Tellem caves to bury their dead; they found their own caves. Nor did they raise the corpses with ropes. Among the Tellem caves in the cliff above them, there were many that no Dogon had ever reached. These would of course be full of Tellem goods. In this corner of the Bandiagara, antiquaries had yet to do their mischief.

As our interview drew to a close, the man in the blanket unwrapped a piece of cloth. He produced a pair of curious objects, which he let me handle; he said they had been found long ago in a Tellem cave. They looked to me like ritual hoes, each about a foot and a half long. The wood handles were whittled with ridged bands, like the ritual sticks Dogon make as ladders for their ancestors. Fixed through the head of each stick was a curved iron blade, similar to the ones Dogon attach to wooden shafts to make real hoes. These strange implements were too small to be functional, but the workmanship was excellent. They were definitely Tellem, not Dogon, said the elder, and he was not sure what they had been used for. I had no reason to doubt his words; he was not trying to sell me the objects. Enthralled, I took pictures. I had seen nothing like these tools before.

DURING OUR MONTH RANGING UP and down the Bandiagara, we had discovered many Tellem sites that the Dutch had never seen; we were almost certainly the first whites to visit them. And we had counted hundreds of Tellem caves that it would be a formidable effort for modern climbers to reach. Yet we were still dumbfounded as to how these pioneers of the vertical had done it. There was no doubt that boulins and baobab ropes were the key to Tellem technique; every boulin we saw in place was deeply scored by rope-grooves. In a wetter past, had there been vines or trees all over the escarpment that facilitated the climbing? The Dutch archaeologists doubted it. Had the lower parts of the cliff broken away, making access more difficult? Unlikely, for if such collapses were frequent, the Dogon would not build their villages beneath the cliff. Somehow the Tellem must have perfected wild techniques that never occurred to us modern alpinists.

And even if we could guess how the Tellem had done it, we still had to wonder why. The standard explanation for cliff dwellings anywhere in the world is defense against enemies. We know from Arab sources that the Mossi and the Songhai raided the Bandiagara area in the fifteenth century in search of slaves. Earlier, the great empire of Mali may have driven such people as the Tellem into a defense reclusion.

But to our eyes, the extreme inaccessibility of so many Tellem sites seemed to outstrip the needs of defense alone. It ought to be just as easy to hold off raiders from a cave 40 feet off the ground that requires moderate climbing to reach, as from a cave 200 feet high that demands an elaborate approach with ropes and boulins. It may be that a simple shortage of caves drove the Tellem to build in more and more difficult sites.

Or maybe—just maybe—the Tellem did it for its own sake, because it was clever and beautiful. By the end of our trip, we wanted to believe that aesthetics alone had driven the Tellem to their mastery.

On our last night in Dogon country, we camped again beside the well at Banani. I wanted to go on my own for a last afternoon hike. I told the others I'd be back by dusk, in an hour and a half. After a month of forced company, it was bliss to be alone. I scrambled to the top of the plateau above Banani and gazed nostalgically up and down the Bandiagara.

Before me stretched a small valley, bathed in amber sunlight. There, in the far wall, stood a small group of Tellem buildings. Somewhere below lay the town of Néni, but the valley itself seemed empty. I hurried down for a last look at ruins.

A superb free-standing granary stood on a boulder before the cave, casting its windowed shadow on the orange rock. Thirty feet above lay other granaries and a sealed wall. I backed down twice before I forced a hard move and reached the cave. The granaries were empty. I walked along the corridor behind them and saw that the sealed building had a small open doorway. I stopped through and waited for my eyes to adjust to the dark.

221

It was not the largest mausoleum I had entered—nothing could match the cave of the skeletons—but it was the best-ordered. On twin natural benches, some seventy corpses lay wrapped in their dusty winding sheets. Many of the skulls were still attached to skeletons. The indigo-dyed cloth matched the Tellem pattern, but I saw two empty wicker baskets that looked Dogon. I was wild with excitement, and a dawning agitation. It was getting late—I could afford only a few minutes inside the crypt.

As I stepped back into the sunlight, I saw a Dogon man walking down the valley below. He was carrying an axe over his shoulder. He stopped and hacked at a tree. In the windless air, I could hear him muttering to himself. I felt a sudden fear. Rather than saunter down into the valley, I knelt behind a granary and hid. I'll wait till he passes through the valley, I thought, before I come out. But the man was taking his time. Then I saw another Dogon coming up the path. At evening the herders and farmers walk back to their villages; below me, perhaps, a man from Sanga was crossing paths with a man from Néni. They met, talked, and parted. I thought, This is silly, hiding here, and what will they think if they see me crouched like a spy? Still concealed, I scuttled forward and rounded a corner, and a chilling sight opened before me.

On a ledge just below stood a huge pile of what looked like wooden stretchers. Nearby was a cache of some thirty blue canari pots. I looked above, and saw walls of stone—not brick—sealing off caves. I had done the worst possible thing: blundered alone into a Dogon tomb. The stretchers were the biers on which the corpses had been carried to the cliff. I was pretty sure the skeletons I had seen were Tellem, but right above me, behind the sealed walls, lay the sacred dead of the Dogon.

As I hid, my breath came in soft bursts. I peered through the granary window, begging the man with the axe to move on. When I shifted one foot, I was sure he could hear the scuff of shoe on rock, or hear my breathing. Another man strolled down the valley. The sun was fading; back at camp they would soon start to worry.

At last the men meandered out of sight. I took a quick look, then scrambled as noiselessly as I could down to the valley. No one had seen me. My pace back to camp was just short of a run. As I came in sight of Banani, I felt a vast relief, and in that very moment, a flood of shame. I could protest that my trespass had been an honest mistake, that I had tampered with nothing in the sacred cave. But I had committed a deep offense against the Dogon, whom I had come to like and respect. Whether or not the men of Néni knew it, I had profaned the peace of their ancestors.

The next day, Oumar seemed unperturbed by news of my misadventure.

He said, however, that if the men in the valley had caught me in the cave, they would indeed have attacked me with their axes.

AS FOR THE TELLEM, after a month of trying to fathom the eccentric brilliance of their doomed culture, we were left only with a deepened awe. Some day, perhaps, the Dogon will guide us to a sharper understanding, by letting us pry beneath the surface of their own towns and tombs. But to do so may violate the integrity of their own culture. It would be wrong to desecrate one mystery in order to probe another one.

As we headed back to Bamako a few days before Christmas, the intensity of our experience tingled in our blood. Through 400 years, the Dogon have pounded their millet and tilled their fields, while above them, from the caves of the Bandiagara, the Tellem enigma stares out across the Gondo plain. Centuries of elucidation lie ahead.

CAMPAIGN IN THE CLOUDS

All day, as I had hiked up a pine-smothered trail and scrambled across prickly slabs of rock, I had seen no one else. It was mid-July in the Italian Dolomites, my favorite range in the Alps. A sovereign sun commanded a fleet of cumulus clouds sailing out of the northwest. The blue wrinkles of a stream wound among the larches in the valley floor, 3,000 feet beneath me. At the moment, other corners of the Dolomites were thronged with tourists, but I had the Forame, a middling peak hidden behind the lordly Cristallo, to myself.

Above the forest, on steep rock, the going grew devious. Winding upwards through a series of chimneys and gullies, I climbed the Forame's north face. Emerging from a short cliff, I moved gingerly across a slope where a skin of scree teetered on raw, scraped bedrock. Ordinarily, I would have needed a rope and a partner here, and an edgy apprehension would have dogged my moves. Instead, I felt only pleasure, for I was following a classic *via ferrata*, or "iron way." A Dolomite invention, the *via ferrata* strings together steel cables, eyebolts, and ladders to secure a route that would otherwise be perilous. With a waist harness, two nylon slings, and a pair of carabiners to attach myself to the cables, I was as safe as I had been hiking through the woods.

I paused for a snack on a sunny ledge. Then the route ducked into the mountain's shadow; here the rock was stained black with dripping seeps, and cavelike hollows, floored with ice, exhaled a breath of winter.

I looked up, and my gaze froze in startled discovery. Blocking my path was a tall, featureless, overhanging cliff. The *via ferrata* circumvented it on the left, but in the middle of that blank precipice loomed an unmistakably manmade construction. In thirty years of hiking and climbing, I had never seen anything remotely like it.

A hundred feet above the scree, a row of rusted iron spikes, each drilled straight into the rock, made a horizontal stitch across the cliff. Each spike was bent up at the end to form a shallow hook. Laid across the row of spikes, not even tied or nailed down, a few decrepit planks still hung in place.

The thing, I later learned, was a *passerella,* a gangway designed to walk across. I tried to imagine how it must have been built, one iron bar at a time, by some fearless engineer who hung from the last spike as he drilled the next one. The *passerella* had served a platoon of Austrian soldiers who lived through the winters of 1915 and 1916 on this north face. On their shaky gangplank, they had stood and hurled *bombe a mano*—crude, heavy hand grenades fitted with wooden sticks for handles—at Italians who clawed up the treacherous scree toward the Austrian line. The whole rationale for the *passerella* was to give the bomb-tossers a better angle for their throws. But on that dark cliff, raked by machine-gun fire from below, the Austrians had had no place to hide.

Like most Americans, I had first come to the Dolomites utterly ignorant of the course of World War I in Italy. On my first hike in 1983, I had been surprised to see coils of old barbed wire strewn across a high meadow. During subsequent visits, I kept stumbling across vestiges from the Great War, weathered ruins and rusted relics stranded in the most inaccessible places.

In 1992, on my fourth visit to the Dolomites, I spent two weeks methodically tracing the front between the Austrian and Italian lines, as it cuts a sixty-mile swath from southwest to northeast across the heart of the range. And I read my history: not an easy task, for virtually no sources have been translated into English. I performed my pilgrimage in two- and three-day loops, using the exquisite town of Cortina d'Ampezzo as my base.

The War to End All Wars raged all across the north of Italy. Though important offensives were fought in the valleys, it was on the mountaintops that the struggle pivoted. Nowhere were the deeds of the alpinist-soldiers more extraordinary than in the Dolomites, which comprise, with the Chamonix aiguilles, the steepest mountains in Europe. Among these soaring crags and towers young men waged the ultimate in mountain warfare ever witnessed on the surface of the earth.

The story of the war in the Dolomites is a tale of anonymous heroism, sacrifice, and misery, all the more poignant for the grim stalemate in which it ground to a halt. Remarkably enough, the traces of that war still abound, spilling across the genial trails where grandmothers stroll and children picnic. Had such a war been fought in the United States, every acre would have been declared a historic park, every cartridge shell gathered for the museums, as at Gettysburg or Little Bighorn. But in the Dolomites—in part because the bitterness of World War I lives on in the breasts of the villagers—the ruins have been left to molder and decay, as if in hopes that the greening earth might swallow them and heal the wounds that still fester in the ethnic paradoxes of this sublime land.

Thanks to the excellent hut system of the Dolomites, as I wandered along the front I never had to carry more than twenty-five pounds on my back. It's hard to walk more than four hours without coming upon a *rifugio*, and except in tourist-mad August, there's never a shortage of space. At dinner in each high hut, I ate wienerschnitzel or rostbraten, drank pints of good strong beer or sampled the Tirolean red wines. The decor of a backcountry *rifugio* leans to a venerable kitsch. At the Valparola hut, a stuffed chamois stood ready to pounce upon my table, while a spread-winged eagle (symbol of the Tirol) eyed my stray french fries. Two stuffed squirrels contemplated pinecones held in their paws. The dinner music was lilting Tirolean waltzes on the accordion. The *Gemütlichkeit* in the hut was infectious: I traded trail gossip with total strangers.

Upstairs, I slept under a giant down comforter, listening to the wind whistle in the shutters. There was only cold water for my ablutions, but the room had its own washbasin. It has always surprised me how few Americans know about the Alpine huts. At the Locatelli hut near Monte Paterno, as I browsed through the guest register, I had to go back 1,325 names to find my last previous compatriot.

Had I simply been on holiday, out for good hiking, the two weeks would have seemed a lark. But my chosen quest—to trace the ruins of the war—deepened the traveling by planting it in the somber ground of history. Always the paradox assailed me: that I walked in delight through scenes from a Stygian nightmare.

For to hike the Dolomite front is to imprint one's soul with an epic saga that the world is in danger of forgetting. Never for me had a landscape become more charged with historical meaning. Never had a battlefield brought home to me so vividly the horror—and alongside it, as the soldiers themselves testified—the eerie beauty of war.

TO THE BRITISH WHO THRONGED to Italy's aid in 1915, the war seemed morally black-and-white. It was the gallant Italian soldier, with a mandolin under his arm and a passion to reunite his torn country, against the ravaging Hun. Steeped in Victorian smugness, one English journalist at the front reported, "With a shock we faced the stark brutality beneath the German veneer of sentiment and culture"; another inveighed, "For ways that are dark the heathen Chinee is a babe compared with an Austrogoth." The eighteen-year-old Ernest Hemingway, badly wounded as a Red Cross ambulance driver on the Italian front, saw the war through just such spectacles.

For the soldiers themselves, it was never so clear-cut. Two-and-a-half years of lying in trenches within easy shouting distance of the enemy inculcated not contempt but respect. A profound ambivalence lay at the core of a struggle so desperate no one could afford ambivalence. My hotelkeeper in Cortina, a sullen old man named Siro Alverà, told me one night that his father had won the silver medal in the war—for saving an enemy soldier who cried out for help. "Because it was humanitarian," Signor Alverà said quietly. "Because he was brave."

The ambivalence seeped into the most courageous acts. In June 1916 a young Italian single-handedly held off a determined Austrian charge, shooting two of the oncoming soldiers dead and putting the others to flight. The next day he was cheered as a hero by his comrades, but he fled their applause and returned to the trench he had defended. "I saw my dead," he wrote his family, "and, poor things, they were two fine young men, strong and beautiful. Fate had brought them to die by my bullet. I was indeed sorry, and I almost wept seeing them so beautiful . . . and dead on account of me."

For no soldiers on any European front was the war more contradictory and absurd than for the conscripts from Cortina d'Ampezzo. Since 1509, with the settlement of a war between Venice and the Habsburgs, Cortina had lain within the Austro-Hungarian Empire—but only just barely. The border passed a mere six kilometers southeast of town; on the road to Venice today, an old customs house called Dogana Vecchia still marks the former boundary. Almost nobody in Cortina speaks German, but only thirty-two kilometers to the north, in Dobbiaco, German is the first language. "People from Dobbiaco said we were Italians," Signor Alverà told me with a wan smile. "People from San Vito di Cadore [eleven kilometers to the southeast] said we were Austrians."

The truth is that the villagers of Cortina were neither. They were *Ampezzani*, shepherds and farmers whose roots trace back to the eleventh century, speakers of their own language, a dialect of Ladin (it is still heard in the streets and taught in the schools). The overriding fact all across what is called the South Tirol is that the country is neither Italian nor Austrian; ethnically it cries out to be a sovereign country. The analogy with the recent chaos in Yugoslavia—an artificial country dissolving under the stress of war into its bedrock cultures, insular and xenophobic—suggests itself.

The war began in late July and early August 1914, with Austro-Hungarians fighting Serbs and Russians, the Germans attacking Belgium. For nearly a year Italy stayed out of it, though since 1882 she had been the third member of the Triple Alliance with Germany and Austro-Hungary. The world assumed Italy would eventually team up with her partners to the north, but meanwhile her leaders negotiated secretly with the British and nursed colonial ambitions of their own.

By the end of summer 1914, all the able-bodied men in Cortina had been drafted into the Austrian army. They were spirited all the way to Russia and Galicia (on today's border between Poland and the Ukraine), to fight an enemy with whom they had never had the slightest quarrel. Luis Trenker's thinly-veiled novel, *Kampf in den Bergen (War in the Mountains)*, the most moving account of the Dolomite front I know of, vividly captures the Cortina men's response to Italy's joining the fray on May 23, 1915. Trenker's hero Dimaï returns from leave with the news. "Italy has declared war," he tells his comrades.

The unworldly Tchams bursts out with hurrahs: "My god, victory is ours!"

"Imbecile!" Dimaï answers with a bitter smile. "It's against us that Italy has declared war."

While Italy slumbered, a wary Austria had built up its southern frontier against just such a turn of fate. Stretched thin by the war in Russia, however, her troops had withdrawn to the Dolomite mountaintops. The Italian army marched into Cortina and took the town without firing a shot. Through the rest of the war, the wives and children of the men fighting for Austria were forced to wait on Italian officers; their very homes were turned into barracks.

Returned at last from the Russian front, the Cortina men bivouacked in the mountains they knew better than any Austrians, charged with attacking their own homes, where their families were held hostage. They begged their officers not to ravage the town, and for the most part the commanders showed restraint. Yet Cortina was shelled from the north and bombed from the air. In 1990, as contractors built an underground garage in the center of town, they came across an unexploded 305-caliber bomb that had reposed in the dirt for seventy-four years.

ON THE EASY PATH THAT LEADS from the Rifugio Auronzo to the Forcella Lavaredo, a traffic jam of hikers creeps along the most popular walk in the Dolomites: graybeards with piolet-tipped canes, ladies in low heels and skirts, couples walking dogs or pushing baby carriages. On a warm July morning I was bemused to share the trail with a gang of teenaged Italian boys, their boom box turned high; at intervals they stopped to throw rocks at cows.

This trail was originally the hand-built road by which the Italian soldiers supplied the Forcella, a gentle saddle of immense strategic importance. I paused on the pass, tuned out the chatter and the mob, and saw the splendid vista with the eyes of 1915. Immediately on my left, the triple fangs of the Tre Cime di Lavaredo, whose north faces plunge sheer 2,000 feet to the talus; on my right, Monte Paterno, a labyrinth of spiky towers; at equal height, across a mere kilometer and a half of shallow valley, the blissfully placed Rifugio Locatelli, the busiest hut in the Dolomites.

There in 1915 stood a smaller hut, headquarters of an Austrian command. Facing it on the Forcella sat the heavy Italian artillery, cannons homing in on their target. On the morning of May 25, a huge cheer went up among the Italian troops. Five shells in quick succession had found the hut, smashing it in and setting it on fire: a pillar of black smoke stained the sky. It was only the second day of the war.

Seventy-seven summers later, I left the throng on the Forcella to climb Monte Paterno. A swirling mist swallowed the mountain as I traversed a tunnel drilled along the mountain's west face; from its dark passage, vertiginous bunkers gaped in sudden portals. Higher up, the trail swooped over pinnacles and tiptoed along the precipice. I heard the distant voices of other climbers, invisible in the fog.

The hut the Italians had shelled and burned belonged to Sepp Innerkofler, the finest guide in the Sexten Dolomites (as these northeastern massifs are called) and one of the great climbers of his day. In July a new Austrian captain, who knew nothing about mountains, ordered Innerkofler to try to storm the Italian position on the summit of the Paterno.

The guide was forty-nine years old when the war broke out, but he had hesitated not an instant before enlisting, along with his sons of eighteen and twenty-two. Innerkofler knew how dubious an armed assault on the northwest ridge of the Paterno would prove: he had "put up" the route in 1896 and climbed it often since. Failing to dissuade his captain, he obeyed with a dark fatalism. Innerkofler chose five men to climb with him, mostly seasoned Sexten guides. His son Gottfried begged to be included. Sepp refused, saying: "Your mother must weep for only one of us." Father and son embraced and said goodbye.

At four in the morning of July 4, Innerkofler led the difficult climb in the dark. The other men could not keep up with him, and as he neared the summit he was alone. Some say the light of dawn outlined his silhouette and gave him away to the Italians. From a niche just ten feet below the summit, Innerkofler hurled his three stick-handled grenades. Above him hid an Italian named Piero De Luca, also an expert climber. Choosing his moment, De Luca came into view. In Italian patois he cried out, "So you don't want to go away?" With both hands De Luca threw a heavy rock. Innerkofler had no chance: the stone caught him square and knocked him from his niche.

Later the Italians retrieved the guide's body from a high chimney and buried it under stones on the summit, in honor of their noble adversary. After the war Innerkofler's sons retrieved the body and reburied it in the cemetery in Sesto, his home town.

Wreathed in the cold mist, I reached the summit and found the simple iron cross proclaiming, "Hier fiel Sepp Innerkofler . . . am 4 Juli 1915." I sat on the stones nearby and pondered the guide's martyrdom. For two more years the war raged between the ruins of his hut and the Forcella Lavaredo. The Italians seized the pass where the hut stood, only to lose it in counterattack. The Austrians won and lost the Forcella Lavaredo. Men died by the score, but the front shifted only a few feet here and there.

It was the pattern of the whole Dolomite war, to the despair of later historians. No linked chain of victories, like Sherman's march through the South, gave the struggle logical coherence. On the Marmolada, the Cristallo, the three Tofane, and a half-dozen other mountains, brilliant but ultimately indecisive battles took their bloody course simultaneously with the struggle around the Paterno.

It was not even, for the most part, a war of heroes: Innerkofler was the exception. A few days before my jaunt over the Paterno, I had visited the serene Italian cemetery at Pian di Salesei, tucked in a bend of an obscure valley, presided over by cows who grazed the adjoining fields. A plaque told me that the cemetery held the remains of 5,404 soldiers who had fallen on the Dolomite front. Four thousand seven hundred of them remain *ignoti*—unknown.

It was a war of faceless death, of bold deeds that no one recorded, of tales of suffering that blur with each year of fading memory. In Cortina in 1992, the only surviving veteran of the Dolomite war still lived, a man named Teofilo Gillarduzzi. Then ninety-two years old, in poor health, he had forgotten everything he knew of the great struggle.

THE DEBRIS FROM THE WAR, however, lingers on: in all its ramshackle eloquence, it speaks directly to the heart of the observant wanderer today. An old axiom of war decrees that whoever holds the high ground controls the battle. This was true with a vengeance in the Dolomites, where a single sharpshooter atop a pinnacle could decimate a whole platoon in the trenches below, where a well-placed cannon could lob shells into the midst of a barracks eight kilometers away. And at the onset of the war, the Austrians had the daunting advantage of occupying nearly all the summits; the Italians had to fight upwards, the Austrians merely to hold the heights.

On the Cima Grande, whose easiest route requires a rope to climb today, the Italians hauled a spotlight taller than a man to the very summit, where it illuminated the enemy lines through midnight bombings and lit up the tangles of barbed wire that were all but invisible by day. By dint of ropes and strong shoulders, Italian alpinists carried a cannon in pieces to a crest four-fifths of the way up the mountain, reassembled it, and fired off some 800 *granate*, hefty shells that took their toll.

The virtuosi of the front were the special mountain troops, the *Alpini* among the Italians, the *Alpenjäger* of the Austrians. As I traced their handiwork, I began to wonder whether they labored for art's sake as well as from tactical necessity. Here I found a cable bridge across the void, there a sentry shack wired into a vertical dihedral, or barbed wire strung like fixed rope across a piton-studded traverse. The relics of the soldiers' craft seem to body forth the fantasies of some band of crazed architects in a nether circle of Dante's hell.

The linchpin of the Austrian position near the Tre Cime was the Torre di Toblin, a sheer tower of rock just north of Innerkofler's ruined hut. The Austrians used it as a shield for their barracks, and climbed its cold north face to man a watchtower on top.

In 1979 a *via ferrata* was engineered up this 500-foot precipice. With my waist harness, slings, and carabiners, I climbed the Toblin by the *via ferrata* the morning after my traverse of the Paterno. The wall is nearly perpendicular, and some of the steel ladders overhang; secure or not, I felt a giddy exhilaration on the route. Alongside the *via ferrata*, the rotting timbers and rusted eyebolts of the Austrian ascent-line conjured up for me the watchman's daily ordeal. The whole of this World War I route is mind-boggling, but its showpiece comes near the top. Across a broad rock chimney, the Austrians managed to wedge a ten-foot timber end-to-end. On top of this dizzy platform in midair, they erected a wooden ladder; thirty feet up at the highest rung, where the chimney walls relent from the vertical, the ladder touched rock for the first time. Hanging from the modern cable fifteen feet away, I was seized with vertigo as I gazed at the broken remnants of this staircase in the sky.

That so much physical evidence of the Great War remains strewn across the landscape is something of a miracle. In the mass poverty that followed the war, villagers razed barracks for the wood, keeping the good planks for building, the rubble for firewood. Farmers plowed away the barbed wire; others salvaged it to use as reinforcing rods in concrete. Gypsies camped on former battlefields and scavenged everything in sight to sell as scrap.

Then, as Mussolini built Italy back into a military power in the 1930s, there arose a new demand for metal. It became the patriotic duty of every villager in the Dolomites to ransack the front for iron. A bounty of two *lire* was offered for each World War I helmet salvaged and sent to the factories. Since the war, small cemeteries, each linked to a nearby battlefield, had graced the landscape. The searchers for scrap iron kept coming across the skeletons of unknown soldiers. Mussolini offered five *lire* for every skeleton turned over for proper burial, but the penury of Italy was so dire villagers dug up corpses from the cemeteries to claim the small reward.

Recent efforts to preserve and restore the Dolomite battlefields have confronted a strong resistance among the villagers. "There was too much suffering," says Loris Lancedelli. "The older people don't want to remember the war." A genial and earnest man in his forties, Lancedelli has launched a one-man crusade to save the heritage of the Dolomite campaign.

Lancedelli's father, Rolando, who runs a small inn above Cortina, was one of the men whom Mussolini's appeal sent scavenging the slopes. As a small boy, Loris accompanied his father. The fascination of the lost objects soon seized the father; he stopped selling the relics and began collecting them. For Loris, the outings became a lifelong quest.

In the foyer of his parents' inn, I saw for the first time what the crude, square, barbed-wire-encased *bomba a mano* looked like. Loris showed me a heavy iron helmet pierced with a fatal bullet hole, a shovel-head riddled by bullets, a cannon-fired grenade that he had cut open to reveal the deadly pellets of lead that burst as shrapnel upon impact. The most beguiling artifact was a gift from a soldier to his fiancée. Linking small-caliber bullets with tiny wires, the man had made a pair of pendant earrings. In like fashion, Rolando Lancedelli has taken the brutal cannon shells he found on many a high alp and engraved and colored them with deft scrollwork, as New England whalers used to carve their scrimshaw.

In such sea changes I saw crystallized the strange blend of death and beauty that had tugged at my feelings since my first day's walk along the front. The soldiers had felt it, too. The lead pellets screaming from a burst shell looked "like a rose in the air," they reported. The arcs of nighttime artillery fire seen from a distant camp were "appalling, but almost beautiful."

The sheer ubiquity of war debris bespeaks the extremes to which men went to kill each other in the Dolomites. Without even looking hard, I found seven or eight cartridge shells, some so pristine I could read "1915" stamped on the end, and Lancedelli could tell from the factory mark whether they were Italian or Austrian. I found many pellets of lead shrapnel, buried like gray marbles in the packed dirt of the trail. They seemed to me to have a curious numen, and one evening I made the mistake of offering a pellet to Signor Alverà, my hotelkeeper. He took the object in his fingers, groaned, and held his hand to his forehead. Then he began a halting account of his thirty-six months as a prisoner of war in World War II. "My father lost the First War," he said sheepishly. "I lost the Second. I think we are not a good family for war."

Everywhere—on summits of sharp spires, in the moss beneath stunted pines—I came across iron shrapnel, scattered by cannon shells. Holding a jagged piece of brown metal in my palm, I could all too easily imagine it tearing a hole through my body. Yet it was tempting to pick up and fondle these artifacts, like flint flakes or potsherds at an Anasazi site.

The beauty of the war's traces kept piercing my intellectual grasp of its horror. In July, the landscape drowns in wildflowers: blazing magenta rhododendrons, the deep blue stars of gentians, cushions of pale blue forget-me-nots, clumps of yellow arnica, and bursts of violet campanula. Time and again I would spy a thorny brown weed in the grass, only to realize it was a tendril of barbed wire sprouting from the earth.

Even a discarded sardine tin, the key still wound in the half-peeled lid, seemed an object of fascination. The men hung their used cans from the barbed wire that guarded their trenches: a tinkling in the night signaled the crawling approach of a soldier in the wrong uniform.

Seen from above, the grassed-over zigzags of trenches seemed to promise archaeological wonders, like the barrows and middens of Stone Age man. The ruined shacks with their bleaching boards had the gothic patina of gold-rush cabins. Even a black leather boot sole, soggy with age but each stitch-hole intact, had a melancholy power: What else had come apart here, besides a man's boots?

ON A WARM OCTOBER day a few years before I had climbed the long *via ferrata* that traverses the west face of the Tofana di Rozes.

Here lies one of several bold Dolomite routes that was first climbed during the war, not for sport but to attack an enemy outpost. As I hung from the cables, I marveled at the nerve of men who had dodged bullets as well as falling stones as they clung to the nubbins of this then-unknown wall.

The *via ferrata* was conceived in the cable-and-ladder systems by which the soldiers gained their airy bunkers. The very look of the Dolomites to-day owes everything to the war. Nearly all the roads, and most of the trails, were built to ferry countless tons of matériel to the front. Before the war, farmers had rigged simple rope tows to haul hay and wood down from high pastures; by 1917, they had constructed swooping aerial tramways to haul cannons and men. The *téléphériques* that now whisk tourists to mountaintop sun decks where they drink beer in their swimsuits had their genesis in the cable cars of the war. In the main square of every town in the Dolomites, no matter how small, a plaque or monument names the World War I dead. I paused one afternoon in the sleepy village of Pieve di Livinallongo, chilled by the revelation of its memorial. The town must harbor fewer than 200 citizens today. One hundred thirty-six of the valley's men had perished in the war, of whom fully seventeen were from the family Crepaz. The name is neither Italian nor Austrian, but Ladin. It was not for their own country that the sons and fathers Crepaz had died.

FOR MORE THAN A YEAR, as soldiers for the Austrian side, the men from Cortina fought in the mountains just north and west of home. Sometimes they volunteered for dangerous missions just to gain a ledge or spire from which they could glimpse their beloved town; with binoculars, a man might pick out his own farmstead. "If the wind blows from the south," they told one another, "we might even hear the bells of Cortina." But at Christmas, when their comrades opened letters from home, there was no mail for the Cortina men: the Italian post office did not forward missives to the Austrian front.

What gnawed at the men's souls most sharply was the knowledge that their wives and children assumed they were still fighting in Russia or Galicia—if they were still alive. Inevitably, some broke under the strain, fled the lines, and tried to reach Cortina. Some of them were arrested, tried as deserters, and executed. From his boyhood, Lancedelli remembers the Austrian cemetery at Fiames, five kilometers north of Cortina. West of the road ranged the graves of a thousand soldiers, interred in sacred ground; east lay the remains of thirty-seven "deserters," impugned by the separation, estranged from honor even in death.

As tragic as the plight of the Cortina men proved, their lot was preferable to that of the Russian prisoners sent to the Dolomites to build

Austrian roads. The oldest people in Cortina remember them still. On a front where even the Austrian soldiers were underfed, the Russians starved. They begged their captors for bones and scraps of food, but died in droves.

All of my Dolomite holidays had occupied the months of summer or early fall. The soldiers had stuck it out through two winters in their miserable quarters. And the winter of 1916–1917 was the kind that could break the staunchest of spirits.

On the Marmolada, the highest peak in the Dolomites and the only one with a major glacier, the Austrians had built the most extravagantly baroque of all the wartime edifices. They called it the *Eisstadt*—the Ice City. Burrowing beneath the surface of the glacier, using crevasses as hallways, they carved a network of rooms out of the ice, stabilizing them with wooden walls and floors. The *Eisstadt* had a woodshed, munitions and gas storage rooms, a telephone center, a bomb-testing cavern, and barracks for 135 men. I had once spent a month inside a snow cave on an Alaskan glacier; it was not a pleasant domicile. The soldiers spent two years in their Eisstadt. Almost nothing of this mad city remains, for in seventy-five years its ruins have sunk deep into the glacier. The mountain guides say, though, that at the end of a dry August you can peer into certain crevasses and spy a stranded plank or skein of wire.

In November 1916, the snow started falling. Before the winter was over, nine meters of snow had accumulated, a near record. The *Eisstadt* became a trap. All over the Dolomites avalanches poured from the ridges: some 10,000 soldiers found their tombs beneath blocks of ice. On the Marmolada, 400 perished in a single snowslide. The resourceful armies learned to aim their shells at high cornices and unleash avalanches on enemy camps. The supply trains, so vital to the front lines, could not operate: countless men died of hypothermia. According to Lancedelli, fully half the fatalities in the whole Dolomite campaign came during that terrible winter.

The death toll from the war can never be accurately calculated. Too many *ignoti* died; too many were never buried. Even today, in obscure patches of forest, hikers occasionally stumble across skeletons from the Great War. Lancedelli's mother once found a pair of old boots in a grassy field: out of them protruded a pair of leg bones.

Though the Dolomites are a range of savage, soaring peaks, it was on two of the gentlest that the most important struggles of all took place. Thanks to an accident of border geography, the single summit the Italians held at the onset of the war was the south peak of Monte Piana. But the Austrians held the north peak, and for more than two years, the bitterest combat raged across a green plateau where sheep once grazed.

You can drive to the summit of Monte Piana, as nearly all today's visitors do. I chose instead to climb 1,500 feet from the Valle di Rinbianco on the southeast. It was another perfect day, with a cobalt sky and a light breeze that cut the heat. Embarking from an ancient dairy farm, I zigzagged up a trail toward the Piana plateau. This path had been the Italian supply route, and I admired the careful craft that had terraced hairpins up a slag-strewn gully so that wheeled vehicles could lug the machines of death to the plateau. When I emerged on top, I felt empathically prepared: like the *Alpini* seventy-five years before, I had climbed a pastoral trail, lulled by the scent of flowers and the cadence of birdsong, only to plunge—so I could imagine—into the apocalypse of hand-to-hand combat. The trenches, tunnels, barbed-wire fences, and barracks bespoke the struggle. Some 7,000 soldiers had died here.

The Col di Lana is a featureless peak that looks transplanted from one of the more humdrum ranges of Colorado, but it lay at the most strategic corner in all the Dolomites. By the second year of the war, thwarted time and again in their charges on Austrian lines, the Italians had perfected a fiendish new technique: tunneling beneath the enemy to blow up his strongholds. On Col di Lana, a ninety-two-meter tunnel allowed the Italians to lay 5,500 kilograms of explosives beneath the very trenches of the Austrians on the summit. On April 18, 1916, they blew the top of the mountain off, killing 110 soldiers and wounding another 170 in an instant. Yet even this stunning coup failed to clinch the struggle for the mountain. By the end, 8,000 soldiers had died on the Col di Lana, the bloodiest battlefield of all.

The burnt cone the explosion left has healed little over the years: Col di Lana looks like an extinct volcano. The day I hiked up the mountain was the worst of my two-week sojourn. A pelting rain turned to snow as I climbed, with the wind lashing out of the east. Despite my rain gear, I was soon soaked to the skin. The scars of the war are muted on the Col di Lana, the trenches muffled in grass, the fatal tunnel sealed with dirt. On the summit I hunkered on the lee side of the tiny chapel that commemorates the debacle of 1916, and tried to eat lunch. Soon I was shivering with the first hints of hypothermia. This in July! I felt an awe for the soldiers who had wintered over here in far worse conditions, with sharper threats than cold to worry about.

The labor of the Italian tunneling was infernal: working around the clock in six-hour shifts, men knelt, naked from the waist up, caked with a white muck of dolomite dust and water, as they forced the *perforatrice*, a giant rotating drill, against the unyielding stone. A train of men behind the drillers passed sacks of debris back to the last portal. The drill gained fourteen and a half meters a day: the Lagazuoi tunnel took three months to finish.

A week after my rain-soaked ascent of the Col di Lana, I turned my headlamp on and entered the 700-meter tunnel through the Tofana di Rozes, emerging at the Castelletto, a sharp spur of the mountain that had sheltered the crucial Austrian sniper's nest. The soldiers here had heard the Italian drilling. The dishes on their makeshift tables rattled with the vibration. The sound—a grinding "rrr rrr tschrr tschrr"—left the Austrians nerve-racked and sleepless. But the men were trapped on their eyrie, surrounded by enemy, and there was little they could do. They found themselves holding their breaths on the hour and half-hour, assuming the blast would be timed by the vertical minute-hand. In Trenker's novel, Dimaï tells his fellow soldiers, "As long as they keep on drilling, comrades, we have nothing to worry about. It's when they stop. . . . "

On July 9, 1916, the Castelletto blew to pieces. Some forty Austrians died under the boulders. As I prowled across the small saddle where the explosion had gone off, I could see the broken boards of the barracks peeping from beneath tons of shattered talus. On the side of a huge boulder, I found a haunting memorial: beneath a small iron cross commemorating one of the dead, someone had hung an old tin can filled with apparently human bones.

A year after the Castelletto, the crest of the Lagazuoi burst in a tremendous explosion, but only after the Austrians had evacuated it. The 1,100-meter tunnel (longest of the war) by which the Italians crept toward this colossal deed has been preserved as a tourist path, secured with handrails. Yet as I snaked up its helical passage, each time I emerged at a portal to peer suddenly out over the vertical void, the severity of it all took my breath away.

Even the great explosions settled little. All the Italian gains in the Dolomites were negated in 1918 by a single disastrous defeat, at Caporetto, far from the mountains in what is today Slovenia. By 1918, the Dolomite front itself, once pivotal to the war, had become irrelevant to its larger course. In the end, the Allies won because Germany and Austria were spread too thin on too many fronts. After the war, diplomats shoved the border north to the Brenner Pass, where it rests today.

The sleep of the *Ampezzani* still stirs to nightmare at the memory of all the futile bloodshed. As Signor Alverà said to me one night, "The only result was death." Even Loris Lancedelli, for whom every bent nail found on a meadow has value, shakes his head in sorrow. "Too many men died," he says, "for a meter of earth that meant nothing."

HIGH ON THE FORAME, above the *passerella*, I paused on a patch of steep scree. At my feet lay a telltale scattering of objects. A sodden tangle of gray-green cloth, snagged in barbed wire; part of a black boot sole; the leather buckle of a belt; a small glass flask, broken in half, purple with age; and there, all but hidden among the pebbles, a single bullet, sans cartridge. It seemed unarguable that an Italian soldier had died on this spot. The bottle might have held rum or marsala, with which the *Alpini* warmed their lonely bivouacs. Gray-green was the color of the Italian uniform.

I picked up the bullet, put it in my pocket, and headed on. The summit of the Forame, only a few meters above, meant something to me, though less than it had to my vanished predecessor.

In the distance, crest after Dolomite crest ranged toward the azure horizon. The sun was warm on my shoulders, the air tasted rich in my lungs, and the mountains brimmed with peace.

LOST CITY OF THE
LUKACHUKAIS

"The Lost City of the Lukachukais—now there is a legend to conjure with!" wrote Ann Axtell Morris in 1933. "Of all Southwestern enigmas, it is the most mysterious. And of all Southwestern treasures, it is the most desired."

As Morris told the tale, in 1909 a pair of Franciscan missionaries set out from Farmington, New Mexico, determined to penetrate the red-rock wilderness across the Arizona border, beyond the soaring monolith of Shiprock. Among these canyons and mountains, which few Anglos had ever seen, lived unacculturated Navajos, whose souls the fathers hoped to save.

One night, as they sat beside their campfire, the Franciscans were startled by the disappearance of their Navajo guide. Minutes later, the man returned, carrying a huge ceramic jar under his arm. One of the padres recognized the jar as a masterly Anasazi pot, fired at least 600 years before.

The padres asked their guide where he had found the jar. The Navajo would neither tell them, nor allow the Franciscans to purchase the object. But he told them of a trailless box canyon, seldom visited by Navajos, at the head of which, on a high ledge, stood a huge, pristine Anasazi ruin. From this site, the pot had come.

239

By the 1930s, when Ann Morris first committed the legend to print, the Lost City of the Lukachukais had become an archaeologist's El Dorado. The writer's husband, Earl Morris, one of the leading Anasazi scholars of his day, spent years looking in vain for the Lost City.

In another version of the legend, the fathers had seen the cliff dwelling from afar, comparing it favorably to the wonders of Mesa Verde, but had had no time to approach the ruin. On subsequent journeys, they had never been able to find the site again.

Morris's fruitless search had pushed him to explore the Lukachukais further. On rugged, month-long expeditions in 1930 and 1931, he had dug in a dozen caves, finding the pit houses, baskets, and spear-throwers of the Basketmaker people, Anasazi who lived before 750 A.D., ancestors to the more visible cliff dwellers. Morris's pioneering work in the Lukachukais promised to be some of the most important research yet performed in the Southwest.

But the legend of the Lost City receded further into myth. And Morris himself, after his death in 1956, took on a legendary aura of his own. His portrait on the cover of Florence and Robert Lister's biography of the man, in battered fedora and denim shirt, is rumored to have served as the model for Indiana Jones.

Long an enthusiast of remote Anasazi ruins, I had followed Earl Morris's footsteps across the Southwest, from Canyon de Chelly to Aztec Ruins to the Ute Mountain Tribal Park south of Mesa Verde. The legend of the Lost City had gotten under my skin. In obscure documents, I had found further clues to the whereabouts of the elusive cliff dwelling. I decided to round up a few cronies and make my own search for the Lost City.

By 1996, there was virtually no chance that a ruin as grand as Cliff Palace could have escaped detection for a century. But the Lukachukais, spreading across an out-of-the-way corner of the vast Navajo Reservation, remained one of the least-visited regions in all the Southwest. A glance at the maps made it clear that the range promised months of blithe exploring.

On the one hand, I hoped to find, if not the Lost City itself, the wellsprings of the legend. On the other, I would be happy to tread once more in the footsteps of Earl Morris. And in any case, deep in the Lukachukais, I would be hiking canyons still all but unknown to Anglos and to archaeology.

BEFORE HEADING INTO THE DESERT, I stopped in Boulder, Colorado, to meet Joe Ben Wheat. Eighty years old, a retired professor of anthropology at the University of Colorado, Wheat is one of the few colleagues still alive who knew Earl Morris well.

"Earl was a great guy," Wheat told me, "but he wasn't a bit like Indiana

Jones. He was very careful and precise with language. Even in casual conversation, he measured every word.

"In the field, Earl had the instincts of a pothunter and the scientific control to make archaeology out of what he found. He just had this quiet ability. He knew who he was."

It was Morris's influence that had persuaded the young Wheat to become an archaeologist. "In his own quiet way, Earl generated excitement. You could feel the force of his intellect."

Yet from Wheat's recollections and the Listers' biography, I gleaned a picture of Morris as a melancholic who felt he had fallen far short of his goals. No one ever dug more sites than Morris, but, like many another archaeologist, he found writing an onerous task. Toward the end of his life, he was plagued with guilt over the fieldwork he had failed to write up.

Indeed, Morris never published any account of either his 1930 or his 1931 expedition in the Lukachukais. Much of the content of his Basketmaker discoveries thus died with him. And in this silence from the grave, the mystery of the Franciscan legend deepens—for Morris himself, as far as I could learn, never wrote a word about the Lost City.

My perusal of maps and museum notes had convinced me that the place to look for the phantom village was in a canyon called Tsegi-ho-chon. In the 1920s, Indians had told John Wetherill, the only trader in northeast Arizona, about this canyon full of ruins. Wetherill would serve as Morris's guide in both 1930 and 1931. And Charles L. Bernheimer, the wealthy New Yorker who bankrolled the 1930 expedition, wrote that the Navajo name signified "Ugly or Difficult Rocks." During my own trip, I was to receive a much richer understanding of the name.

With a pair of friends, *National Geographic* photographer Ira Block and horsepacker/amateur archaeologist Fred Blackburn, I headed south on dirt roads from a gas station on Highway 160, to make a two-day reconnaissance of Tsegi-ho-chon. Simply finding the canyon proved tricky: we got lost twice before pitching camp at sunset on the north rim of the defile.

During a long, marvelous next day, Fred, Ira, and I hiked fifteen miles up and down Tsegi-ho-chon and its tributaries. In these lower stretches of the canyon, an inch-deep stream meandered between parabolic walls, some 100 to 200 feet high, carved over the eons out of sweeping red sandstone.

Navajos today run sheep through the lower canyon, which is grazed to a dry stubble. Here and there we found what Fred called *jedi*—bright rags affixed to posts or fences to act as mystic scarecrows, charming the coyotes away from the sheep.

We found four small cliff dwellings tucked into south-facing alcoves in side canyons. But the glory of Tsegi-ho-chon was its rock art, carved and painted on the canvases of the enclosing walls. The oldest figures (usually those highest off the ground) had been limned by the Anasazi. Particularly impressive were a number of hulking humanoids with broad shoulders, triangular bodies, and huge dangling hands and feet. These, we knew, had been inscribed during Archaic and early Basketmaker times, before 500 A.D.

But there was also an abundance of Navajo rock art, more than I had ever seen before. Athapaskan nomads from the Canadian subarctic, the Navajos had entered the Southwest around 1400 A.D., a hundred years after the Anasazi had abandoned the Four Corners. Navajos may have penetrated the Lukachukais as early as the eighteenth century. Certainly much of the Navajo rock art we saw looked old. The artists' favorite theme was horses, lovingly etched down to the hairs on the manes. I was beguiled by a series of eerie *yei b' cheis*—sticklike supernatural beings in charge of corn and fertility.

At the end of our jaunt, we discovered a shortcut into the middle Tsegi-ho-chon, saving six miles of approach. As we walked back in the late sun toward our car camp, footsore but exhilarated, meadowlarks and white-throated swifts darted before our path. The cottonwoods were just beginning to bud, and a few globe willows in full leaf blazed like green balloons floating in the air.

Our reconnaissance had saved us a lot of unnecessary toil. We had glimpsed the upper canyon. Sixty-five years after Earl Morris's last visit, our own probe into the Lukachukais was about to begin.

A FEW DAYS LATER, we retured to Tsegi-ho-chon in full force. Joining Fred, Ira, and me were Bryan Harvey, a young videographer with whom Ira hoped to make a film about our trip; Dennis Gilpin and Kelly Hays, husband and wife archaeologists who had worked elsewhere in the Lukachukais but never explored this canyon; and Wilson King, our Navajo guide. We had recruited Wilson out of Cove, an idyllic little town on the other side of the Lukachukais to the south. Though his home lay only about eight miles from the head of Tsegi-ho-chon, Wilson had never been in this part of the country, nor had any of his friends. So tortured is the Lukachukai slickrock that it can take a journey of 100 miles to go from one canyon to another only a few miles apart as the crow flies.

Fred used his two horses to pack our considerable baggage: besides Ira and Bryan's camera equipment, I had brought a full rack of rock-climbing gear and two ropes, hoping to use my skills as an alpinist to reach the more inaccessible cliff dwellings. I knew from many previous trips to the Southwest that the Anasazi had been climbing geniuses, whose dwellings sometimes lay on ledges you could figure out virtually no way to reach today.

We loaded up Shamrock, a chestnut Missouri Foxtrotter, and Rico, a dappled gray-and-white Appaloosa, then set out on foot up the canyon. As soon as we passed beyond the range of our reconnaissance, we recognized an alarming fact. The inch-deep, steady stream we had strode along a few days before issued from a spring in the valley floor. Above the spring, the canyon was dry as dust. For four miles we hiked onward, increasingly conscious of a dawning thirst, as we found not a single drop of water. All across the Southwest, the previous winter had delivered almost no snow, and everyone was predicting a tough summer for cattle, sheep, and crops. We began to worry whether we would find *any* water—the irreducible sine qua non for desert survival—during our week-long journey.

The splendor of the canyon distracted us from our water anxieties. As we headed south, the surrounding walls grew taller, until 300 feet of surging rock—fins, towers, bulging domes—separated us from the rims above.

In six miles of travel, we discovered half a dozen Anasazi sites. Several of these were intriguing, and in one we had a sudden shock of recognition. The ruin, we realized, was the same one Morris had called Archers Cave. For the first time, we correlated our own position with the footsteps of our predecessors in 1930.

Archers was covered with both Anasazi and Navajo rock art: black, white, and yellow handprints; a great painted white bird that Kelly swore was a macaw, indicating Anasazi contact with Mexico; a memorable Navajo battle scene, replete with firearms and dead bodies; *yei b' cheis*, one of which Wilson recognized from the ephemeral sand paintings he had seen Navajo shamans craft; the inevitable horses; and even a 1920s jalopy, detailed down to the bulging headlamps.

The most striking feature about the ruin was a two-story front wall festooned not with windows but with small loopholes. Morris's party had named the site after these holes, imagining ancient warriors shooting arrows through them, but Dennis and Kelly argued that the loopholes more likely served as viewing tubes through which hidden dignitaries could watch some sacred ceremony in the plaza below.

We pushed on into the waning afternoon. At last a trickle of water appeared, seeping out of the arroyo bank on the right. But it was not a good place to camp. We hurried on up-canyon, mistakenly believing we would find water above. Instead Tsegi-ho-chon dried up once more.

At last we stopped to establish base camp. The site was sublime, at the junction of two tributaries with the main canyon, on a bench covered with sagebrush and greasewood. Two geologic anomalies—a toothlike pinnacle of sandstone, and a slender "needle's eye" arch—guarded our camp.

But there was no water. In the end, for the next week, Fred and Wilson

243

had to ride daily a mile back down-canyon to the fugitive trickle, where they filled every water bottle we had.

That night, we sat around a small fire of greasewood branches, which burn hot and smokeless. Coyotes howled in the darkness. I felt a deep contentment in the knowledge that only a handful of Anglos before me had ever camped in this convoluted canyon, which we had only begun to discover.

LINGERING LATE AROUND the campfire, I was treated to Wilson's explication of all the shades of meaning embodied in the name of our canyon (which Bernheimer had breezily glossed as "Ugly or Difficult Rocks").

"Tsegi-ho-chon," Wilson said, pronouncing it with a Navajo inflection that defies transcription. "It means literally, 'It doesn't work any more.' But it also means, 'The rock that has been destroyed,' or 'The rock that has ruins in it.' Or even just, 'It's been ruined.'

"I guess I'd translate 'Tsegi-ho-chon' as 'Inside of a rock that was being ruined.'" Wilson stuck another greasewood branch on the fire. "Basically, it's like a scary place."

The next morning, we loaded daypacks with lunch, clothing, and bottles full of precious water from the trickle, then headed up the main fork of the branching canyon. Fred and Wilson followed on horseback.

As we pushed south, the canyon narrowed around us and the walls soared to a height of 400 feet. In the distance, a deer traversed the draw; then a coyote loped across a slickrock slab, seemingly oblivious to us. Farther along, seven wild burros peered over the bushes to watch us pass. The day before, as we entered the canyon, a Navajo woman he met along the trail had told Fred about the burros. "They've been there for years," she said. "Nobody can catch 'em." Near its head, the valley made a sudden turn to the left. In a glance, I could see that Tsegi-ho-chon ended in a true box canyon, where vertical walls prohibited escape.

But it was not the canyon itself that took my breath away. One hundred fifty feet above us on the left, ranging across a long, concave ledge sheltered by a gigantic overhang, stood the rooms of a spacious Anasazi town. All the ruins we had seen coming up the canyon were dwarfed by this lordly village.

At first, the ledge seemed impossible to reach: beneath it, the rock caved away in yet another overhang. But as I approached the only part of the cliff that was less than vertical, I found exactly what I was looking for.

A series of shallow, cupped steps led up the sixty-degree precipice. The first several steps had been improved by moderns wielding metal tools. The remainder, above, had weathered over more than 700 years to mere scallops that would barely take the toes of one foot.

It was an Anasazi hand-and-toe trail, carved by some ancient engineer wielding a quartzite pounding stone. And it had once served as the ladder to the village, up which men, women with pots on their heads, and bare-foot children had scampered daily.

Nervously, I set out to climb the eroded staircase. Forty feet up, I nearly quit, for a piece of cliff had broken away, leaving three feet of blank rock. But the sight of the lofty city was too enticing. I pushed delicately on, until I reached the lip of the ledge.

My friends below heard my jubilant cries, and their envy forestalled more than a cursory visit. I climbed back down the hand-and-toe trail, dashed the two miles to base camp, retrieved a rope, and hurried back to the high cliff dwelling.

By early afternoon, after I had belayed each of my colleagues up the hand-and-toe trail, all seven of us stood in the magnificent ruin. There followed three hours of rapturous discovery.

We counted some forty rooms, of which a remarkable ten were kivas, underground chambers possibly reserved for religious rites. "This has to be the ceremonial center for the whole damned canyon!" Kelly exclaimed.

The ruin, to be sure, was no Cliff Palace. (The crown jewel of Mesa Verde boasts four-story towers and some 200 rooms.) But the site was so dramatic that I could well imagine early travelers such as the Franciscan priests sight-ing the stone-and-mud town from afar—perhaps from the mesa opposite—and being able to divine no way of getting to it. Perhaps here was the ruin that had given birth to the legend of the Lost City.

It was not so much the size as the exquisite preservation of the site that dazzled us. Of all its rooms, the masterpiece was a big, rectangular kiva with an intact roof made of wooden poles, shredded juniper bark, and mud; six pristine "banquettes," benchlike storage niches in the walls; and a perfect chimney, deflector slab (to regulate drafts), and hearth in the floor. None of us had ever seen a better preserved kiva.

Dennis was beside himself. "Holy mackerel," he whispered. "This is staggering. I feel this is exactly what the kiva looked like in 1275. This is just a treasure trove of information."

The rock art was as rich as what we had found at Archers Cave. And on one wall, we saw an inscription from the Bernheimer expedition, with the initials:

J. W. — E. H. M. — 30.

We had found the record of Earl Morris's visit, sixty-six years before—as well as that of his peerless guide, John Wetherill.

THAT EVENING IN CAMP, looking over my notes, I figured out that the cliff city on the high ledge had been named Promontory Ruin by Morris's 1930 team. But once again, the ambiguity of the record befuddled me. Had Morris speculated, as I would six-and-a-half decades later, whether an early glimpse of Promontory had inspired the legend of the Lost City? The only day-by-day account of the 1930 expedition I had been able to find was Bernheimer's typescript diary, which I had discovered in a museum archive. And Bernheimer never mentioned the Lost City.

The diary, however, disclosed other tantalizing hints. Before the 1920s, the Lukachukais had been off limits to all Anglos. In Tsegi-ho-chon, the expedition had felt sure, as Bernheimer wrote, that they had managed "to penetrate a canyon no white people had ever entered." Yet the party's Navajo guide told them about "a hunter by the name of Lang" who had tried to probe Tsegi-ho-chon around the turn of the century, only to be chased out by Navajos.

This scrap of diary entry set off bells in Fred's head. The passion of our horsepacker's life is to find inscriptions scrawled on Anasazi cave walls by the first Anglo visitors. Fred knew Charles Lang well—in fact, he had interviewed Lang's son when the man was in his nineties. But Lang himself, who had been a crony of John Wetherill, remained an enigma. What Fred wouldn't give to find some firsthand account of that daring solo thrust into the Lukachukais! Had Lang been the first white man to see Promontory Ruin?

In any event, it seemed likely that only a handful of Anglos had climbed up to Promontory since 1930. One of the finest Anasazi ruins any of us had ever seen lay in such an obscure place that it went years at a time without a visit.

Alone among the seven of us, Wilson had entered the ruin with misgivings. In fact, I had overheard him mutter, "I hope these guys forgive me."

The relationship of Navajos to the Anasazi ruins that are scattered all over their reservation is a complex one. These "houses of the dead" are not simply taboo for Navajos; an immense power for both good and evil haunts the crumbling room-blocks.

Beside the campfire, Wilson told us what had happened to him the year before. Hired as a worker on an archaeological dig in the path of a proposed highway, on his first day Wilson had unearthed the skeleton of a fifteen-year-old Anasazi girl. Two months later, he woke up one morning unable to walk. "I had to crawl across the floor," he said quietly. "It hurt so bad.

"I went to a medicine man in Red Rock. He said there was lots of stuff that needed to be done on me, so the thing wouldn't affect my wife and kids." The medicine man performed a rite, and suddenly Wilson could walk.

"He said, 'It will go away now, but it will come back again.'" Wilson paused. "After my leg got better, my wife lost our child when she was five months pregnant."

We sat in silence around the fire, until I asked our guide how today's visit to Promontory Ruin had felt to him. It was the first cliff dwelling Wilson had ever entered. "The place jumped on me," Wilson said, choosing his words carefully. "I thought, 'Should I go up, or stay down below?' It seemed OK to go up.

"But then when you found that leg bone—" Wilson nodded at me. In the midden, or trash dump, below one of the rooms at Promontory, I had stumbled upon the thigh bone and vertebrae of a human. An ancient burial had eroded to the surface.

"When I go home," Wilson went on, "I'll change clothes, and wash everything I have before I handle my kids. And I won't tell a lot of people about the place—just a few friends. I'll keep it to myself."

Just before I had belayed him down the hand-and-toe trail, Wilson had complained of a sharp pain in his knee. He was sure it had been caused by visiting the ruin. Now, taking Ibuprofen every few hours, he kept the pain at bay.

A dyed-in-the-wool rationalist, I privately dismissed Wilson's tales as coincidence or even superstition. But there was no mistaking the man's somber mood. Later, I would have reason to rethink my skepticism.

ON OUR FOURTH DAY in Tsegi-ho-chon, Dennis and Kelly had to hike out to attend a conference. We were sorry to see them go, with their archaeological expertise. Among their insights into the ruins we had seen was the recognition that, in terms of the dwellings' masonry style and the designs on the hundreds of potsherds we had found in the dirt, this canyon owed everything to the influence of Mesa Verde, fifty miles to the northeast. Surprisingly, the great Kayenta centers, equally near, such as Betatakin and Keet Seel, seemed to have exerted little pull on the Lukachukais.

The remaining five of us still had much to explore. On horseback, Fred and Bryan circled far to the east, up a tributary that was actually larger than the main canyon. They found four beautiful arches and windows in the sandstone, but no way to escape what amounted to another, colossal box canyon. High in one draw they came across a wild bull, gone feral like the burros many years ago. Rico and Shamrock shied and retreated in the face of this monarch of the wild.

Meanwhile, Wilson and I set out in another branch of the eastern tributary to find a way to the tableland above. We knew that Morris in both

247

1930 and 1931 had started his expeditions near Cove—Wilson's home town—on the far side of the Lukachukai divide. To get to Tsegi-ho-chon, they had climbed up to Cove Mesa at 7,000 feet, then looped far to the north before entering the labyrinthine canyon roughly where we had. But on one jaunt, their Navajo guide had chased a runaway horse almost all the way back to Cove, then on his return found a difficult but rideable shortcut back into Tsegi-ho-chon near our base camp.

For three miles Wilson and I pushed up the tributary. There was no break in the enclosing precipices. Then, with binoculars, I spotted a chute that seemed to split two vertical cliffs.

It took a nasty bushwhack to reach and climb the chute, but it "went." At the very top, I saw a few steps hacked out of the bedrock with picks—classic Navajo trail work. It seemed unlikely that a horse could navigate this treacherous passageway, but evidently horses had.

We sailed up onto Cove Mesa. A stiff breeze chilled us, but the views were stunning—east to the great volcanic plug of Shiprock, west all the way to the buttes and towers of Monument Valley. Hawks spiraled on thermals above us. We crossed a pair of old Navajo driftwood fences, then began to see recent prints of sheep. Wilson, homesick to be so close to his wife and children, tried to think which of his acquaintances ran herds so far up on Cove Mesa.

Pushing on south, we came in sight of a small shack. A man puttered about the yard. In true Navajo fashion, he ignored us as we approached. Later he admitted he was startled, even alarmed, to see strangers coming from the north, where no one ever appeared.

Wilson chatted with the man in Navajo. At last he invited us in and served us cups of spring water and coffee. We shared our lunch with him. His name was Jonathan Lee, out of Two Gray Hills; he was spending a month on Cove Mesa, tending a relative's herd of thirty-five sheep.

We had hired Wilson not for his familiarity with the country, which he knew no better than we, but for his take on what we saw and for his service as a liaison to the locals. We had an official hiking permit from the Navajo Nation in Window Rock, but that scrap of paper carried little value in the outback. Had I, an Anglo, arrived alone at his windy shack, Jonathan Lee might have been downright hostile. As it was, the talk between Wilson and Jonathan partook of the dark and the supernatural: about a strange, bare-chested runner with long white hair many had seen but none had talked to; about a giant snake that lived a few miles to the north on the mesa, the ground around whose den was riddled with big cistlike holes into which a man might fall.

Late that afternoon, Wilson and I forced our way back into Tsegi-ho-chon by the middle tributary. It took a blind, thrashing bushwhack and some tricky climbing—definitely not a horsepacking route. Just as I began to wonder how many humans had preceded us into this brush-choked gorge, we came to a pourover—an overhanging lip of sandstone in the valley floor that portended a dead end. But on the right, across a frighteningly steep slab, led a pecked trail of Anasazi steps.

The ancients had been everywhere.

FOR OUR LAST FULL DAY in Tsegi-ho-chon, I had saved my most ambitious effort. Not far from camp, we had spotted three high caves, 200 feet above the valley, 100 feet below the rim of Cove Mesa. With binoculars, I could see that the ceiling of each cave was covered with soot—a dead giveaway that the Anasazi had used them, probably as living shelters. At the mouth of one of the caves, we saw masonry and roof beams: Fred thought the half-hidden structure might be a kiva.

In all likelihood, no Anglo or Navajo had ever been to these caves—for it would obviously take a technical climb to get to the ledge that linked the three sites. After reconnoitering the base of the 200-foot cliff, I saw that there was only one conceivable approach. A steep corner in the sandstone snaked up left, then right, to the ledge. Unlike the staircase that led to Promontory Ruin, however, this corner was devoid of pounded hand-and-toe holds.

With my ropes and high-tech climbing gear, I thought I might be able to scale the corner. I tied Wilson into the other end of my lead rope, anchored him to a juniper tree, and taught him how to belay, while Bryan filmed and Ira photographed. Wilson looked apprehensive.

As soon as I left the ground, I realized the climb was going to be dangerous. There were plenty of holds, but the sandstone was so rotten, great chunks came loose in my hands. I managed twenty-five feet of ascent: because of the poor rock, what looked like easy climbing turned out to be hard and scary.

I reached a small platform from which the corner angled at seventy degrees up to the right. Here I had hoped a vertical crack would allow me to place protection. But I saw at once that the corner was seamless, without even a pencil-thin crack.

There were holds, but all it would take was for one piece of sandstone to prise off under my weight, and I would plunge all the way down to Wilson's useless belay. It was what climbers call a "death route."

The only reasonable course was to back off. In that instant, as I raised my leg, I felt a hot stab of pain shoot through my right knee. "Damn!" I yelled down. "I've pulled a ligament, or something." In the first twenty-five feet of climbing, I had made an awkward long step, shifting all my weight onto a small hold high under my right foot.

Now, as I climbed down to the ground, feeling inept and vexed, the pain grew worse. Making the awkward step, I must have pulled or twisted something in the knee.

I left my gear in a forlorn pile at the base of the cliff while we scrambled up to one last Anasazi cave—this one a "pure" Basketmaker site that, Fred thought, might well harbor burials under the drifted dust. My knee felt worse and worse.

"So how the hell did the Anasazi get up there?" I asked Fred, miffed at my failure to reach the three high caves.

"Log ladders," he answered. "That'd be my guess."

An hour later, packing up my climbing gear, I noticed an old dead tree lying at the foot of the corner. Sorting out my hardware earlier, I had stepped across the tree without even looking at it.

"My God, Fred, look!" I blurted out. "You called it!" For the dead tree was indeed an Anasazi ladder. Ancient notches in the wood, chopped with a stone axe, had served as footholds. So perishable are these ladders that in years of prowling around the Southwest, Fred and I had found only three or four apiece.

But we knew that the Anasazi had been virtuosi of dead-tree-ladder technique. Archaeologists had found these notched logs hundreds of feet off the ground, propped insecurely on some mortared platform. No doubt a series of such logs had given the Anasazi access to their three high caves. Only this, the initial log, had survived the decay of the centuries.

As I limped back to camp, I marveled at Anasazi daring. And I recognized for the first time that in one odd sense stone-axe-cut dead trees were superior to the snazziest modern rock-climbing gear. With all my nuts and friends, I still had to climb the rock itself, which here was treacherously loose. With an Anasazi ladder, bad rock didn't matter: you climbed the log, not the cliff.

In the dangerous corner that led up to the three high caves, the ancients had eschewed a hand-and-toe trail, probably because the rock was so friable. Instead they had hauled custom-made ladders into place. Even so, the daily ascent and descent must have been terrifying.

THAT EVENING, OUR LAST IN Tsegi-ho-chon Canyon, the five of us huddled around the campfire, warding off the chill of a sharp wind out of the northwest. Staring at the red coals, I pondered the three high caves I had failed so utterly to reach and explore.

The obvious question such ruins provoke is—Why? Why build and live in eyries so difficult and dangerous to reach? All over the Four Corners, especially during the last century before the 1300 A.D. abandonment, the Anasazi retreated to such cliff dwellings, ones that could be entered only by hand-and-toe trails or log ladders.

The obvious explanation—that the retreat was defensive, in response to some new threat to the people's existence—seems after all to be the likely one. Yet among archaeologists, the defensive theory has spurred decades of bitter controvesy.

From the discovery of Cliff Palace in 1888 on, scholars postulated that the Anasazi had holed up against raids by nomadic invaders such as Navajos, Utes, and Apaches. Yet excellent research during the last thirty years argues that none of these nomads reached the Southwest before 1400 A.D.—a century after the Anasazi abandonment. In the face of these findings, the defensive hypothesis lapsed for a while into limbo. Within the last decade, however, it has come back to the fore.

The Anasazi, we now believe, did indeed retreat into high cliff dwelling in response to a marauding enemy. But that enemy was themselves. During extended thirteenth-century droughts, the water table of the farmland dropped, and the big game were hunted into near-extinction, fragmenting the Anasazi into bands that may have raided and killed each other. There is new evidence even of cannibalism among the people.

The high caves I had tried in vain to reach had stirred me with their majestic inaccessibility. Yet I had to recognize that, whatever beauty hung about those cliff dwellings, it was a beauty born of a daily, gnawing fear.

That last night, the pain in my knee throbbed. When I had pulled up my trousers leg to look, I had discovered a splinter embedded in my knee-cap. Using his Swiss Army knife tweezers, Fred had dug it out. We were both disturbed to find that the splinter had gone straight in half an inch. During my rough bushwhack with Wilson the day before, the splinter had evidently pierced my trousers and entered my knee without my feeling it.

"I wonder if you haven't got an infection," Fred mused. Two days later, in the emergency room in Cortez, Colorado, his hunch was confirmed. The splinter had been the conduit for a deep anaerobic infection. Left untreated, the doctor warned, the infection could go into the joint, and I might even lose the leg. I was put on massive doses of antibiotics, but it was three weeks before the swelling subsided and the pain went away.

Though he was kind enough to say nothing, I knew that Wilson had a different understanding of what had happened to my knee. It was no coincidence that I had felt the pain suddenly as I had started to climb to the high caves. Just as Wilson had awakened one morning in Cove, unable to walk, after he had dug up the skeleton of the fifteen-year-old Anasazi girl, so my hubris in attempting to reach the forbidden caves had everything to do with my own crippling.

That night I had to take a strong pain-killer to sleep. The wind increased to a gale, and the temperature plummeted. At 2:00 A.M. I woke hearing rain on the tent fly, but when I opened the door, a driving sleet hit me in the face.

In the morning, our snowstruck camp looked like something out of an arctic survival tale. With numb fingers, keeping our backs to the gale, we packed up the horses, cramming the panniers with frozen tents and soggy sleeping bags. Only three days before, we had hiked in T-shirts and shorts!

I could barely walk. Popping another pain-killer, I faced into the storm and started the long hobble out to civilization.

Despite the pain and the storm, I left the Lukachukais full of richly contradictory feelings. For a week we had had one of the most spectacular corners of Arizona to ourselves. Yet the place, Fred, Wilson, and I agreed, was distinctly spooky. We had not unraveled the legend of the Lost City, but in Promontory Ruin we might well have plumbed its source. (Yet there are many other canyons in the Lukachukais, and a man could spend his lifetime exploring all of them. . . .)

As for the timeless conundrum of the Anasazi achievement—we left that behind us, too, shining like a star wreathed in a cloud. What dwellings, what artifacts, what clues to lost meaning lay inside those three high alcoves, unseen by anyone since the last ancient climbed down the teetering ladders more than 700 years ago? We had pushed hard into the Lukachukais, only to halt in awe at the edge of a mystery—a mystery that had once, for the Anasazi, been as plain as daily life.

LA PROVENCE IGNORÉE

Below me to the left, a soaring fin of rock peaked in a tiny ledge. If I could reach that perch, I could stare into the very bottom of the abyss. It was a sunny day in September, and the trail on which I strode westward might have made for a pleasant half-day's hike. But always on my left hung the chasm, one of the most tortured I had ever beheld; like a dark crime half-remembered, it nagged at my equanimity, demanding that I face it head-on.

I left the trail and scrambled through tough, wiry bushes that tore at my clothing. Down toward the fin, then along its airy gangplank, the limestone gritty and sharp under my fingers. I swung around a corner over the void, and suddenly the rock I was grasping with my right hand came loose. My balance pivoted on the edge of falling, but I held on with my left hand.

I sat down on the ledge to catch my breath. Having climbed mountains for thirty-four years, I might have thought I was used to the precipice beneath my feet. But the moment of lost balance—not quite a near-fall, but closer than one likes to flirt with—reminded me of the natural world's terrifying indifference to human aspirations. My hands shook as I gazed down the thousand-foot gorge to the turquoise river pounding through the distant gloom.

With two companions, I had been hiking the Sentier du Bastidon above the Grand Canyon of the Verdon, in the middle of Provence in southeastern France. It was our mission to spend two weeks probing the wild, the ragged, the semi-mythical at the heart of one of the strangest and most splendid regions in Europe. Ours was not the Provence of the topless beaches of the Côte d'Azur, of the papal palace of Avignon, of the Promenades at Nice and Cannes. Ours was the Haute Provence, a land of stern crags and lonely valleys; a land gentled by vineyards and olive groves, but haunted everywhere by ancient ruins and laconic legends; "a fierce, sad, formidable country," in the words of the English traveler James Pope-Hennessy.

Though seldom precisely defined, the Haute Provence covers a region roughly bordered by the town of Briançon on the north, by the Italian border on the east, by the low coastal massifs of the Alps on the south, and by the Rhône Valley on the west. This sprawling quadrangle enfolds some of the most convoluted topography on the continent, ranging from slot canyons slashed through limestone plateaus—the "Gorges," as they are called, of Cians, la Nesque, Valabres, Daluis—to the high, glaciated summits of the Alpes Maritimes. Across such prodigies of geography, inhabitants ranging back to the Paleolithic have left their runes, among them the troglodyte dwellings of Lamanon, the miracle-working Fountain of the Vaucluse, the iron chain linking mountaintops above Moustiers hung by a Crusader to thank God for his deliverance from the infidels, and the hundreds of *cabanons pointus* (pointed huts) near Forcalquier, built by farmers out of dry stone cleared from their fields in a fashion that defies gravity.

Most enigmatic of all are the prehistoric testaments to vanished pagan faiths. On a previous trip to the Haute Provence, I had stumbled across a dolmen in the woods: a huge, hutlike enclosure made out of six giant slabs of granite. Dolmens and rows of standing stones, lost in the forests all over Haute Provence, date from the late Stone Age, from 3000 to 4600 B.C. But as to who built them, and why, even the canniest archaeologists can only guess in the dark.

On yet another trip, I had spent two days hiking in the Vallée des Merveilles, near the Italian border. Here, in the Bronze Age (after 2200 B.C.), ancient artists wielding stone drills pecked out on schist and sandstone boulders an astonishing open-air Louvre of mysterious images. The more than 30,000 engravings seem to celebrate some taurine cult, for again and again the *corniforme* emblem of a bull's horns appears, even worked into sticklike humanoids as a kind of visual pun. Deepening the mystery is the fact that the high valley is a foreboding place, a notorious center for storms and snow, and names strewn on the landscape since before the Middle Ages associate the region with death and the devil.

"WE" COMPRISED, BESIDES MYSELF, Gérard Kosicki, a photographer and ex-ski champion from Grenoble for whom the Haute Provence is a limitless back yard, and the perspicacious and skeptical Matt Hale, with whom for three decades I had climbed in Alaska and cavorted on other continents.

We spent six days struggling to wrap our minds and our senses around the Grand Canyon of the Verdon, a natural wonder few Americans know about. One of the two or three deepest canyons in western Europe (through thirteen twisting miles, its limestone walls hang from 1,000 to 3,000 feet above the surging river), it is also one of the sheerest. In all the United States, nothing compares to Verdon except the Black Canyon of the Gunnison, in Colorado. Our own Grand Canyon in Arizona, though deeper by twice than Verdon, is far less precipitous.

As every schoolboy knows, John Wesley Powell led the first descent of the Colorado River through the Grand Canyon in 1869, when Arizona was still, from the Anglo point of view, utter wilderness. By 1869, it would seem, every inch of France had been explored. Yet the first descent of the Grand Canyon of the Verdon did not take place until 1905.

This bold deed was the work of a small team led by E. A. Martel, often called the father of speleology. In *La France Ignorée (Unknown France)*, a blithe and romantic memoir of his prowlings into the *incognita* all over his native country, Martel recounts his party's four days of peril and exhaustion, as, in effect, they invented the sport of canyoneering as they struggled downstream.

Martel's team set out in three wooden canoes built in the United States. By the end of the trip, one was trashed beyond salvage, the other two grievously smashed and patched together. The men paddled, made desperate portages, waded and swam roped up, climbed the cliffs, and scrambled over *chaos*, as the French call piles of giant boulders. In places the river dove underground for hundreds of yards at a stretch.

It was August, but the canyon was full of terrors. At their first bivouac,

> We are at the bottom of a veritable shaft; our arms, extended, almost touch the walls that shoot up, overhanging, 400 meters in the air; the intersections of their ledges, from one side to the other, hide the sky from us; up there the sun sparkles and warms; down here, it is almost night, in our prison of water that roars frightfully; it is an overwhelming, unimaginable spectacle.

By now, the Verdon has become a center of tourism and sport, and the sheer numbers of visitors have done much to tame its wildness. At the Point Sublime, we stood behind a guard rail with ladies in heels and lapdogs, peering into the profound. On the terrace of the Chalet de la Maline, we drank beer and gazed across the blue void. At the cliff called L'Escales, we watched bare-chested youths from East Germany rappel one or two pitches down, then climb back up on hard but well-protected routes (a bolt every ten feet), while tourists recorded their contortions on videocam.

So far, we were merely playing at the edges of the awesome canyon. We agreed to save for last an all-day hike into the bottom of the gorge and through the labyrinth of its mystery.

Meanwhile, we set out to plumb the region's history. Castellane, the village at the head of the Grand Canyon, and Moustiers-Ste-Marie, its twin at the bottom, were Roman outposts built by the conquerors of Gaul under Augustus Caesar. There is no record of the Roman response to the dramatic canyon that links the towns, but it was probably disgust and annoyance. Caesar's legions avoided the Verdon gorge, building the road between the towns well to the north, where it looped pastorally in and out of gentler valleys.

One day we walked a piece of the ancient roadway above the trickling stream of the Bau. The bedrock limestone underfoot bore the grooves and gouges of cold iron wielded two millennia ago. The old path wound through olives and poplars, past disused fields, up to a gentle saddle where we came upon the crumbling walls of an abandoned town.

Châteauneuf-les-Moustiers, founded in the eleventh or twelfth century, lasted all the way through World War I before the town gave up the ghost. The warm, bright day seemed at odds with the Byronic gloom of the ruins. We were only three miles north of the crowds gaping from the Point Sublime, but we had the forgotten village to ourselves. For hours we poked through roofless buildings, fighting ten-foot-high wild rose bushes that had taken over the kitchens and bedrooms of twenty-five generations of upland shepherds. Sagging roof beams, shaped with medieval axes and black with age, hung in midair, still bracing the ravaged walls. Cobblestone lanes sprouted a furry cushion of weeds. The Romanesque church, bare to the sky, still bore the faintest trace of frescoes inside the apse, where Christ-in-Majesty would have sternly blessed the villagers.

Someone still cared about this ghost town, for in the cemetery I found the grave of one Emilie Pierresnard—born 1894, died 1989. Had she been the last living soul who as a child had curdled milk into goat cheese in Châteauneuf? And yet someone else cared less—for a stone campfire ring sat on the grass, covered with a metal grate for broiling steaks, and to my shock I saw that the firewood was roof beams wrenched from the ruins.

Following a hint in an obscure guidebook, we pushed on along the Roman road as it wound toward the headwaters of the Bau. Soon we walked in the cold shadow of a stern north-facing cliff. Suddenly we stood beneath a huge natural cave. We clambered past collapsing walls of masoned stones and entered the alcove. Deep inside the dim grotto stood a bizarre chapel, built (claimed our guidebook) by the Knights Templar, the sect of militant Crusaders founded in the early twelfth century.

The off-center portal, the humble altar, the floor polished to a sheen by centuries of furtive worship, the very eeriness of the cave—all this conjured up vividly the secret rites of highland bands of Catholic mystics plotting the overthrow of Jerusalem and the death by sword of whole armies of infidels. The place still had about it an ominous aura, and yet we loitered for hours in its chill severity.

All across the Haute Provence, it is the stamp of the medieval that strikes you, most forcefully in the scores of *villages perchés*, towns dating from the tenth through thirteenth centuries, whose grimly defensive architecture bespeaks a gnawing, immemorial fear. The houses huddle close, gapped by crooked alleys, their backs to sunny fields. The church looms over the rooftops, its bell clanging like a reminder of fate. Often a village clings to some spiky summit, or spills in steep lanes along a craggy ridge.

It was not easy for me to discover just which invaders the villages had perched in fear of. "Sarrasines," says *Michelin,* alluding, I assume, to the Moors who conquered Spain. Another guidebook speaks of Allemani rampaging down from the north. "Barbarians," sums up Pope-Hennessy with a British sneer.

For the aesthete, the *villages perchés* form some of the most beautiful towns in France. The temptation is to idealize the inhabitants, as well: the writer Peter Mayle (*Toujours Provence,* etc.) has struck gold turning the Provençal peasant into a stubborn but wise eccentric.

My own inklings are more pessimistic. The ancient villages of Provence seemed to me all too often to embody what Marx called "the idiocy of rural life." Over this perception, Matt and I wrangled for two weeks.

As we drove one day through the twin perched villages of Rouaine and Rouianette, I couldn't resist scoring a point. "Hey," I told Matt, "this is the place of that old Castellane proverb."

"Read it to me," said Matt, who was driving.

My book had translated the original Provençal into French. I rendered a version in English: "'If you want to make an ass of your daughter/ Marry her to Rouaine or Rouainette./ And if they won't have her,/ Marry her to Brans or Villars.' Clever, huh?"

"Read me another one," Matt said.

"How about this? 'If Destourbes were made of bread,/ The Roc of cheese,/ And the Verdon of wine,/ Castellane would never take it all.'"

"Something must be lost in translation."

Yet another day, we stopped in a bar in St-Etienne-les-Orgues—"St. Stephen of the Orgies," Matt deliberately misconstrued—to ask directions to the Jas de Fraches, a remarkable building with tranverse arches made all of mortarless dry stone. Four men playing cards, very drunk on a Tuesday morning, took turns squinting at the picture of the Jas in a book I had. They shook their heads, trading queries in a *patois* so thick I caught only every third word. None of them had heard of the place or ever seen the building.

Too late to visit, I located Jas de Fraches on a good map. It stood only twelve miles from the card-players' bar. "The idiocy of rural life," I sighed.

"Look," said Matt, who works for the government, "if you go into a bar in Washington, not one person in ten could tell you where an important Civil War site like Fort Marcy is."

"Nonsense."

"I guarantee you. Maybe one in a hundred."

"It's different. These guys have lived their whole lives. . . . " I lapsed into reassessment. "Where is Fort Marcy, anyway?"

All Haute Provence is crisscrossed with hiking trails. The most ambitious of these are the numbered *Grandes Randonées*, paths on which you can walk for days or weeks, staying at night in huts or country *auberges*. In the Vallée de la Clarée north of Briançon, we followed the GR 57 out of Laval, up past the larches to timberline. Tiny signatures painted on the rocks—a "57" neatly lettered on vertical bands of red-white-red—kept us on the route. We came to a basin filled with cold pools of snowmelt; the tufted grasses invited us to loll and eat our lunch.

In the afternoon we contoured for hours south through alpine meadows, under frowning peaks, stone-stepping over brooks that crossed our way. It was the first Sunday in September, and down in the valley below—mere dots in the distance—a mob of picknickers and fishermen squeezed the orange of summer for the last drops of their yearly holiday. Up on the GR 57, however, the loudest sound was distant cowbells, and we crossed paths with only three other parties.

In late afternoon we came to the Refuge de Ricou, a ramshackle little hut with a picnic table under a striped umbrella, where we sat, took off our boots to wiggle our toes, and sipped beer in half-liter mugs. The sun was dodging in and out of thunderheads in the west, above the jagged skyline of the Chardonnet. During the last warm hour of the day, we sprawled in placid contentment, watching the picknickers below, already in shadow, pack up and head for dreary home.

Later we wandered through the sleepy village of Plampinet, which seemed unchanged since the seventeenth century. On the wall of the church we saw a *cadran solaire,* one of hundreds of colored sundials all over the Haute Provence painted on church walls in olden times by traveling artisans. Each came with its motto. I read Plampinet's out loud: "'Rappellez-vous de vôtre dernière heure et vous ne pecherez jamais.' I like that. 'Remember your last hour, and you will never sin again.'"

Matt, who had won a French prize in high school, pointed out that "pecherez" was missing a diacritical mark.

"That's true," I said. "Shouldn't there be an *accent aigu* on the first 'e'?"

"Or a *circonflexe*. What it really says is, 'Remember your last hour, and you will never fish again.'"

The next day, in the pristine Vallouise, above the pretty town of Les Vigneaux, Matt and I climbed a vertiginous trail the local guides had built only three years before. The *via ferrata,* invented in the First War in the Italian Dolomites, has only begun to catch on in southern France. An "iron way" is a route engineered, by means of metal cables, ladders, and gouged footholds, up a cliff that would otherwise suffer only expert alpinists.

No *via ferrata* anywhere in France is more *sportif* than the one Matt and I followed up the Falaise de la Balme. For 1,200 vertical feet, at an average angle of eighty degrees, the route snakes its way up an exhilarating wall of mottled brown rock. Secured by a harness, two nylon slings, and two carabiners each, we ascended in gymnastic safety.

So steep was the Balme, that if you dropped a pebble from near the top, it would bounce only once or twice before landing in the trees a thousand feet below. At every step, we glanced between our feet at the vertical void. As climbers, we were reminded in our very fingertips of the all-out commitment, the dread mixed with hope, that had come on the serious routes of our youth. Yet thanks to the *via ferrata,* the Balme amounted to a morning's giddy play.

The pièce de résistance of the route comes near the top. On dead-vertical rock, the holds inch up a frightening channel between overhanging prongs. A bulge with no good holds forces you to arch out backwards over empty space. Without the *via ferrata,* even in our prime, Matt and I might have been stumped by this impasse. As it was, we simply leaned out on the cable and walked up the overhang. Even with iron to hold onto, I felt the old *frisson* of the primal precipice.

In the Tetons or Yosemite, if you even suggested building a *via ferrata,* climbers and rangers alike would ride you out of the campground. In the

Alps, the notion fits an age-old sensibility. The mountains are to be culti-vated, not preserved in all their ragged squalor; an iron way makes much the same sense as a formal garden or a plowed field.

Kosicki took us one day to his favorite perched village, called Péone. To reach it, you must drive up the Gorges des Daluis, a relatively small but frightfully sheer chasm cut by the river Var out of grotesque cliffs of red schist. The narrow road hugs the right-bank precipice, hundreds of feet above the black stream in the depths. It seems unfathomable—Saracens, Allemani, or no—that thirteenth-century peasants might have forced their way up the gorge to build one of the highest and strangest towns in France.

Though Péone appears in none of the guidebooks, it is an unforget-table place. The houses, rising as high as four stories, seem to lean against each other. Dizzy aiguilles of conglomerate rock—blanketed today with wire mesh so that women hanging out laundry are not brained by falling stones—hover above the village. The tortured lanes have homely names—Street of the Oven, Street of the Clock, the Narrow Street (they are all narrow).

By the time we had arrived, a violent thunderstorm with drenching rain had seized the region. Huddled in doorways, we watched flash floods pour down alleys whose cobbles were contoured to feed the streams down the center, away from the houses.

We took refuge in the town's only café. The proprietor was cooking lamb chops in the fireplace. Four jovial local men drank red wine as they waited for lunch. I got up the nerve to ask them what the name Péone meant. All eyes turned to a confident fellow with a mustache. "I wrote it down once," he said, "but now I have forgotten." His cronies laughed. (I gave Matt a telling look, which he declined to return.) Later the man fetched me a brochure about the town. "It's very well written," he ven-tured. "I wrote it myself."

After lunch I asked our waitress how many other Americans she had seen during the summer. She made a "zero" sign with thumb and forefinger.

Driving down the Gorges des Daluis verged on the terrifying. The ra-vine was flooding everywhere, cascades of red water pouring like magma from gullies, stones bouncing across the roadway. We parked in a tunnel to wait out the worst of it, but the storm continued. At that moment, we learned later, a huge mudslide on the pass leading back to Castellane bar-ricaded the road. Motorists forced to turn back eventually gave us the news. We contemplated options. A few days before, I had read in the regional paper about the stricken village of Boulc, near Die to the northwest. The previous January, torrential rains had unleashed mudslides that wiped out the only road to Boulc. Engineers declared the thoroughfare unrecon-structable. For eight months the 106 villagers had had to hike a forest trail to communicate with the outside. Now they were demanding that the government build a tunnel. Otherwise the village would die.

We loitered in a cafe in Annot, watching the rain come down in sheets, while around us old-timers played cards and drank their *pastis*. I thought of Boulc, felt grateful to have escaped Péone, and realized in a visceral way just how close to medieval isolation a *village perché* might still lie.

Yet by late evening the sky had cleared, and the crew from Ponts et Chaussées—Bridges and Highways, a kind of local fire-and-rescue brigade— had bulldozed clear the pass. We drove back past Rouiane and Rouianette and collapsed after midnight in warm, dry beds.

Though our days were filled with rambles in the hinterland, we made sure to pamper ourselves each evening. In Briançon, Barcelonette, Castellane, La Palud-sur-Verdon, and Forcalquier, we slept in comfy, moderately priced hotels. We drank a local peach aperitif called Rinquinquin, and downed many a bottle of cheap, good Muscat blanc, Bandol rosé, and reds such as Vac- queyras and Gigondas. At breakfast we dawdled in some town-square café over croissants and café au lait.

Our last dinner, at the Hostellerie des Deux Lions in Forcalquier, was our best. We dined on Provençal specialties: lamb kidneys, piglet stew, fish from a local lake, seasoned with thyme, sage, fennel, and basil. We tasted the regional cheeses, including *chèvre* in chestnut leaves. And we finished up with a Lethean elixir called Marc de Cordelier, the *digestif de la région*.

Two days before, we had at last come to grips with the Grand Canyon of the Verdon. Along several miles of its most tortured windings, "we touched on the sorcery" of the place, to borrow a line from Martel. In the late 1920s, the Touring Club de France decided to improve the route of Martel's brave push and render it accessible to the average *randonneur* with a head for heights. The labor required was phenomenal: today, Martel's most redoubtable passages are circumvented by long tunnels blasted through bedrock; by *passerelles* or gangways carved out of cliffs where you sidle for- ward gripping a cable; by ladders, bridges, and trails beaten through the boxwood jungle.

We left the sunny Chalet de la Maline, where a few days before we had guzzled beer on the porch, and zigzagged our way down an endless trail into the gorge. As we descended, the gloom of the chasm seemed to reach up and swallow us. The thunder of the river filled our ears long before we came to its banks. A rickety iron bridge took us further into the shadows, under the dank north-facing opposite cliff.

The trail kept surprising us: sometimes it climbed through the box- wood to traverse above some overhanging grotto on a skimpy ledge of dark earth; sometimes it snaked beneath giant leaning slabs to emerge on yet another improbable polished shingle of shore. A shaft of sunlight here and there, angling between distant rims, demanded the homage of our basking under it; only two hours into the canyon and we craved its lucid hint of the sane world above.

At the sinuous, polished chute called the Styx, the elemental fierceness of the canyon came home, as I gauged the width of the walls at only 20 feet, while staring up 1,200 feet to a tiny blue strip of sky. The trail ends at l'Imbut, where Martel faced his worst ordeal, and which even the Touring Club was unable to domesticate. As I stood on the shore, my gaze transfixed by the sight of the river plunging into an evil hole beneath a gargantuan stone, Kosicki said to me, in that mystical way photographers lapse into, "It is all about water. Water is why we have the Verdon. Listen to the water, and think of Martel."

It worked. The roar took over my mind. Time stopped. A fear, not unlike the nasty shock of finding oneself halfway up a precipice with too little strength left in one's arms, irrationally claimed my attention. I inched away from the fatal pool.

We had only scratched the surface of the Verdon. Martel himself had led a second descent the year after his first, his team swimming in kapok life jackets instead of paddling canoes, coming close once more to death— yet he had written, "One must traverse the Grand Canyon twenty times before daring to say *that one has seen it.*"

On our last day in Provence, we set out to visit the Romanesque chapel of St-Pons, of which I had seen a photo and read a scrap of text. Built in the twelvth century beneath a vertical limestone cliff facing north, in as severe a spot as the most fevered ascetic could wish, the church was reported still to be the goal of pilgrimages.

A medieval fog had descended upon the countryside. At the trailhead, in the tranquil village of Valbelle, we found an old man wearing a gray coat and beret, watching birds with his binoculars. I asked him who Saint Pons had been. He shook his head shyly. "No one knows," he answered. "Il n'y a pas de documents."

"But there are still pilgrimages?"

"Yes. They go up there," he pointed into the mist, "carrying flambeaux."

"When?"

"In May."

Out of the old man's earshot, I grumbled, "How can they have pilgrimages and not know who Saint Pons was?"

"Perhaps," said Kosicki, defending his compatriot, "the man knows, but he does not want to tell you."

The trail wound up through the forest, growing less and less distinct.

Our clothes got soaked from pushing through wet bushes. The fog blew in and out, disclosing the orange cliff above—and then abruptly we saw the chapel. I had once spent a month searching for Romanesque churches in Catalonia: none occupied a more savage eyrie than St-Pons.

When we got there, we saw that the bridge leading to the church spanned a void; cunning stone arches braced it from beneath, allowing the pilgrim to pass to the tiny grass plot—a ledge between the huge overhang above and the precipice below—where the shrine had been built.

Inside, the font, the altar, and the polished stairs still spoke of services held eight centuries ago. Alas—as in so many holy places—the walls were scratched and charcoaled with graffiti, dating back at least to 1889. Yet even some of these "Kilroy was here" scrawlings were reverent, like the plea of one Aillaud Albert in 1933: "St-Pons Guérissez-nous." ("Saint Pons, heal us.")

Just beyond the chapel, the ledge blanked out in vertical precipice. We found a natural tunnel in the limestone and crawled fifty yards from end to end, emerging on a hidden ledge below. My scrap of text said that an old legend promised a year free of colic to any person completing the crawl. Yet surely the magic of the place went deeper than that.

Saint Pons, I said to myself, speak to us! Tell us who you were, and what your chapel has to do with the wild enigmas at the heart of the Haute Provence.

As we hiked back down through the woods, an eagle soared in circles above us, flitting in and out of the mist. His shrill keening cries portended something—if only we had had the wit to hear it.

Acknowledgments

where we came very close to making the discovery of the Iceman eleven years before a pair of German hikers blundered upon the lost voyager from the Copper Age.

Close in the chambers of my gratitude to Atwood and Rasmus lodge my three genial editors at *Smithsonian*, Jack Wiley, Marlane Liddell, and Jim Doherty, as well as editor-in-chief Don Moser. Not least among the delights of writing for *Smithsonian* is the opportunity to dive into a subject virtually every other magazine would deem too esoteric: e. g., a profile of the Victorian polymath, novelist, and self-taught archaeologist Sabine Baring-Gould, all but forgotten today. Other editors I've been particularly happy working with and getting to know include Erla Zwingle and Jennifer Reek at *National Geographic*, Kim Brown at *Travel & Leisure*, Mark Bryant at *Outside*, Harriet Choice at Universal Press Syndicate, Mike Curtis at the *Atlantic Monthly*, David Schonauer at *American Photo*, Chris Bergonzi of the late lamented *Ultrasport*, Ted Moncreiff at *Condé Nast Traveler*, Sue Zesiger at both *European Travel & Life* and *Civilization*, Greg Henderson and Peter Esmonde at Discovery Channel Online, Christian Kallen at Mungo Park, and old pal Steve Roper at *Summit*. The many companions of the larks and labors chronicled in this collection, too numerous to list here by name, often deepened my understanding of what I was witnessing even while they provided much of the pleasure of the voyage. I feel compelled to single out, however, my long friendship with Jon Krakauer (crony in three of the adventures in this book) as contributing to my development as a writer.

Since 1984, when Jon started writing for a living, he and I have formed a nonstop two-man support group. Every few days for the last dozen years, we've called each other to commiserate about our freelance fiascos, to pass on tips about new markets, to ask each other's advice, to gossip about our rivals in this parlous trade, and to congratulate each other's occasional triumphs. We send each other everything we write in manuscript. The value of our Scribblers Anonymous brotherhood, for me at least, has been incalculable. (During our first years, when we both took on a fair amount of what can only be called hack work, Jon or I would typically send the typescript off to the magazine in the same mail as a copy for the other's perusal. The cover note to the editor would read, "Here's _____. Hope you like it. Thanks for the good assignment." My note to Jon took a different tack: "Here's my latest piece of dreck, dashed off in two hours. Good enough for _____, don't you think?" I was always terrified I'd put the respective notes in the wrong envelopes; but so far as I know, neither of us ever slipped.)

Finally, I must express my pleasure at being published since 1986 by The Mountaineers Books, which represents everything that a press that

266

cares about its authors should be. In particular, the enthusiasm, sensitive criticism, and plain hard work on the part of Margaret Foster and Donna DeShazo in putting *Escape Routes* together have reminded me that, when all is said and done, the life of a freelance writer has its share of sheer delight.

ABOUT THE AUTHOR

DAVID ROBERTS did his first climbing as a teenager in Boulder, Colorado. While still an undergraduate at Harvard, he began climbing in Alaska, ultimately leading or co-leading thirteen expeditions and making first ascents of the Wickersham Wall of Mount McKinley and the peaks of the Revelation Mountains.

After teaching for nine years at Hampshire College, he became a freelance writer and over the past fifteen years has written for *Outside*, *Backpacker*, *Smithsonian*, *Men's Journal*, *Summit*, *National Geographic*, *Atlantic Monthly*, *American Photo*, *New York Times Magazine*, *Reader's Digest*, and many other publications. He is the author of *Moments of Doubt*; *The Early Climbs: Deborah* and *The Mountain of My Fear*; *Once They Moved Like the Wind: Cochise, Geronimo, and the Apache Wars*; and *In Search of the Old Ones: Exploring the Anasazi of the Southwest*. He lives in Cambridge, Massachusetts.

THE MOUNTAINEERS, founded in 1906, is a nonprofit outdoor activity and conservation club, whose mission is "to explore, study, preserve, and enjoy the natural beauty of the outdoors. . . . " Based in Seattle, Washington, the club is now the third-largest such organization in the United States, with 15,000 members and five branches throughout Washington State.

The Mountaineers sponsors both classes and year-round outdoor activities in the Pacific Northwest, which include hiking, mountain climbing, ski-touring, snowshoeing, bicycling, camping, kayaking and canoeing, nature study, sailing, and adventure travel. The club's conservation division supports environmental causes through educational activities, sponsoring legislation, and presenting informational programs. All club activities are led by skilled, experienced volunteers, who are dedicated to promoting safe and responsible enjoyment and preservation of the outdoors.

If you would like to participate in these organized outdoor activities or the club's programs, consider a membership in The Mountaineers. For information and an application, write or call The Mountaineers, Club Headquarters, 300 Third Avenue West, Seattle, Washington 98119; (206) 284-6310.

The Mountaineers Books, an active, nonprofit publishing program of the club, produces guidebooks, instructional texts, historical works, natural history guides, and works on environmental conservation. All books produced by The Mountaineers are aimed at fulfilling the club's mission.

Send or call for our catalog of more than 300 outdoor titles:

The Mountaineers Books
1001 SW Klickitat Way, Suite 201
Seattle, WA 98134
1-800-553-4453 / e-mail: mbooks@mountaineers.org